616·97

To my part.
whose enduring love,
has transfori.

Acknowledgements

My thanks to all those who have contributed thoughts and information to my posts on Gay in the 80s; they all help paint a more detailed picture of that period. Particular thanks to David Hunt in North Carolina and Martin Goodsell and Catherine Booth in the UK for providing various source materials. Also to Tanya Solomons for editing services. I am especially grateful to Kevin Franklin, whose design expertise has transformed my original document into this book.

And last but by no means least, to the many thousands of queer activists around the world and over the decades, whose actions – small and large – have contributed to better lives for innumerable queer people.

Contents

5

6

Gay in the 80s – From Fighting for Our Rights to Fighting for Our Lives   © Colin Clews

Ready for the 80s?

"I'm ready for the 80s... ready for the time of my life"

(Ready for the 80s, The Village People, 1979)

Why the 80s?

On the face of it, the 1980s doesn't seem like the best decade for queers around the globe. In the UK there were events like the trial of Gay's the Word bookshop, Operation Spanner (the prosecution of gay men for having consensual sex in private) and, of course, Section 28 of the Local Government Act, which banned the use of public monies for 'the promotion of homosexuality as a pretended family relationship'.

In Australia there was the continued criminalisation of homosexuality in a number of states, and the sustained police harassment that went with that. And in the USA there was the rise of the New Right, epitomised by Ronald Reagan, who manifested homophobia on a jaw-dropping level – not least in his belligerent passivity in the face of the AIDS crisis.

At times it seemed like our slow but steady progress down the road to Gay Liberation had not only stalled but actually gone into reverse. This was particularly so in the early years of the AIDS crisis when a relentless onslaught of fear, vicious homophobia and the loss of so many loved ones came close to breaking our spirits. At the same time, our enemies gleefully claimed that AIDS was, quite literally, a godsend and a warning that granting us equal rights would simply spread the disease further.

Yet, in spite of that, it's my view that – in the Western world, at least – the 80s was very much the tipping point for our communities. By that I mean that, despite the continuing and predictable hostility from the usual quarters, we achieved a very real sense of place in the world – and that place wasn't on the margins. By the end of the 80s we had seen some very tangible outcomes. We were no longer alone in fighting for queer rights: they were on the policy platforms of some of the major political parties (even if those parties were incredibly reluctant to follow through on it); trades unions increasingly took up our fight and increasing numbers of regional legislators introduced anti-discrimination laws and policies. Elsewhere our profile – and participation – in areas such as film, television, literature and music increased immensely. And the various elements of our own communities – our media, our social scene, our support and advocacy organisations, for example – also grew significantly.

Just how we achieved this in the face of sustained opposition is difficult to say; my

9

guess is that it was the result of a number of factors that played out both separately and synergistically. For example, I suspect that the radical idealism of Gay Liberation gradually transformed into a more pragmatic engagement with mainstream politics. That, in turn, brought in other people to fight alongside us – the aforementioned political parties and trades unions in particular – and this began to pay dividends in the longer term.

The emergence of HIV and AIDS undoubtedly played a role. It spawned a greater sense of solidarity within our own communities; for example, a number of lesbians have told me that it led to them working more closely with gay men. I suspect it expedited the growth and effectiveness of our community organisations, not least because we realised that it was no longer just our rights that were at stake – it was our lives. It reinforced the value of our social venues: as points of information and support; as places of re-spite from the homophobic, AIDS-phobic outside world; and as sources of much needed funds to support the various community initiatives established to support people with or at risk of HIV/AIDS.

It also dragged many previously apolitical queers out of the closet. With an AIDS diagnosis it became increasingly difficult to deceive your parents, your friends or your work colleagues – especially in the early days when common symptoms included facial lesions and severe physical wasting. This was summed up in the first AIDS joke I ever heard:

Question: *What's the worst thing about having AIDS?*

Answer: *Trying to convince your parents you're Haitian. (Haitians were perceived as another high-risk group in the early days.)*

Not only were thousands of people involuntarily 'outed' to those around them, but the tabloid media also raised our profile by continuing to refer to the disease as 'the gay plague'. Quite simply, if you're going to have a widespread 'gay plague' then you've got to have widespread gays!

The development of the queer social scene – driven, in part, by the discovery of the so-called Pink Pound/Dollar – also helped strengthen our communities and increase our visibility. For example, by the end of the decade corporate sponsorship of events such as London's Lesbian and Gay Pride, Sydney's Gay and Lesbian Mardi Gras and numerous Gay Pride/Freedom events in the USA was demonstrating that some people

10

were interested in us – even if it was only as a source of profit. With Margaret Thatcher championing monetarism – that is, valuing everyone and everything in terms of their monetary worth – this must have confused some conservatives (although still not enough to put their mouths where our money was).

But even when governments hesitated, corporations keen to tap the pink market were strengthening our queer voices by taking out expensive adverts in our newspapers and magazines. Similarly, the increasing recognition of this market was one of the factors that drove the development of queer cinema and literature. For example, in 1983 *The Bookseller* – the trade magazine for the UK book industry – predicted that the 80s would be 'the decade of the gay novel'. Also in the UK – and somewhat incongruously, given the political climate of the time – a new television channel, Channel 4, was launched with a specific brief to address the needs of under-served populations such as queers.

The establishment of Channel 4 by a government that exuded and exploited homophobia is a perfect example of the complex and often contradictory political dynamics of that decade. Plans for a fourth British television channel had been mooted since the 50s, before finally coming to fruition in a hostile political environment three decades late. In much the same way, the fight for queer rights had been fought for several decades before consolidating in the AIDS-induced homophobia of the 80s.

Positive things happened in seemingly the most unlikely of circumstances, and they did not always happen in a logical, linear or predictable fashion. Our communities grew stronger, in part, as a consequence of proactive and prolonged campaigning on issues such as equal rights in employment and parenting. But we also grew stronger as a result of our response to adversity: AIDS being the most obvious, global example but there were many other 'local' campaigns like the fight against Section 28 in the UK, against Proposition 64 in California and against police raids on gay clubs in Sydney.

In March 2012 I began writing about these events in my blog *Gay in the 80s;* partly because I believed that the 80s was a pivotal decade in queer history and partly because it was also a pivotal decade in my own personal history. At the beginning of January 1980, I was a necessarily closeted residential childcare worker in Leicester, England. By the close of the decade I was poised to take on the management of a multimillion dollar budget for HIV/AIDS services in Sydney, Australia – the centre of Australia's AIDS pandemic.

I had lived and worked in both the UK and Australia during the 80s and also undertaken some life-changing visits to the USA. I'd been a queer activist, queer journalist, AIDS activist, AIDS counsellor and AIDS educator. I'd had furtive meetings with gay Chinese asylum seekers in Leicester; waved placards at dawn beside busy Los Angeles intersections; played cat-and-mouse with police as a member of the London Lesbians and Gays Support the Miners group and, quite literally, talked a young man to death in Sydney.

It was all part of being an activist in the 80s: responding as best we could to the challenges that were thrown at us on what felt like an almost daily basis.

My experience across three countries has given me a fascinating insight into both the similarities and the differences between those countries and how they played out in terms of advancing the position of queer people in their respective societies. One particularly intriguing example was the widespread and defiant activism of Australian queers, despite their being sexual outlaws (homosexuality was only gradually and slowly decriminalised across Australian states in the 80s and 90s), in contrast to their seemingly more complacent UK counterparts: technically legal since 1967 but still subject to immense harassment.

For example, in 1984 the future of the UK's Lesbian and Gay Pride week was thrown into doubt due to low levels of support: less than two thousand people attended the national Pride march – the only event of its kind in the entire UK. Meanwhile, in that same year, tens of thousands of queers were out on the streets for Sydney's Gay and Lesbian Mardi Gras, despite homosexuality still being a crime for which men could be – and were – jailed.

Of course it doesn't just come down to community attitudes; it's also about the political systems in which we live. Both Australia and the USA have federal systems of government, which meant that many of our battles had to be fought on a state-by-state basis. The USA also has a system wherein its citizens can propose and vote on specific issues through ballots and referenda – a measure that has been used repeatedly to block or repeal the rights of queer people and people with AIDS [2]. It was California's Proposition 64 – to bar people with HIV from certain areas of employment (among other things) – that got me banner waving beside those Los Angeles freeways.

In theory, the UK's centralised model of government should mean that battles

12

needed to be won only once – but sexuality seems to be a notable exception to this. Such was the case with the 1967 Sexual Offences Act, which conditionally decriminalised homosexuality in England and Wales but not in Northern Ireland, Scotland, the Isle of Man, Jersey or Guernsey. It wasn't until the 1980s that a variety of campaigns – as well as a ruling from the European Commission on Human Rights – finally got the provisions of the 1967 Act implemented across the rest of the UK.

And yet, despite these national differences, I think that the overall dynamic of queer history across these three countries is very similar during the 80s. My sense is that this is largely down to our increased visibility during that decade – and the positive and negative consequences that flowed from that. For example, one positive is the true size and nature of our communities became increasingly apparent, challenging the oppressive stereotypes as well as identifying a sizeable political constituency. On the other hand, it also meant that our enemies – citing the spread of the mythical 'gay agenda' as well as HIV/AIDS – re-doubled their efforts to drive us back down.

I hope this book will help give a greater insight into the dynamics of that period, as well as an idea of what life was like for queer people at that time. It is organised into five broad areas; these are:

- **Increased Visibility** – the various ways and areas in which our profile increased
- **The Growth of Queer Communities** - the different areas in which our communities grew.
- **Mainstream Politics** – looking at the progress of queer civil rights in the mainstream political system
- **Under Attack** – the various ways in which our communities came under attack
- **HIV/AIDS** – an attempt at a comprehensive overview of the AIDS crisis

There's no scientific rationale behind the designation of these groups; they're based entirely on my opinion. Nor are they mutually exclusive: for example, HIV/AIDS had an impact in every one of these areas. My aim is simply to establish some kind of frame of reference to look at the diverse activities and events that occurred in the 1980s.

13

References:

1. For example, on 9 November 1986, Britain's *News of the World* opined,
   "Some Labour councils encourage AIDS with grants to homosexual centres. So do Labour education authorities telling children that homosexuals living together are as stable as married couples."

2. See, for example, Stone, Amy L. 2012. *Gay Rights at the Ballot Box,* University of Minnesota Press, p.18.

Chapter One

Increased Visibility

Part One – Coming Out: Making the Personal Political

Coming out – that is, being open about one's sexuality – is the essential first step in increasing queer visibility and has been a mainstay of queer politics since the birth of the Gay Liberation movement. In 1978 legendary gay activist Harvey Milk had called for people to come out in order to demonstrate to those supporters of anti-gay ordinances that it was their own sons, daughters, brothers and sisters who would be affected by these measures.

Two years later, the UK's Campaign for Homosexual Equality made a similar call: *"To get rid of anti-gay stereotypes, along with residual guilt about being gay, many more people must come out – become more openly gay."* [1]

In this case it wasn't about anti-gay ordinances; the call was made in their report *Attacks on Gay People*, which documented a shocking list of what we now call hate crimes. Such a term didn't exist back then; anti-queer violence was very much seen as a justifiable response to the merest hint of our presumed degeneracy.

As our communities became increasingly organised and therefore increasingly visible, those who stood against us dragged out and developed the dangerous stereotypes that fuelled so much of the homophobic violence. So every additional person who came out constituted a challenge to that negativity and sent an important message to young or isolated queers and all the others who were still some way from self-acceptance. Even in those countries that didn't have specific votes on queer rights, coming out meant standing up to be counted in an environment where politicians and tabloid newspapers frequently whined about 'wasting' taxpayers' money on queer services – as if queer people weren't taxpayers too.

Such was the perceived value of coming out that, on 11 October 1988, the world witnessed the first ever National Coming Out Day. Founded by psychologist Robert Eichberg and political activist Jean O'Leary, one of its functions is to reassure those who are considering coming out that they are not alone. But the timing of its launch – the first anniversary of the Second National March on Washington for Lesbian and Gay Rights – also underscored the political dimension to coming out.

Coming Out Day was one of the initiatives that grew from the energy of the National March. Organisers felt that our communities had too often reacted defensively to anti-queer campaigns and events and that there was a need for a more proactive approach. In the words of the present organisers, National Coming Out Day is *"a reminder that one of our most basic tools is the power of coming out"*. (2)

Making the Political Really Personal: Coming Out at Home

The increasing emphasis on the importance of coming out was matched by the increasing number of books and articles discussing the best way to do it. I know, because I think I read most of them prior to my own coming out to my mother during my annual Christmas visit in 1982!

I saw my decision to come out as very much a 'political' act; I was just beginning to get into my stride as a gay activist and had read Harvey Milk's exhortation on the importance of coming out. I was coming out for 'the cause' rather than for myself – or so I told myself. Not that that made it any easier to do.

I had intended to do the deed shortly after arrival on 21 December. The timing was dictated by the train timetable: not having a car, I was reliant on public transport to get me out of there in the case of a bad reaction. This meant that my 'coming out deadline' was the time of the last train out of Bishop Auckland on Christmas Eve.

After bottling out of a number of attempts desperation finally pushed me into delivering the news on the afternoon of Christmas Eve. As an old Tarzan movie played on the TV I called my mother into the lounge, reminding myself that the key message of all the coming out guidance was to 'keep it positive'. In practice this meant not introducing the topic with statements such as 'You're not going to like this but ...' or 'I've got something awful to tell you' and, instead, emphasising how important it was to be able to share a very important part of your life. And so, by the time my mother was seated in the armchair beside me, I had a very well-rehearsed script in place.

Sadly, none of my reading had advised me what to do in the event of bursting into tears in mid-disclosure, which is precisely what I did. As I sat sobbing in the armchair, the only thought that went through my mind was: *"This is not what it says in the book!"*

My unanticipated departure from the script notwithstanding, we did finally get through the episode. My mother's response was brief but to the point: she didn't understand it but I was still her son and that was all that mattered. My first reaction was relief that she wasn't going to banish me from her home. It was followed swiftly (but

16

briefly) by a sense of indignation that the many hours invested in my coming out speech and subsequent question and answer session had been largely wasted!

But that feeling passed quickly and the event was brought to a swift termination by the arrival of my aunt, who lived next door. I suspect it came as a bit of a relief for both of us, although I soon came to realise that it also marked the closure of any further discussion on the issue. Feeling brave enough to raise it the following day, I asked if she had anyone questions relating to the previous day's discussion. She hadn't. A lengthy, pregnant pause followed then finally a change of subject. It was the same the following day – and the day after that too. I asked the same question but the only change was the length of the pregnant pause, which became shorter and shorter as we both became more adept at returning to our respective comfort zones. In the end I returned to my own home feeling like I had 'technically' come out but the information had been quickly filed away – preferably never to be retrieved again.

It never really became possible to share that important part of my life with my mother until I finally met my life partner, at which point it was unavoidable. Nonetheless, we were still restricted to 'edited highlights' – stories of our travels or theatre visits – rather than anything that indicated a relationship, such as discussions about having kids.

Over the years I have come to realise that this 'information lockdown' is a common experience for other queer people too and I think this generates a lot of ambiguity. On the one hand we're not being rejected but, on the other, an absolutely fundamental part of who we are is. In consequence, we struggle to rationalise it or manage the practicalities of it and end up either rejecting those who claim not to reject us or colluding with it by self-censoring our interactions with them.

The Stars Come Out (Reluctantly)

Of course it wasn't just mere mortals like me who were struggling with the concept of coming out. There were many among the rich and famous who struggled with the notion of declaring their sexuality. For some of them it had always been an open secret: everyone in their industry knew but the public at large were kept in the dark in order to preserve their masculine or feminine image. But the 1980s brought two new avenues by which celebrities could be outed – the palimony suit and AIDS.

In 1981, for example, Billie Jean King's former secretary and travelling companion Marilyn Barnett brought a palimony suit against her, claiming that the two had been in a relationship. King denied the relationship and won the case, but still lost most of her commercial endorsements.

The following year 'flamboyant' entertainer Liberace began the fight against a $133 million palimony suit from former employee Scott Thorson, again denying that there had ever been a relationship. The case dragged on until December 1986 when, just two months before his death from AIDS, Liberace's lawyers finally agreed a payout of $95,000 – on condition that the terms of the settlement were not publicly disclosed. Even after his death, the fight to hide Liberace's sexuality continued: his representatives repeatedly denied that he was gay or that he had died from AIDS while his doctor recorded the cause of death as 'cardiac arrest due to heart failure brought on by subacute encephalopathy [brain inflammation]'. It was only after the intervention of the local coroner, citing medical inconsistencies and the failure to report a death due to infectious diseases, that tests were undertaken to confirm an AIDS diagnosis.

Liberace certainly wasn't the first – or last – celebrity to be 'outed' by AIDS; others included Queen frontman Freddie Mercury, actor Rock Hudson and one of Margaret Thatcher's ministers, Lord Avon. As usual, the tabloid press latched on to these as yet another opportunity for sensationalism: the confirmation of Hudson's diagnosis, for example, generated headlines such as *'I Saw Rock Wed Man'* [3], *'I Lost Rock to James Dean says Liz'*, [4] *'AIDS Killer Stalks Hollywood'* [5] and *'Kiss of Death'* [6].

Even when celebrities hadn't died of AIDS, some newspapers were keen to try and suggest they had, usually to make a point about their sexuality. Such was the case with British television presenter Russell Harty. Both the *News of the World* and *The Sun* had pursued him, initially with allegations about his use of underage male prostitutes then, subsequently, with suggestions that he was dying of AIDS. Their tactics included having a reporter masquerade as a junior doctor and demand to see Harty's medical notes and the bribing of local children in the village where Harty lived. They even tried to bribe the local vicar.

In 1988, when Harty became ill with Hepatitis B *The Sun* snidely reported that he was dying from 'a disease transmitted in the same way as AIDS' [7]. They rented a flat opposite the hospital in which he was being treated and trained a telephoto lens on the

18

window of his room. Even after his death, they remained unapologetic. When Harty's friend, the author Alan Bennett, claimed at his funeral that *"the gutter press finished him off"*, *The Sun* ran an editorial that said:

"Stress did not kill Russell Harty. The truth is he died from a sexually transmitted disease. The press didn't give it to him. He caught it from his own choice. And by paying young rent boys he broke the law. Some – like ageing bachelor Mr Bennett – can see no harm in that. He has no family. But what if it had been YOUR son Harty had bedded."

But while it seemed that the media were ready to jump on the tail of every celebrity who had (or could be suggested to have) AIDS, one high roller's illness and death managed to escape such scrutiny.

Roy Cohn had served as Chief Counsel to Senator Joe McCarthy during his 'witch hunts' of communists and homosexuals in 1950s America. These had ended the careers (and, not infrequently, the lives) of many hundreds of people. For example, Cohn and McCarthy had created the so-called 'Lavender Scare' to convince then US President Eisenhower that communist governments were blackmailing closeted US government employees to obtain government secrets. Eisenhower consequently banned homosexuals from federal government employment.

And yet Cohn himself was actively homosexual. But he was also given immense political power, which he used ruthlessly to bring down political enemies as well as conceal his homosexuality. He had no qualms about furthering his own career by bringing down other gay men through the Lavender Scare and he used his powerful political influence to protect himself from a number of malpractice suits (he was finally barred from legal practice shortly before his death).

It is widely acknowledged that he could have used his influence to achieve more funding for AIDS treatment and research but he failed to do so. Unsurprisingly then, when he died of AIDS on 2 August 1986, his death was one of the few that was not mourned by queer people. Indeed, I remember reading one AIDS activist's comment that *"It couldn't have happened to a better person."*

For other celebrities, AIDS raised a different problem.

Since the 1970s, David Bowie had used shock tactics to increase his profile at every opportunity. He adorned the cover of his 1971 album *The Man Who Sold the World* in full drag and flowing locks. In queer politics terms this is known as 'gender fuck' and it was taken directly from the tactics of the Gay Liberation Front: men challenging gender stereotypes by wearing 'female' attire.

Then the drag persona mutated into Ziggy Stardust, an androgynous character in skin tight body-stockings and heavy make-up who flirted onstage with lead guitarist Mick Ronson. In 1972, while still promoting the Ziggy persona, he told a *Melody Maker* reporter, *"I'm gay, and always have been, even when I was David Jones."* [8] The image was duly honed over the next few years by the publication of photographs of Bowie being intimate with the likes of Mick Jagger, Lou Reed and Andy Warhol. But by 1976 his story had already changed – possibly to accommodate the very obvious presence of his wife Angie. That year he told *Playboy* magazine that he was bisexual. And there was even a rumour that he had met his wife because, *"they were fucking the same bloke"* [9].

But in 1983 he told *Rolling Stone* magazine that declaring his bisexuality *"was the biggest mistake I ever made"*. Just in case this wasn't clear enough he went on to add that he had always been *"a closet heterosexual"*. Quite what prompted this major turnaround has been the subject of much speculation. Some have argued that the homophobia that accompanied the emergence of AIDS made him realise that being gay was no longer a good marketing ploy. Bowie has never made such a statement, although in an interview in 2002 he did allude to the hostility he experienced in the USA, which he described as *"a very puritanical place"*. And, as if to distance himself from the gay community and gay politics, he said, *"I had no inclination to hold any banners nor be representative of any group of people"* [10]. But he was, apparently, happy to appropriate some of their tactics to increase his profile.

A year later, in 1984, Bowie's good friend Elton John took even more drastic measures, marrying his recording engineer Renata Blauel in a very public Valentine's Day wedding in Sydney; a wedding that Australia's Channel Nine News described as *"the most unexpected wedding of the year"*. The marriage ended in divorce in 1988, at which time John came out as gay, although not before becoming the victim of a series of unfounded allegations made by *The Sun* newspaper in 1987. These included claims that he had enjoyed sexual relationships with male prostitutes and that he had had the voice boxes of his Rottweiler guard dogs surgically removed. None of the allegations were true and John successfully sued the newspaper, issuing a total of 17 writs.

20

What's in a Name?

The extent to which people came out (or, as we have seen, 'went back in') is very much linked to how they perceived the likely consequences of being gay. Centuries of stigmatisation and persecution obviously had a huge impact on that process but things began to look a little more positive with the birth of Gay Liberation. As gay people became increasingly visible it looked like the stigma was finally beginning to fade – albeit very slowly.

Then along came AIDS. Labelled initially as 'GRID' – Gay Related Immune Deficiency – and reported thereafter as 'the gay cancer', 'gay bug' and 'gay plague', it didn't take a great deal of imagination to conclude that AIDS was simply a consequence of being gay. It wasn't of course, but the reality – that it was certain sexual practices, rather than membership of particular groups that might lead to the transmission of the AIDS virus – simply didn't sell newspapers.

In consequence, the misconception of 'gay = AIDS' served to further increase the anxiety of those already reluctant to acknowledge any of their behaviour as homosexual and many chose to deal with this through denial – of both the behaviour and the risk. In practice this seems to have involved selecting certain characteristics that 'made' someone gay then reassuring yourself that you didn't have them. Needless to say, it was usually a bit of a selective list, based in the first instance on characteristics you were pretty certain you didn't have. It could include anything from the old stereotypes of limp wrists and 'effeminate' behaviour to the desire (or otherwise) to become emotionally involved. As AIDS educators were to discover, many men could engage in regular penetrative sex (fucking and being fucked) with other men without perceiving their behaviour as in any way homosexual.

Of particular concern was the fact that large numbers of men were having high-risk sex with other men while believing they were safe from the risk of HIV infection simply because *'they weren't gay'* [11]. All sorts of reasons were given for this: one of the most common I came across during my time as an AIDS educator was the notion that only the passive partner (that is, the one being fucked) was 'gay'. This seems to be a rather sad take on the old joke, 'I'm not gay but my boyfriend is', although there was certainly nothing funny about it in this context.

Such was the resistance to acknowledging any kind of risk that some men changed their definitions even further. When AIDS educators talked about 'men who have sex with other men' in order to avoid using the word 'gay', the response came back that they weren't having sex; they were simply 'messing around with their mates'. The fact that 'messing around' included behaviour that we would define as fucking was deemed to be irrelevant.

When two members of my AIDS education team visited one of Sydney's many surfing beaches as part of their outreach work, they found another example of this selective thinking. In one of the cubicles in the men's public toilet they found a scrawled phone number, along with the message, *"Desperate for cock. Surfies only. No poofs."*

As an AIDS counsellor, I saw the consequences of this high-intensity denial first-hand. One of my clients was a married man who had contracted AIDS after many years of anonymous sex with other men. He was in his early 60s when he was referred to me and had been having regular sex with other men since he was 18. In spite of this, he left me in no doubt that he hated 'poofs'; never missing an opportunity to vent his spleen about 'filthy queers', 'dirty homos' and so on. He didn't know that I was a 'homo'; such was his blinkered view on the type of people we were. Somewhat ironically, this intensely homophobic man had had far more male sexual partners than I had!

Nonetheless, his hatred was so intense that he had raised his children and then his grandchildren to despise gay men too. And now, having contracted HIV through sex with another man, his condition had progressed to the point where he would soon require hospitalisation – and family explanations would be necessary. Prior to this point his illness had been managed as a private patient of an immunologist, thus avoiding the necessity of him having to attend the AIDS outpatient clinic in the public hospital (along with all the poofs). But the private hospitals didn't take AIDS in-patients; they had to be managed on the AIDS ward of the public hospital and everyone knew – or quickly found out – which ward was the AIDS ward.

And then there was the issue of his wife – with whom he'd also been having regular sex prior to his diagnosis. Fortunately for all concerned it transpired that he had not passed the virus on to her, although even this was established only after some considerable bending of medical rules as she had been tested without her knowledge or consent. Had her test come back positive, a whole new can of medical and ethical worms would have burst open.

Throughout this process my client laid responsibility for his situation entirely at the feet of the filthy queer who had recklessly infected him. My role was essentially one of allowing him to vent his emotions. These were generally channelled as homophobic anger but would undoubtedly have been fuelled by fear – about the progression of the disease, about the possibility that his family might discover that he was 'a filthy queer' himself and, of course, their likely responses to that, particularly at a time when his health was failing.

We never discussed the option of him 'coming out' to his wife or other family members: I suspect that, for him, acknowledging that he might be 'queer' would have been even worse than telling them that he had AIDS. And I couldn't – and, indeed, wouldn't – encourage him to lie about the source of his infection; as well as being professionally unethical it was also, quite simply, untenable. His wife knew that he wasn't a haemophiliac, that he hadn't had any blood transfusions and he clearly wasn't the type to have experimented with injectable recreational drugs. Thankfully for me, the rules of patient confidentiality meant that I was not allowed to discuss a client's condition with anyone other than my professional colleagues without the client's permission: in other words, I was never faced with the possibility of difficult discussions with my client's wife.

As it transpired I left my counselling role before this particular client was ever hospitalised so was not party to whatever events unfolded as a consequence of that. My guess would be that the wife probably guessed the real source of her husband's infection but they colluded – consciously or otherwise – to conceal this from the rest of the family. She would already have been blaming herself for not being a good enough wife on the grounds that her husband had been forced to turn to men to have some of his needs met (even though he had been having sex with other men long before they were married). This is a common response from women on discovering their male partners have also been having sex with men [12]. Given the homophobia engendered within her family, I have no doubt that they – including her husband – would have blamed her too.

The Man from China – Found Out and Fearful

In the early 80s I trained as a probation officer at Leicester University School of Social Work; a course that included a three month placement at Leicester Prison. This led to the interesting position of my being the contact person for the University's Gay Society while also working in one of the most homophobic environments imaginable.

In practice, being the contact person usually involved fielding a range of telephone enquiries from students with various levels of anxiety about their sexuality. For many young people the freedom and exposure to new ideas that came with leaving home for university was often the catalyst for self-questioning and the first tentative steps towards coming out. In consequence, I was used to receiving mysterious phone calls from unidentified individuals who would tell me that 'they'd seen my name in the Student Union newsletter' then leave it to me to fill in the details.

One winter afternoon I received such a phone call in the prison itself. That alone indicated that the caller was keen to talk to someone, but the ensuing conversation also suggested that they were desperately fearful. One of the first questions I was asked was, *"Is this telephone being tapped?"* – a question that I was asked at least twice more despite my reassurances. As was the norm for such conversations, we talked in vague terms: he'd seen my name in the Student Union newsletter, he wondered if we could meet up somewhere for a chat, was I really sure my phone wasn't tapped and so on. He did, at least, reveal to me that he was Chinese.

I suggested we meet up at the School of Social Work once I'd finished for the day at the prison. This provoked another anxious response: would I still be wearing my prison officer's uniform, as this might attract attention? I reassured him that probation officers didn't wear a uniform but he still remained anxious. He asked me questions as to who might be in the school building, what they might think of us meeting there and what we would say if we were questioned. But finally, and after much reassurance, he agreed to meet later that day.

Once we actually came face to face he seemed to relax a little, although still obsessed about who might see us and what they might think. So it wasn't long before we moved on to a cafe on one of the main thoroughfares out of the city.

It was little more than a 'greasy spoon' type of establishment – very much the norm in those pre-coffee chain days. Formica tables, functional chairs, linoleum flooring and large, steamed-up windows, which my nervous Asian friend glanced at repeatedly throughout our conversation. Not the most relaxing environment for a confidential chat about one's sexual orientation but it was clear that the guy needed to talk and, after the umpteenth check of the windows, he started.

24

He told me that he was from the People's Republic of China and was currently studying at the university. He'd known he was gay long before he came to the UK but had been forced to conceal it because of China's persecution of gay men and women. In Chinese law, homosexuality was seen as both a mental illness and 'hooliganism' which, in those days, was subject to a range of punishments including periods in jail or labour camp, public humiliation and incarceration in mental institutions (13).

In order to avoid suspicion and also comply with family expectations, he'd married a local woman. It was clearly a marriage of convenience for both of them: from his description it was pretty obvious that she was a lesbian and under the same pressures as he. Sex was never discussed, let alone attempted; neither partner being under any delusions that this was anything other than a pretend marriage.

Eventually he was granted permission to come to the UK to study – something that must have been a bit of a relief for them both.

When he arrived he was given a specific allowance to cover his food and study materials and was accommodated with other Chinese students – 'so they could keep an eye on each other', he said. But for a gay man who had grown up under such a sexually repressive regime, even early-80s Leicester seemed a bit of a paradise. He 'made friends' with another student on his course and he used some of his allowance to buy the occasional gay newspaper.

At some point during his stay he received news that his wife had died so he sought permission to return for her funeral. It was refused. Presumably, to the bureaucratic mind he had no good reason to return. She was dead now so why waste time when he could be getting on with his studies.

Throughout our time in the cafe he continued to glance at the windows: he was worried that one of the other Chinese students might walk past and recognise him, he said. Then he explained why he was so worried about being spotted.

He had felt that the other students were beginning to suspect him, not necessarily of being gay but up to something, nonetheless. The basis of this suspicion, he felt, was the fact that he kept himself apart from the other students whenever possible. Initially he tried to tell himself that he was just imagining it; that trying to conceal what little gay life he had was making him paranoid. But then, out of the blue, he received a letter from the Chinese Embassy telling him he was to return home immediately. No explanation was given. And this only a few months after his own application to return for his wife's funeral had been so bluntly rejected.

Now *I* was beginning to glance over at the steamed-up windows – although I had no idea what I was looking for! And my Chinese companion was becoming increasingly anxious about someone seeing him.

We talked for a little while longer. He told me that his 'friend' was from somewhere in the Middle East and was convinced that if he could just find his way there everything would be fine. It seemed like a bit of a 'happily ever after' fantasy to me: there seemed to be no consideration of the practicalities of getting there – nor the likely reaction of his family to their son's penniless Chinese boyfriend. Nor, indeed, did the boyfriend seem to be offering any kind of practical assistance.

So, under increasing pressure and in the absence of anything more constructive, my Chinese friend had done a runner from the student house. This was a true indication of just how desperate he must have been: this act would also have put him in breach of his visa conditions and, in consequence, made him an 'illegal'. Now the British would deport him – if the Chinese didn't drag him home first.

And there's no doubt that the Thatcher government would have deported him: asylum applications on the basis of sexual orientation would have been rejected out of hand. Even Amnesty International didn't see persecution on the grounds of sexual orientation as a valid human rights issue until the 1990s.

So now he was renting a room in a boarding house and working as a dishwasher in a Chinese restaurant in order to pay the rent.

Somewhere along the line he had been told that the then West German government had a policy of accepting all asylum seekers from communist countries. That appeared to be the only ray of hope and he had contacted the West German Embassy in London. They had, as I understood it, issued him with an entry visa. However, it was time limited and, by time we met, there were only a couple of days left.

He explained that he had already made one attempt to get to West Germany but – evidently – without success. Given that this was well before the days of cheap flights, he had taken a ferry across to mainland Europe with the intention of continuing to West Germany over land. Unfortunately, he only got as far as the Netherlands where he was turned back because he didn't have the right paperwork to enter that country. And, of

26

course, he'd used up some of the little money he had on the travel costs so he now had a financial setback as well.

At some point in our conversation his edginess got the better of him and he asked if we could go somewhere less public. I suggested the School of Social Work again but he wasn't keen and suggested, instead, we go back to his boarding house. And despite everything he had just told me, I suddenly wondered if there was an ulterior motive.

It's quite hard to make a decision in those circumstances. On the one hand this man may have been fighting for his freedom and his future – if what he said was true. On the other, I could be some gullible sap who was being set up for something nasty.

In the end I decided to give him the benefit of the doubt. He surely couldn't be planning to rob me: if he had any intelligence at all – which he undoubtedly did – he would know that, as a student, I didn't have a lot of money. It also seemed a rather elaborate set-up for that – or, indeed, any sort of physical or sexual assault. And even though I was pretty skinny back in those days, I really felt I could handle any possible attack from this diminutive, slightly stooped man.

I was further reassured when he told me where the boarding house was: I knew that area like the back of my hand, having lived there for three years while undertaking my first degree. It was on a busy road in a pretty safe area.

Nonetheless, I still felt obliged to give him a little warning that he'd better not be thinking of any funny stuff; I knew my way around this area better than him, I knew people who lived on that street (an absolute lie) and so on. He, in turn, reassured me that his motives were pure and he just wanted to avoid discovery by one of the Chinese students. And so we left the cafe and headed off to the boarding house, continuing our conversation as we went.

I asked him what I could do to help and he said there was nothing I could do. So I asked him why he had contacted me. He said it was because he wanted to meet someone who was 'brave enough' to publicly declare himself to be gay. That in itself had given him some reassurance that it wasn't 'wrong' or 'sick' to be gay.

With my ego expanding at a rate of knots, we arrived at the boarding house and went to his room. He didn't have a gang of thieves waiting to mug me, he didn't pull out a knife and threaten me with it, he simply gave me the one chair in the room then sat on the edge of his bed and we talked further.

27

He told me he intended to try the ferry again the next day, hopeful that he might get a different response from Netherlands immigration officials. I didn't think there was much chance of that and asked why he didn't fly direct to West Germany. I already knew the answer, of course, but he told me anyway – he didn't have enough money for the air ticket.

So I took a deep breath ... and offered to pay for it. And he instantly refused. So we talked around the issue again, in the vain hope that I might be able to identify some other possibility that I'd missed previously. It didn't work.

Then suddenly he lunged at me from the edge of the bed! He grabbed my head in his hands, kissed me on the forehead ... then sat back down again!

This sudden turn of events left me a little shaken and I struggled to find the right response. *"If you ... You said ... I told you ..."* I don't think I ever finished a sentence. The reality was that it (whatever 'it' was) was over and done with. There was no follow up action; he was back on the edge of the bed, remorseful and apologetic.

He told me something similar to what he'd said earlier: this time he'd just wanted to kiss a man who was quite open about being gay. He promised it wouldn't happen again – and I believed him (although still felt obliged to make all sorts of indignant noises about what I'd do if it did!).

The evening was now beginning to wear on, and I had still to catch a train back home to Nottingham, so I made one more offer to pay his airfare. I would, I added, need to see some sort of proof that he was who he said he was before I did so, of course.

He obliged by showing me his passport, which I inspected thoroughly – even though I didn't really know what I was looking for. I think I was able to confidently conclude that he was, indeed, Chinese but I honestly can't remember anything else – including whether or not there was a West German visa therein. Nonetheless, I reiterated my offer. And this time he accepted, reassuring me that he'd send me the money from West Germany as soon as he was able to.

Things finally seemed to be looking up and I told him we would need to meet again the next day as my cheque book was at home (we didn't have cash dispenser machines in those days). For some reason this proved to be an insurmountable obstacle for him. He wanted to leave Leicester first thing the next day and couldn't wait around until 9:30 a.m. when the banks opened. He politely thanked me for my concern, declined my offer

28

and advised me that he would stick to his original plan with the ferries.

Nothing I could say would persuade him otherwise so, in the end, I simply had to take my leave. He walked with me to the railway station, which was only a couple of blocks from the boarding house. By this time it had started snowing quite heavily with large, fluffy snowflakes that had already formed a significant covering on the ground.

He walked into the station and up to the ticket barrier with me. Then we said our final words: I asking him to reconsider, he politely declining and thanking me for my time and concern. Then he turned around, walked through one of the station's large Victorian archways and out into a dense flurry of falling snow. It was such a cinematic image I half expected film credits to start rolling before my eyes!

I never saw or heard from the man again so have no idea what happened next: nor was I ever able to establish the veracity of his story. On the one hand I think that the whole thing was too elaborate to be concocted. On the other, I question some elements from time to time. For example, if the West German embassy in London really felt that someone was deserving of a visa for asylum wouldn't they also help them get there too – or help organise a transit visa through the Netherlands?

But I wasn't hurt – physically or emotionally – nor was I exploited in any way. All it cost me was some of my time, which I was happy to give to anyone who was experiencing difficulties around their sexuality. That's a very small price to pay for something that may have had life changing consequences.

But, of course, I do still wonder what happened to him.

References

1. Campaign for Homosexual Equality Commission on Discrimination. 1980. *Attacks on Gay People*. London.

2. Anon. *National Coming Out Day*. [Online] Human Rights Campaign website. Available at
    http://www.hrc.org/resources/entry/national-coming-out-day
    Accessed August 2014.

3. Williams, Peter. I Saw Rock Wed Man. *News of the World,* London. 4 August 1985.

4. Ellis, Richard. I Lost Rock to James Dean says Liz. *The Sun*, London. 31 August 1985.

5. Ellis, Richard. AIDS Killer Stalks Hollywood. *The Sun*, London. 29 August 1985.

6. Willows, Terry. Kiss of Death. *The Star*, London. 27 September 1985.

7. See, for example, Morrison, Blake. Birthday Boy. *The Guardian*, London. 7 May 2009.

8. Watts, Michael. Oh You Pretty Thing. *Melody Maker*, London. 22 January 1972.

9. Sandford, Christopher. 1996. *Bowie: Loving the Alien*. London: Da Capo Press, p48.

10. Collis, Clark. 2002. *Dear Superstar: David Bowie*. [Online] Blender.com, August. Available at
    http://www.bowiewonderworld.com/press/00/0208dearsuperstar.htm
    Accessed August 2014.

11. See, for example, Hood, D. 1994. *Report on Bisexual Activity/Non-Gay Attachment Research (BANGAR)*. National Centre in HIV Epidemiology and Clinical Research, Sydney, Australia.

12. Gochros, J. 1989. *When Husbands Come Out of the Closet*. New York: Harrington Park Press.

13. US Immigration and Naturalization Service Resource Information Centre. 2001. *China: Information on Treatment of Homosexuals*. Washington D.C.

Part Two - Painting a Clearer Picture of Queer Reality

While discrimination and harassment has been a feature of queer life for centuries, the 1980s was the first decade where this began to be extensively documented. For example, by the end of the decade, statistics on homophobic violence were routinely collected by government agencies in the UK, USA and Australia.

One reason for this was an increasing number of queer organisations, as well as better administration on their part.

In the UK alone, the early 80s saw reports on issues such as workplace discrimination (for example, the Campaign for Homosexual Equality (CHE), 1981, and London's Lesbian and Gay Employment Rights Group, 1986); lesbian mothers (Rights of Women Lesbian Custody Group, 1986), the experience of young people (Joint Council of Gay Teenagers, 1980, London Gay Teenage Group, 1984), homophobic violence (CHE), 1980, and homophobia within police forces (Gay London Police Monitoring Group (GALOP) annually from 1984 onwards).

At the same time, more non-queer organisations were also taking up queer issues: for example, trades unions were increasingly fighting for queer equality and, in the process, evidencing the nature of discrimination.

In the UK, significant numbers of Labour-controlled councils not only funded organisations but actively researched the needs of queer people themselves. Probably the best known example of this is the Greater London Council (GLC), which funded projects such as the Rights of Women Lesbian Custody Group but also undertook their own research; most notably the 1985 project *Changing the World: A London Charter for Lesbian and Gay Rights.*

This involved extensive research into a range of areas including health, ageing, parenting and adoption, employment and the law, and culminated in the publication of a charter with 142 specific recommendations for action in these and other areas.

The continued growth of queer media during the 80s also offered increased outlets for the dissemination of information on both the individual and collective queer experience.

The increasingly detailed picture that was being painted in the 80s certainly wasn't pretty but it was crucial in informing the campaigns for change. The extent of the discrimination, the frequency of the violence, the depth of institutionalised homophobia, now so clearly evidenced, all offered a powerful retort to those who dismissed queer rights as trivial or irrelevant.

Violence

Violence has been an intrinsic part of the queer experience for centuries and the emergence of HIV/AIDS triggered an upsurge. In his 1986 book *AIDS and the New Puritanism*, for example, Dennis Altman recalled an episode while working on an AIDS helpline. A call came in from a young man, concerned about possibly contracting AIDS – because he and his friends had just beaten up a man with the disease [1].

One of the first studies to look at anti-gay violence in the UK was the Campaign for Homosexual Equality's 1980 report *Attacks on Gay People*. This identified more than 250 cases of assault in Great Britain and Northern Ireland over a three year period – and speculated that there were a lot more that had gone unreported. Its findings included the fact that:

"... about one in eight [attacks] led to the death or disablement of the victim." [2]

These experiences were certainly not unique to the UK. In the USA, for example, a 1989 analysis of hate crime data concluded that 92 per cent of lesbian and gay survey participants had been the subject of verbal abuse or threats and 24 per cent had been physically assaulted [3]. In Australia, a 1980 survey by the New South Wales Anti-Discrimination Board found that 54 per cent of respondents had experienced verbal abuse and 35 per cent physical violence [4]. A 1988 survey by the Gay and Lesbian Rights Lobby in Sydney found that three quarters of all assaults on lesbians and gay men resulted in physical injuries, but only half were reported to the police [5].

A reluctance to go to the police was a common finding. For example, the CHE report stated:

"... it is clear that most attacks are not reported. One reason is that victims are afraid they themselves will be 'on trial' as much as their attackers. This fear is to some extent justified. In extreme cases victims who reported assaults have been charged with sexual offences, being drunk and disorderly or even 'wasting police time'." [6]

In Australia:

"Attempts by NSW police to gather data on violence in the mid to late 1980s proved

useful as an initial step in getting 'the community' to report incidents, but the long mistrust between police and gay men was seen as a factor that led to under-reporting."
[7]

The mistrust was well-founded; a 2005 coronial inquest into the deaths of a number of gay men near a well-known Sydney beat (a meeting place for men looking for sex with other men) during the 1980s recorded a catalogue of police disinterest and antipathy. This included failure to undertake basic procedures such as taking crime scene photos but also losing vital evidence such as samples of hair found in the hand of one of the victims [8].

In the UK, the first annual report of the Gay London Police Monitoring Group (GALOP) included a number of case studies, including that of 'Larry':

"GALOP was contacted by Larry the day after he received a black eye and a fractured skull. He had been in a well-known gay pub in South London when eight straight men started attacking the customers. Larry went outside where there were two police vans and three police cars.

When Larry asked a policeman to stop the fighting and protect the customers being attacked, the policeman had said: 'What do you expect? You're a queer in a queer's pub.' Larry reminded the police that his taxes paid that policeman's wages. Larry was then told to 'fuck off, before I nick you for drunk and disorderly."[9]

In the Hands of the Law

Police hostility and failure to act was common, but so too were deliberate strategies to procure arrests. British [10] and Australian [11] police both used attractive young policemen in plain clothes to flirt with gay men at well-known cruising spots.

The memoirs of a former Sydney policeman, for example, include the following:

"At these toilets and in the case of Greens [sic] Park, the poofs would stand at the urinal and play with themselves hoping the person standing beside them would react favourably. The Peanut Squad used young police in jeans and a casual shirt to act as agents provocateur, in that they stood beside the person at the urinal and waited to be propositioned." [12]

In the UK, a 1984 GALOP report described the experience of 'Douglas' who was approached by a young man wearing a fitted T-shirt and tight jeans on leaving a well-known gay pub in London's Earls Court. The young man smiles at Douglas and ...

"They begin a conversation; the young man questions Douglas very directly: does Douglas want to fuck or does he just want a blow job. Douglas is hesitant to talk about sex immediately and suggests they go back to Douglas's place south of the river. The young man says that is too far to go – he has a place around the corner. They walk up Warwick Road and when they reach Nevern Square Douglas has his arm put behind his back and the young man and a third man identify themselves as police officers and Douglas is arrested. At Earls Court police station he is charged with persistently importuning." (13)

'Importuning for immoral purposes' was an offence created in Victorian times to prevent 'stage door Johnnies' harassing showgirls as they left the theatre. Despite the fact that 'stage door Johnnies' had disappeared many decades ago the 'offence' was retained – and used exclusively against gay men. The tactic was so common (the 1984 GALOP report alone contains another five case studies) it was known within the queer community as 'the pretty police' and, obviously, it used allegations of importuning for sexual favours in order to gain convictions.

But police were happy to arrest people for far tamer 'offences' than that. On 24 January 1984, for example, police – wearing rubber gloves – entered the Royal Vauxhall Tavern pub in South East London and arrested 11 men for *"being drunk on licensed premises"*.

In 1986, police arrested two men leaving a pub in London's West End and charged them with *"insulting behaviour contrary to the Metropolitan Police Act 1839"*(14).

The 'insulting behaviour' was kissing (which the defendants denied doing anyway). Despite being acquitted of the charges, the men were still bound over to keep the peace for 18 months.

In London's crowded Piccadilly Circus two young gay men wearing gay badges were arrested for obstruction. When they asked why they had been singled out from the many hundreds of people present, the arresting officer had replied, *"Well. You're woolly woofters, aren't you?"* (15)

Further north, in Manchester, the notoriously homophobic Chief Constable James Anderton conducted a vigorous harassment campaign that included attempts to charge nightclub patrons with 'licentious dancing'.

34

All of these actions took place in the UK where homosexuality was – technically at least – no longer a crime, thus necessitating the revival of outdated legislation in order to sustain their attacks. In Australia, on the other hand, where decriminalisation was only just getting underway in the 80s, police persecution was a much more straightforward affair. It involved raiding gay men's clubs and charging the patrons with 'indecent assault' (that is, having consensual intimate contact with each other).

Such was the case with Club 80, a gay men's club in Sydney, which was raided by police on a number of occasions in 1983. In January of that year 300 men were detained on the premises during a raid, then 30 of them were taken to the local police station, with six men eventually being charged. Despite a 1000-strong protest rally on 5 February, the police returned on 26 February, charging a further 11 men. In May, the club was declared a 'disorderly house' and closed.

By August another men's club had been raided, another 11 men charged and two gay discos were closed for alleged licensing breaches.

In the USA, the *Report of the Independent Commission on the Los Angeles Police Department* documented a history of entrenched homophobia.

This included the facts that police were more aggressive in enforcing minor infractions against suspected homosexuals than against presumed heterosexuals and that they were not averse to assaulting men just for the sake of it:

"It's easier to thump a faggot than an average Joe. Who cares?" [16]

Even in the supposedly enlightened city of San Francisco, rabid police homophobia surfaced as late as 1989 in the form of the so-called 'Castro Sweep'. The Castro District is well-known as San Francisco's long-standing queer heartland. Yet in October of that year, the Bay Area Reporter described how police had responded to a peaceful demonstration by the AIDS Coalition to Unleash Power (ACT UP) with *"bloodied heads, mass arrests and the spectre of fully armed riot police marching through the heart of the Castro, sweeping demonstrators and confused passers-by from the streets and sidewalks."* [17]

The incident began when police insisted that ACT UP protestors march on the sidewalk and not the road. When ACT UP's tactical coordinator stepped off the sidewalk to talk to the commanding officer he was thrown to the ground, handcuffed and taken away. When marchers reached Castro Street they found their way blocked by lines of police in riot gear. With nowhere else to go, the protestors sat down in the middle of Castro Street.

35

Within a matter of minutes police swept down the street, clubbing people at random and threatening to arrest anyone who did not get off the street immediately. By the end of the evening 53 people had been arrested and 10 civilians and four police officers had been injured. The scale and aggression of the police response left the community in shock.

Responding to Violence and Police Harassment

On the face of it, it seemed like little had changed in relation to the levels of violence and police harassment as we entered the 80s. But things were beginning to change – and quite rapidly in some cases – because our communities got better organised to take a stand against these types of hostilities.

In London, for example, the Gay London Police Monitoring Group (GALOP) was established in 1982 in an attempt to monitor police and hold them accountable for their actions. Despite a lack of legal powers – the Metropolitan Police were accountable only to the UK government's Home Secretary – their mere existence flagged up to the police that they were being watched and that every individual episode of police harassment was being documented and publicised.

Eight years later, as a consequence of police inaction over the April 1989 murder of a gay man [18], a number of gay activists including Peter Tatchell and Simon Watney established the direct action group Outrage!

In Sydney, activists responded to the repeated club raids by challenging the government head on. In September 1983, more than 20 gay men gathered at Sydney Gay Centre and signed Statutory Declarations that they had had sex with another, named, man. Two of them – Lex Watson and Robert French – then presented theirs in person to the head of the New South Wales vice squad and waited to be arrested. The plan was that if they got arrested the other men would then submit their declarations.

But they weren't arrested and were sent home while the head of the vice squad pondered what action should be taken. Shortly afterwards, the two men were advised that no action was to be taken against them. Indeed, there were no further police actions against any of Sydney's gay men's clubs either and nine months later, on 8 June 1984, homosexuality was finally decriminalised in New South Wales.

In 1988, the Gay and Lesbian Rights Lobby, Lesbian Line and the Gay and

36

Lesbian Counselling Service together launched the Streetwatch project to collect and analyse data about the physical and verbal abuse of queer people as a first step towards tackling the problem.

In Los Angeles, a Lesbian and Gay Advisory Board was established in February 1989 in an attempt to address the rampant homophobia within the Los Angeles Police Department. Founded by long-time activist Ivy Bottini, it was (and remains) an official body of the LAPD.

In San Francisco, the Police Department moved swiftly and decisively to repair the immense damage to community relations resulting from the Castro Sweep. Senior police officers were suspended, demoted or assigned other duties, new policies on police liaison with queer communities were brought in, and a number of people received payment for damages from the city.

Lesbian and gay self-defence classes were set up in cities across the UK, USA and Australia. And, borrowing a strategy adopted by women's groups, people were encouraged to carry whistles and use them when they felt they were in danger.

Attempts were also made in some cities to establish self-defence groups to patrol queer neighbourhoods, such as Sydney's Oxford Street and its environs. These seem to have reflected a global trend at that time of citizen vigilante groups, the most famous of which was the Guardian Angels. And like many of the Guardian Angels groups, the queer self-defence groups were also short-lived, not least because of concerns that they might actually attract, rather than deter, people who were looking for trouble.

Employment: Out At Work – Then Out of Work

In September 1981 the UK's Campaign for Homosexual Equality's 'Commission on Discrimination' released a second report – this time a study of workplace discrimination entitled *What About the Gay Workers: A Report of the Commission on Discrimination* [19]. It included an extensive list of cases where lesbians and gay men had lost their jobs because of their sexuality, beginning with *Eight Famous Cases*.

The 'Famous Eight' included Ian Davies, a Principal Area Officer in Social Services who had been dismissed following conviction for 'gross indecency' and Tony Whitehead, a trainee manager at British Home Stores who was forced to resign following his appearance in a television documentary about homosexuals. Despite the fact that neither Whitehead nor his employers had been named in the programme, his employers argued that their customers might be offended. No complaints were ever received from customers.

The year before the publication of the CHE report I had been working as a residential childcare worker. I had been open about my sexuality at interview but, on appointment, was advised by the Service Director not to come out as people would immediately assume I was a child molester and my position would become untenable. This ultimately proved to be a bitter irony since this same Service Director – a man named Frank Beck – achieved national notoriety in 1991 when he was sentenced to a record five life terms of imprisonment for the sexual assault of more than 100 children in his care.

But this perception of queer people as predatory or exploitative was widespread within the caring industries. And even though my own experience told me that there were large numbers of queer people working in this field, there was relatively little openness; due largely to the perceived vulnerability of our patients/clients and the prevailing stereotype.

Such was the case in 1980, for example, when an employment tribunal in Scotland heard the case of John Saunders, a handyman who had been sacked by the Scottish National Camp Association, simply because he was gay. His employers ran residential camps for young people and claimed they had received 'confidential but anonymous' information that Saunders had 'homosexual tendencies'. Saunders did not deny this when questioned about it – and was promptly sacked. His employers refused to provide details of the anonymous information they had received, nor were they able to produce any evidence of wrong-doing, complaints or accusations against him. A psychiatrist examined Saunders and reported that he was *"no more likely to wish a sexual relationship with children than a heterosexual"*. Nonetheless, the employment tribunal dismissed his appeal on the grounds that 'a reasonable employer' might consider a homosexual person 'a risk' (although the nature of this risk was neither specified nor quantified).

The following year Susan Shell – a night care attendant in a girls' hostel – was sacked by Barking Council simply because she was a lesbian. The council is recorded as having said:

"It is the responsibility of social services departments to encourage the socio-sexual norms of marriage for the young people in their care, and it was not prepared to debate the philosophy of homosexuality." [20]

The employment tribunal ruled in the Council's favour. Similarly, in 1982 Judith Williams was dismissed from a youth worker role simply on the grounds that she was a lesbian. Her employer had decided that this made her 'temperamentally unsuitable' and not a 'mature, stable adult who identifies with the conventional adult model normally accepted by society'.

In 1984, the Conservative-led Rugby Council declared that they would remove sexual orientation from their equal opportunities policy. Various councillors issued statements of breath-taking ignorance, including one who declared all homosexuals to be *"vile and perverted people"* and Council leader Gordon Collett, who stated: *"We're not having men turn up for work in dresses and earrings."*

On 28 September 1984, *The Sun* newspaper ran an editorial congratulating 'the brave little town' of Rugby for standing up to *"the sick nonsense"* of gay rights. It concluded with: *"Let's ALL follow Rugby in fighting back."*

But even when organisations did include sexual orientation in their equal opportunities policies, queers could still be at risk from entrenched homophobia. *What About the Gay Workers?* noted that:

"In many cases employers are not open about their reasons for discrimination. There can be few workers, whatever their sexuality, whom a determined management could not find some reason for dismissing." [21]

That was certainly the case of a gay friend of mine who worked as a residential childcare worker in Nottingham in 1982. His boss, unaware that he was gay, actually bragged to him that she would find a way around any equal opportunities policies in order to sack any employee she discovered to be gay.

Queer Parents
Fostering and Adoption

The myth of queer people as child molesters continued to influence decision-makers throughout the 80s, regardless of the lack of supporting evidence and the abundance of challenging evidence.

For queers seeking to adopt or foster children in Australia, the situation was simply impossible until the beginning of the 21st century, with every state and territory maintaining a ban despite most of them having stringent anti-discrimination policies in place for all other aspects of queer life.

In the USA, the situation varied enormously on a state-by-state basis; influenced in part by the existence or otherwise of anti-sodomy laws, which effectively served as a marker for the level of discrimination against all homosexuals, male or female. Perhaps unsurprisingly, it was the state of California that saw Rebecca Smith and Annie Affleck become the country's first openly lesbian couple to legally adopt in 1986.

In the UK there was no legal ban on adoption and fostering by queer people but the sustained homophobia of the Conservative government, culminating in the notorious Section 28 of the 1988 Local Government Act, made most local authorities reluctant to support prospective queer parents.

A 1988 survey of prospective queer parents [22] found that most experienced prejudicial attitudes from adoption authorities. Applications generally took longer and the outcomes were usually much less favourable than those from non-queer people. A number of respondents reported that social workers demonstrated a serious lack of knowledge about queer people and many felt they had to try and correct the erroneous assumptions that social workers made. Even when queer people were successful in their applications, a disproportionately high number were allocated children with severe cognitive or physical disabilities; those who were traditionally hard to place elsewhere. As one respondent put it, it seemed to be a case of "second class children for second class carers".

The fact that Section 28 refers to homosexual couples as *"a pretended family relationship"* made the government's position very clear. This was soon reflected in a 1990 consultation paper on family placement under the 1989 Children's Act, which stated:

"... the chosen way of life of some adults may mean that they would not be able to provide a suitable environment for the care and nurture of the child. No one has a 'right' to be a foster parent. 'Equal rights' and 'gay rights' policies have no place in fostering services." [23]

'Gay rights' was removed from the final policy paper but the term 'chosen way of life' remained.

Michael Dukakis' 'No-Queer' Adoption Policy

But even where there was declared political commitment to queer rights, the reality was somewhat different when it came to implementing them. Nowhere was this more obvious than in the state of Massachusetts under the governorship of Michael Dukakis, the 1988 Democratic presidential candidate.

In 1980 the National Convention of the US Democrats had finally voted to support queer rights. Dukakis, however, chose to tread another path altogether; not only failing to support queer rights but making it very clear that he saw homosexuals as inferior to heterosexuals. This translated into some extraordinarily discriminative behaviour during his time as Governor of Massachusetts, not least of which was his active hostility to queer fostering and adoption.

One particularly notorious example was that of David Jean and Donald Babets, two professional men in a long-term relationship who sought to become foster parents in 1984 [24]. They were subject to an extensive evaluation process that included repeated interviews and home visits and an investigation of their standing and reputations both at work and within the local community. The Department's assessment took twice as long as it usually did but the couple still came through with flying colours so, in April 1984, two young boys aged 3 and 2 were placed in their care, with the written approval of the boys' birth mother.

But a few days later, after informing neighbours and community leaders about the placement, the *Boston Globe* ran a front page headline *"Some Oppose Foster Placement with Gay Couple"*. The paper ignored the couple's pleas not to run the story; their reporter subsequently commenting:

"Babets suggested to me that if I did the story the kids would be taken out of the home. I wasn't persuaded of that. He was."

And Babets was right. On the morning the story was published the couple was contacted by Social Services Commissioner, Marie Matava, to reassure them that the children would not be taken from the home.

In the afternoon, Department officials removed the children from the home.

Governor Dukakis' response was to deny all knowledge of the state making foster placements with queer foster parents. This was patently untrue: the use of gay or lesbian foster parents had been acknowledged in a report that he himself commissioned from the state's Department of Public Welfare in 1976.

41

Then, on 14 May 1984 the state's House of Representatives passed a resolution calling for an outright ban on lesbian and gay fostering, adoption, guardianship, family day care and respite care.

The following day the Secretary of Human Services, Philip Johnston, announced the state's new policy on adoption in which 'non-traditional' placements – single people and same-sex couples – were to be considered only if it could be clearly demonstrated that there was absolutely no other option for the child. It would also be necessary for them to be approved directly by the Department of Social Services Commissioner. And, just for good measure, all future applicants would be required to answer a question about their sexual orientation.

The measures were roundly condemned by every agency and organisation involved in childcare, as well as professionals and professional bodies like the Massachusetts Psychiatric Society, the North East Council of Child Protection and the National Association of Social Workers. And the Deputy Commissioner of Social Services resigned in protest.

This didn't stop Governor Dukakis and the Social Services Department insisting that the new policy was based on recommendations from child welfare experts.

The move pushed the state's foster services into crisis.

Social Services Commissioner Marie Matava admitted the state needed 25 per cent more homes to meet demand. In December 1985, a report of the State Legislative Sub-committee on Foster Care found that 750 children were in inappropriate or emergency accommodation. They also found that 50–58 per cent of state and private placement agencies had significant waiting lists.

Meanwhile, the Reverend Kathryn Piccard, who had been a foster parent for six years and cared for 17 children in that time, was removed from the list of approved applicants after she refused to answer the sexual orientation question prior to being approved for the 18th child.

Nor were there any further placements of children with gay or lesbian households.

In January 1986 David and Donald joined other plaintiffs in a suit against Governor Michael Dukakis and the Department of Social Services claiming the new policy:

"... created an arbitrary and irrational presumption that all unmarried couples and single persons, even those with parenting experience, are always less suitable as

42

foster parents than married couples (even those without parenting experience)."

In the course of the proceedings, the state tried – unsuccessfully – to block a request for access to documents relating to David and Donald's case. To no one's surprise, the documents revealed that the children had been taken away from David and Donald purely for political reasons: no expert opinion had ever been sought.

The battle dragged on for a number of years, during which Dukakis maintained his position that heterosexual couples were the 'normal' and therefore most appropriate option – even during his 1988 US presidential campaign. In 1990 both parties agreed to compromise rather than face even more years of ongoing argument.

The policy was amended so that the third and fourth priorities for adoption now read:

"Placement in family foster care with a married couple with parenting experience and with time available for parenting or with a person with parenting experience and with time available for parenting.

Placement in family foster care with a married couple without parenting experience and with time available for parenting or with a person without parenting experience and with time available."

The new wording hardly welcomed queer carers with open arms but it was accompanied by another change: the decision as to who could and could not foster was put back into the hands of caseworkers. It had taken six years to restore some sense of objectivity to Massachusetts' adoption services.

The Bias Against Biological Parents

Queer people seeking to adopt children weren't the only ones facing obstacles. Even queer people who were the biological parents of children – usually conceiving them during an earlier, heterosexual relationship – faced breath-taking ignorance and prejudice in matters of child custody.

For example, in 1985 Virginia's Supreme Court decided that that state's anti-sodomy laws provided sufficient justification for denying a gay father custody [25].

Two years later, in the case of *S.E.G. v. R.A.G.*, the Missouri Appeals Court didn't even need a specific law to deny custody: it ruled that 'societal prejudice was sufficient reason to deny child custody to a lesbian mother.' This despite the presiding judge,

Gary M. Gaertner, declaring that: *"we are not presuming that she would make an uncaring mother."*

Even when custody was awarded to the queer parent, it often came with restrictions that were so severe they effectively required the parent to deny their sexuality in order to keep their child. For example, a 1986 survey by the UK's Rights of Women Lesbian Custody Group discovered that:

"... mothers had been instructed to, for instance, behave in a 'suitable manner' in front of their children, have no contact with their lovers, and not tell their children they were lesbians." [26]

In other words, custody would only be granted to lesbians if they effectively stopped being lesbians.

References

1. Altman, Dennis. 1986. *AIDS and the New Puritanism*. London: Pluto Press.

2. Campaign for Homosexual Equality Commission on Discrimination. 1980. *Attacks on Gay People*. London.

3. Herek, G.M. 1989. Hate crimes against lesbians and gay men: Issues for research and policy. *American Psychologist*, 44 (6), 948-955.

4. Anti-Discrimination Board of NSW. 1980. *Discrimination and Homosexuality*. Sydney, Australia.

5. Cox, G. 1990. *The Streetwatch Report: A Study into Violence Against Lesbians and Gay Men*. Sydney: Gay and Lesbian Rights Lobby.

6. *Attacks on Gay People*.

7. Allen, George. 2008. *Hate Crimes against Lesbians and Gay Men in New South Wales: Accumulated Knowledge of Victimisation via Five Reports*. Paper presented to the Law and Society Association Australia and New Zealand Conference, 10-12 December, University of Sydney, p3.

8. Davis, Kristen. 2007. *Bondi's underbelly: the 'gay gang' murders*. [Online] Available at www.academia.edu/2439187/Bondis_underbelly_the_gay_gang_murders Accessed February 2015.

9. Gay London Police Monitoring Group (GALOP). 1984. *First Annual Report*. London.

10. GALOP *First Annual Report*.

11. Granland, Ian. *A Story of life's adventures*. [Online] Electronic archives at Australian War Memorial. Available at http://pandora.nla.gov.au/tep/57651] Accessed August 2014.

12. *A Story of life's adventures*.

13. GALOP *First Annual Report*.

14. Gay London Police Monitoring Group (GALOP). 1987. *3rd Annual Report: 1986-87*. London.

45

15. GALOP *First Annual Report*.

16. Christopher, Warren (ed). 1991. *Report of the Independent Commission on the Los Angeles Police Department*. Los Angeles: DIANE Publishing, p91.

17. Averill, Brett. Castro Held Hostage. *Bay Area Reporter*. 12 October 1989.

18. The murder of Michael Boothe was one of ten murders of gay men or transsexuals examined by the independent Lesbian Gay Bisexual Transgender Advisory Group in 2007. The Group's subsequent report highlighted entrenched homophobia and transphobia in the Metropolitan Police Force. In the case of Michael Boothe, the report concluded that the killings might not have occurred if previous attacks had been investigated seriously.

19. Campaign for Homosexual Equality Commission on Discrimination. 1981. *What About the Gay Workers? A Report of the Commission on Discrimination*. London.

20. Davis, L. 1993. *Sex and the Social Worker*. London: Janus Publishing Company.

21. *What About the Gay Workers?*

22. Skeates, J. Jabri, J (eds). 1988. *Fostering and Adoption by Lesbians and Gay Men*. London: London Strategy Unit.

23. Department of Health. 1990. *Consultation paper on family placement under the 1989 Children's Act*, Paragraph 16. London.

24. Ricketts, Wendell. 1991. *Lesbians and Gay Men as Foster Parents*. Maine: University of Southern Maine.

25. *Roe v. Roe*. 1985. Virginia Supreme Court.

26. Rights of Women Lesbian Custody Group survey. 1986. Quoted in *From outsiders to motherhood to reinventing the family: constructions of lesbian parenting in the psychological literature 1886-2006*. Victoria Clarke, School of Psychology, University of the West of England. Bristol. 2008.

Part Three - Reaching a Wider Audience

While coming out and detailed reportage of the queer experience certainly played their role in raising the profile of lesbians and gay men, it was the arts and media where queer visibility really took off. Film, television, literature and music saw a huge increase in the representation of, and participation by, queer people.

And what was particularly important about this was the global availability of these media. The film and television industries were already global enterprises; an increase in both terrestrial and cable television networks created new, overseas markets for the likes of Channel 4's *Out on Tuesday* and Showtime's *Brothers*. In literature, the growth of queer publishing houses and, in the UK, the resolution of importation restrictions following the Gay's the Word trial, also increased the profile and availability of queer materials.

Film
The Mainstream Studios

The 1980s kicked off with one of the largest protests ever seen against the representation of queer people in film. The protests were triggered by the filming and subsequent release of United Artists' movie *Cruising* and they were particularly significant because it was the first time a film had triggered protests by activists around the world. Cinemas in cities as diverse as London, Manchester, Sydney, Melbourne and San Francisco were picketed, while New York saw active disruption of filming as well as subsequent cinema protests.

In 1980, activists likened *Cruising* to *Birth of a Nation*, a film that demonised black people and lauded white supremacists such as the Ku Klux Klan. Leaflets produced by protestors declared that *"people will die because of this movie"* and that *"sexual violence does not come from gay people as the film suggests – but from heterosexual queer-bashers, fascists and police"*.

Protests had begun more or less from the moment shooting started because the book on which it was based already had a bad reputation. Written by former New York detective Gerald Walker about a real series of gay murders in the city, it had been condemned for stereotyping gay men as well as implying that the victims got what they

47

deserved. Even before filming had begun *Village Voice* columnist Arthur Bell claimed that the film would be *"the most oppressive, ugly, bigoted look at homosexuality ever presented on the screen"* and called for his readers to *"give Friedkin and his production a terrible time if you spot them in your neighbourhood"*[1].

And that's exactly what they did. Despite director William Friedkin's assurances that the movie would not be a replication of the book, activists did their best to disrupt the filming. Their tactics included renting apartments next to the shoot location then blasting loud music from the windows and using mirrors to deflect the sun's rays to disrupt lighting set-ups. These were so effective that the entire exterior soundtrack had to be re-recorded in post-production.

When the movie finally hit the screens it brought further criticism. Central to this was that it reinforced the notion of 'contamination'; that is, people who have regular contact with homosexuals will turn into homosexuals. This was an argument that homophobes such as Anita Bryant had used repeatedly throughout the 70s to justify discrimination against gays. Thus, the movie begins with a heterosexual cop (played by Al Pacino) going undercover in New York's gay S&M scene in order to track down a serial killer. In the course of the movie it appears that Pacino's character is starting to develop homosexual feelings himself: for example, on one occasion he is discovered naked and bound to a bed in a gay man's apartment – something that is definitely 'over and above the call of duty'.

The movie ends with very strong suggestions that Pacino's character might be responsible for some of the murders himself. Thus we have the additional inference that by associating with homosexual S&M practitioners, Pacino's character has not only become a homosexual, he has also turned into a psychopath.

But *Cruising* wasn't the only 'homo-psycho' movie released in 1980. *Windows* – also from United Artists – was essentially a lesbian version of *Cruising* in as much as it reinforced the 'all homosexuals are borderline psychopaths' line. In this case the focus is a lesbian whose increasing infatuation with her (heterosexual) neighbour ends up getting nasty. This one failed to attract the attention of activists beyond the USA – possibly because the movie itself didn't get that far either. There were no big names associated with the film and its nomination for five Golden Raspberry Awards – Worst Picture, Worst Screenplay, Worst Actress, Worst Supporting Actress and Worst Director

48

– can also be taken as a good indicator of its quality. Even the director – Gordon Willis – decided never to direct another movie again after his involvement with this one.

The question remains as to whether the protests around *Cruising* or *Windows* had any discernible impact on Hollywood's output. It would be a further 12 years before another film –*Basic Instinct* – triggered protests on a similar scale to those seen with *Cruising*. In the meantime the big studios produced a very mixed bag.

In 1982, Paramount released *Partners. The New York Times* called it:

"Hollywood's latest crime against humanity in general and homosexuals in particular ... stupid, tasteless and homophobic, this sleazy, superficial film implies that gay cops can't be trusted to work with straight cops because they might fall in love with them." [2]

In this case Ryan O'Neal and (surprisingly) John Hurt play a pair of mismatched cops; the mismatch being their sexual orientations, of course. O'Neal is the straight cop forced to go undercover with gay cop Hurt to investigate – again – a series of murders of gay men. Lest there be any confusion about the tone of this 'comedy' the promotional poster declares, *"Benson is a cop who wants to clean up the streets ... His partner just wants to redecorate."* While the movie certainly didn't promote the notion of the psychopathic homosexual, it did present Hurt's character as swooning and ineffectual, struggling to keep his eyes off his 'hunky heterosexual' partner.

1982 also saw the release of *Personal Best* (Geffen/Warner Brothers), ostensibly a film about the on- and off-field relationship between two female athletes. Ultimately it ended up reinforcing the notion that lesbianism is just a phase that young women go through until the right man comes along – in this case a water polo player.

Although the love-making scenes were considered to be realistic rather than sensationalist, and some athletics fans considered the shots of the athletes in competition to be particularly realistic, the film still came across predominantly as a soft porn movie for straight men. This wasn't helped by the use of wet T-shirts in the movie's poster nor the addition of the wording *"as featured in the April edition of Playboy"* to the marketing material.

When it came to men's sexuality, however, it was a completely different story. *Making Love* (20th Century Fox), made in the same year as *Personal Best*, is a movie about two men – one of them married and closeted – falling in love and the

49

consequences for the married man's marriage. The sex scenes are very tame – indeed there is nothing more explicit than the two men shirtless and kissing. Nonetheless, the producers felt it necessary to screen an advance warning to the audience lest they be shocked by the content:

"MAKING LOVE deals openly and candidly with a delicate issue. It is not sexually explicit. But it may be too strong for some people."

No such warning was posted for *Personal Best*, even though the sex scenes are far more explicit than those in *Making Love*. According to *Making Love's* screenplay writer, Barry Sandler, people were squirming in their seats and walking out in disgust at the movie's premiere [3]: yet there were no reports of people doing the same during *Personal Best*, suggesting that, for the men at least, that's exactly what they came to see in the first place.

But, studio warning notwithstanding, *Making Love* didn't treat queers as psychopaths, predators or victims. The gay men were just typical people who happened to be attracted to each other and were able to move on with their lives without killing themselves or each other. This was also the case with United Artists' *Lianna* (1983), where a bored housewife falls in love with one of her college lecturers – who is neither predatory nor unhinged. The film then follows the consequences of that relationship, including the outraged husband denying Lianna access to their two children and the college lecturer returning to her long-term lover. Some of the scenes do have the subtlety of a sledgehammer but, that notwithstanding, the issues raised are explored in a non-judgemental and non-stereotyping fashion without the lesbianism being portrayed as the central problem.

While *Lianna's* somewhat depressing storyline and absence of high profile cast members led to limited exposure, another movie from 1983 – *The Hunger* (Metro-Goldwyn-Mayer) – had a star-studded cast that brought in the crowds. It also brought in significant criticism for its portrayal of queer people – in this case lesbians – as predatory. A film about female vampire Miriam (Catherine Deneuve) who needs to acquire 'new blood' in order to maintain eternal youth, it is most famous for its lesbian sex scene where Miriam seduces Sarah (Susan Sarandon). It's all soft-focus, billowing curtains and Delibe's *Flower Duet* as Miriam and Sarah unleash their passion. And it was this portrayal of the sex scene – essentially, as a straight man's lesbian fantasy – that got lesbian viewers offside, along with the familiar 'homosexual as predator' notion.

Then, in 1985, Steven Spielberg got his hands on Alice Walker's *The Color Purple* (Warner Brothers). Whereas earlier complaints about movie makers had centred on their portrayal of queer people, the problem with Spielberg was that he went out of his way to take the lesbians out of the storyline. More at home with mechanical sharks and little boys with alien chums, Spielberg couldn't bring himself to portray the lesbian relationship between two of the movie's principal characters. The physicality and eroticism of the relationship was filtered down to one passionate kiss. Spielberg has subsequently been quoted as admitting he was wrong to play down the lesbian relationship but also claiming he'd do the same again to ensure the movie's PG rating (and, no doubt, safeguard its $98m box office takings in the US alone). Alice Walker is known to have been disappointed by the exclusion of the lesbianism but has diplomatically said she likes the movie anyway – adding that it is very different from the book!

In fairness to Spielberg, however, it should be noted that not all of his films were completely devoid of homosexuals. 1981's *Indiana Jones and the Raiders of the Lost Ark* includes an early lecture room scene where most of his (female) students are watching Dr Jones in doe-eyed adoration. When the recess bell rings they all file out dreamily – then one male student strides quickly and nervously past Dr Jones' desk, puts an apple on it then rushes, eyes downcast, from the room. It's a blink-and-you'll-miss-it moment; a plot device inserted solely to further underline Indy's irresistible charisma. And certainly nothing to threaten the movie's PG rating.

The Independent Studios

While Hollywood continued to send out mixed messages, there was hope on the horizon in the form of the independent studios, which produced a much wider variety of movies about queers. Most of these played largely on the arthouse circuit but occasionally some of the major cinema chains were adventurous enough to take them on.

In a number of cases, it was queer people at the helm; one of the most notable being Donna Deitch who, in 1984, directed *Desert Hearts*, regarded by many as the 'breakout' lesbian movie of the 80s. Perhaps one reason for this is that the two main characters manage to resolve the various issues around their increasingly strong lesbian relationship without the intervention of a man! While their lesbianism is certainly relevant to the storyline it is society's reactions to that lesbianism that is seen as problematic (the film is set in 1959 America), not the relationship itself.

In terms of distribution, *Desert Hearts* was very much an arthouse, rather than cinema complex, kind of movie, but it still managed to gross $2 292 088 at the box office in the US, putting it ahead of *Windows* ($2 128 395) and *Lianna* ($1 530 839). A year later *Kiss of the Spider Woman*, a joint Brazil/US production grossed $17m in the US, making it one of the most successful (positive) queer-themed movies of that decade. The film is essentially about the relationship between two men who are complete opposites but find themselves sharing a prison cell in an unnamed military dictatorship. Sadly, in order to establish just how different the men are, one of them is portrayed as a shallow, effeminate homosexual while the other is a macho revolutionary. The film does redeem itself to some extent, however, by documenting the gay character's transformation into an insightful and ultimately heroic individual whose stand against the dictatorship ultimately costs him his life. The film was nominated for an Academy Award for Best Film and William Hurt, who played the gay character, for Best Actor.

In that same year, 1985, Channel 4 Films released *My Beautiful Laundrette*, the story of the relationship between two young men – one white working class, the other an Asian entrepreneur. Originally planned for television broadcast, the film was so well received at film festivals that it was decided to release it on the cinema circuit first. Like *Desert Hearts*, *Laundrette* was ground-breaking in that it documented the issues around a same sex relationship – men this time – without problematising the relationship itself. In this case the issues included the fact that it was both interracial and interclass thus introducing racism and class hostilities to the mix.

1985 also saw the first AIDS-themed movies, with Arthur J Bressan's *Buddies*, NBC's telemovie *An Early Frost* (discussed in the Television section of this chapter) and Rosa von Praunheim's lesser-known *A Virus Knows No Morals*.

Buddies was a very low-budget film that was, apparently, written in five days and shot in nine. Its director, Arthur J Bressan Jr was better known for gay porn movies until he worked on *Buddies*; the principal exception to this being *Gay USA*, a documentary about Gay Pride events around the USA in 1977. *Buddies* was the first movie to realistically explore the impact of AIDS on people – not just the people with

52

the disease but the other people in their lives as well. Focusing predominantly on the interactions of two men – one in the late stages of AIDS, the other a young man who had volunteered to befriend him and be his 'buddy' – it communicated very effectively the anger felt within queer communities at the lack of government action at that time.

A Virus Knows No Morals was von Praunheim's angry and cynical take on responses to AIDS – by everyone from people with the virus through liberals and political activists to the medical establishment. Its overall tone was satirical with little attempt to make its characters anything more than parodies. For example, the main character is the owner of a gay bathhouse who does everything he can to block safe sex material reaching his customers but then goes on to develop AIDS himself. In the course of his illness he meets a range of bizarre characters including a woman who wants to have a baby by a gay man *"before they die out"* and a research doctor who declares *"the best defence is shame"*. Unsurprisingly, the film did not do well in either mainstream or arthouse cinemas.

A year later the movie *Parting Glances* would use a more restrained approach – and a bigger budget – to explore the impact that AIDS has on relationships. Whereas *Buddies* has the person with AIDS restricted to a hospital bed, the character with HIV in *Parting Glances* is depicted within his social rather than medical context thus placing greater emphasis on the relationships while still acknowledging the illness. Sadly, both the director of *Buddies* and the director of *Parting Glances* (Bill Sherwood) would be dead from AIDS by the end of the decade.

While *Buddies, Parting Glances* and (especially) *A Virus Knows No Morals* were destined for limited distribution (*Parting Glances* only grossing around half a million dollars in the US, for example), *Longtime Companion*, released in 1989, managed to find its way into mainstream cinema networks. Taking its title from the term the *New York Times* used in its obituaries to avoid acknowledging same-sex partners, it is set over a period of seven years and portrays the impact AIDS has on a group of friends over that period. In so doing, it serves as an overview of the gay community's response to the disease: some are in denial from the outset; others paranoid and others more pragmatic. Unlike *Buddies* and *Parting Glances*, which focus on one individual, *Longtime Companion* sees a number of people diagnosed with and ultimately dying from AIDS, thus allowing a greater exploration of the impact.

With AIDS finally making it as a subject for mainstream movies, it seems ironic

53

that one of the other successful gay movies of that period – *Torch Song Trilogy* (1988) – didn't mention it at all. But this wasn't a deliberate avoidance of the issue: the play on which the movie was based was written pre-AIDS in the 1970s. Nonetheless, the issues explored – including bisexuality, hostile parents, gay parents and homophobic violence – were as relevant then as they are now.

With the exception of *Desert Hearts*, lesbians were poorly represented in mainstream or arthouse movies throughout the 80s. Both *Lianna* and *Personal Best* had reinforced the notion of the unhappy homosexual and Spielberg felt it necessary to cut the lesbianism from *The Color Purple*. Films by lesbian directors – such as Susan Lambert's *On Guard* (1983), Su Friedrich's *Damned If You Don't* (1987) and the works of Sheila McLaughlin (*Born in Flames* (1983) and *She Must Be Seeing Things* (1987) – all had significantly lower profiles. *November Moon* (1985), the story of two women in Nazi-occupied France, was a relatively popular arthouse movie but never broke into either mainstream cinemas or mainstream awareness. Another movie set around the time of the Second World War, this time in Berlin, was *The Berlin Affair* (1985), which featured a relationship between the wife of a Nazi bureaucrat and the daughter of a Japanese diplomat. Again, this one never got beyond the arthouses (although, given its unhappy ending, maybe this wasn't such a bad thing!).

While lesbian filmmakers struggled for wider recognition, a number of men from the fringe/underground school began to increase their profile. John Waters, for example, had been building a cult following since the 60s with 'bad taste' movies like *Hag in a Black Leather Jacket* and *Eat Your Make-up*. He began the 80s with *Polyester* which, despite being one of the world's first scratch-and-sniff movies, did little to raise his profile beyond existing fans. But in 1988 he and drag superstar Divine became known to mainstream audiences with *Hairspray*, in which Divine played Edna Turnblad, the mother of rebellious teenager Tracy Turnblad. Whether it was the absence of Waters trademark bad taste or the presence of famous names like Debbie Harry, Sonny Bono and Jerry Stiller, the film was a global success, pulling in $6.67m in the USA alone (although the later, straighter version with John Travolta in the Divine role pulled in $118m).

Pedro Almodovar made his first low-budget film, *Pepi, Luci, Bom*, in 1980, only a year after homosexuality was decriminalised in his home country of Spain. Just as John Waters' trademark was bad taste, Almodovar developed his as complex storylines;

in this case concerning the relationship between a lesbian punk singer, a masochistic housewife and a vengeful young woman. Like many of Almodovar's early 80s films, *Pepi, Luci, Bom* was not released outside of Spain until much later (1992 in this case). In the meantime he continued to produce films, most of which included lesbian, gay or transgender characters and often featured the as yet undiscovered Antonio Banderas. In 1982, for example, he directed *Labyrinth of Passions*, which includes Banderas as a gay Muslim terrorist who can track down his victims through his acute sense of smell. In 1983 *Dark Habits* featured a mother superior who was a lesbian drug addict. By 1984 his films – and the extraordinary array of queer characters therein – had begun to reach an international audience and his 1988 film *Women on the Verge of a Nervous Breakdown* was nominated for a Best Foreign Language Film Academy Award.

At the same time Derek Jarman, an artist already renowned for his homoerotic works (for example, *Sebastiane* in 1976) continued to produce a range of short and full-length films. These included *The Angelic Conversation* (1985), in which two beautiful young men explore the landscape and each other to a soundtrack of Shakespeare's sonnets, and *Caravaggio* (1986), a contemplation of the raucous life of the bisexual artist.

Documentaries

The output of queer documentary makers that had begun in the 70s increased significantly during the 80s. One reason for this was the introduction of videotape, which dramatically reduced the costs of filming while also increasing flexibility. Another was the emergence and sponsorship of progressive television stations like the UK's Channel 4 (whose impact is considered in greater detail later in this chapter), Gay Cable Network in the USA and Australia's Special Broadcasting Service (SBS).

And as the numbers of documentaries increased, so too did the range of topics. For example, there were a number of documentaries that explored the experience of black or Asian lesbians and gay men. These included *If She Grows Up Gay* (1983), *Orientations* (1986), *Looking for Langston* (1988) and *Tongues Untied* (1989).

Before Stonewall (1984) and *Silent Pioneers* (1985) gave us a greater insight into pre-Stonewall queer American history, the Academy Award-winning *The Times of Harvey Milk* (1984) covered an important episode from our more recent history: the life and assassination of out-gay San Francisco politician Harvey Milk.

Many documentaries captured our history in the making. Thus, the 1979 and 1987 Marches on Washington for Lesbian and Gay Rights were recorded in films such as *Greetings from Washington D.C.* (1981), *March On!* (1981) and *For Love and For Life* (1988). *You Can Fight City Hall: Lesbian and Gay Rights in the Mid West* (1985) and *Rights and Reactions: Lesbian and Gay Rights on Trial* (1987) showed how that fight was being fought at a local level, in this case with Columbus City Council and New York City Council respectively.

In Australia, the Special Broadcasting Service commissioned Richard Turner to explore the struggle for queer rights in Australia with his history of Sydney's Gay Mardi Gras, *We'll Dance if We Want To* (1984).

Another television station helped British queer youth find a voice. Funded by Channel 4 and the Greater London Council, *Framed Youth: Revenge of the Teenage Perverts* (1982) was produced by members of the London Lesbian and Gay Youth Video Project. Despite its obvious 'home-made' style it went on to win the Best Documentary award at the British Film Institute in 1983 and was screened at a number of arthouses around the UK. In 1986 it was shown on Channel 4 – albeit in a late-night slot – prompting outrage from Conservative MPs in Parliament the following day.

A very different piece of queer history-in-the-making was produced in 1985 as the London-based group Lesbians and Gays Support the Miners (LGSM) documented their activities raising funds for Welsh miners and their families during the 1984/85 miners' strike. The end product, *All Out! Dancing in Dulais*, received very limited screening at the time of its release in 1985 but nearly three decades later it was discovered on YouTube by screenwriter Stephen Beresford, who used it to inform his screenplay for the immensely successful mainstream film *Pride*.

Elsewhere other documentaries explored issues such as coming out (*Michael, A Gay Son*, 1980), institutionalised police homophobia (*Watch Out: There's a Queer About*, 1981), the realities of lesbian life (*Home-made Melodrama*, 1982; *17 Rooms or, What Do Lesbians Do in Bed?*, 1984) and the UK's proposed 'Video Nasties' Bill (*What Can I Do With A Male Nude?* 1985).

Of course, nowhere was queer history unfolding on a more epic scale than with the emergence of HIV/AIDS, and this produced a range of documentary responses – from the very personal to the broader perspective. For example, *I'm Still Alive: A Person with AIDS Tells His Story* (1987) does exactly what it says on the tin: it documents the thoughts and experiences of a man with AIDS. *Too Little, Too Late* (1987) explores the impact of AIDS on families of people with AIDS. *Like A Prayer* (1989) is one of many videos from ACT UP's video unit DIVA TV (Damned Interfering Video Activists); this one documenting ACT UP's direct actions against New York's homophobic Cardinal O'Connor. *Common Threads* (1989) uses the AIDS Memorial Quilt to explore and document the experiences of people with and those affected by HIV and AIDS. In 1989 it won the Academy Award for Best Documentary Feature.

The emergence of videotape made film-making possible for a much greater number of people – even if their efforts subsequently went largely unnoticed. This was almost the fate of *All Out!: Dancing in Dulais*, a film that has subsequently been recognised as a valuable record of an important part of queer history. Who knows how many other historic gems lie out there awaiting discovery?

The First Film Festivals

With many works by queer filmmakers still being deemed unsuitable – commercially or content-wise – for mainstream screening and many queer filmmakers disinterested in targeting mainstream audiences anyway, an increasing number of queer film festivals offered an alternative outlet.

London had its first Festival of Gay Film and Video in June 1981. Organised by the London Filmmakers Co-operative the Festival sourced a range of cinematic representations of lesbians and gay men. Some of these were relatively old – such as Kenneth Anger's *Fireworks* (1947), Cocteau's *Testament d'Orphee* (1950) and Genet's *Chant D'Amour* (1950) – but there was also a significant amount of new material, including short films and work shot on Super 8 cameras. Sourced from around the globe the festival included *Thriller* by British director Sally Potter, *The Homosexual Century* from French director Lionel Soukaz, *David Montgomery und Ich* from Berlin-based director Wieland Speck and *Nothing Personal* by Ieuan Rhys Morris in the USA. With one or two exceptions, the bulk of the content was produced by lesbians and gay men and was about lesbians and gay men.

There is no record of a second such event but the first annual London Lesbian and

Gay Film Festival was launched at the British Film Institute (BFI) in 1986. Like so many other film festivals that emerged during the 80s, this actually had its roots in the 1970s, having been preceded by a one-off 'Gays and Film' event in 1977.

Similarly, in Sydney, the Australian Film Institute had been presenting a week-long festival of queer-themed films since the 70s prior to joining with the Sydney Gay and Lesbian Mardi Gras to produce a Gay and Lesbian Film Week as part of the broader Mardi Gras Festival. The New York Gay Film Festival was launched in 1979 but ceased in 1987, before being succeeded in 1989 by Newfest: The New York LGBT Film Festival. But many others did begin in the 80s, including the Los Angeles' Outfest (1982), Vancouver (1988), Berlin (1986) and Boston (1984). And as the network of queer film festivals grew, so too did the opportunities for queer filmmakers to have their films shown.

Channel 4

A significant contributor to queer films in the UK – and, indeed, the Western world – was a television company. The UK's Channel 4 was established in 1982 with a remit to provide programming for minority groups, including queer people.

While it was a welcome addition to the three television channels at that time (BBC1, BBC2 and ITV) the timing of its arrival – the middle of the Thatcher era – meant that conflict was almost inevitable if it was to effectively fulfil its brief. Not only was it charged with providing programming for queers – a group increasingly vilified through the 80s, as epitomised by the passage of the infamous Section 28 – it was initially a subsidiary of the Independent Broadcasting Authority, making it a publicly-owned organisation. The timing and its ownership were largely a historical accident: a fourth UK television channel had been considered from as early as the 1950s but it wasn't until 1982 that the political and commercial manoeuvrings finally resulted in the organisation that was Channel 4.

As part of its budget it had a relatively small allocation for the production of low-cost films that would, it was assumed, be screened on television rather than in cinemas. However, a range of factors – including the creativity of the commissioning editor David Rose and the success of movies like *My Beautiful Laundrette* – led to Channel 4 Films having a much greater impact on contemporary films than could ever have been anticipated. In essence, Channel 4 completely funded or part-funded a range of films that garnered critical success. These included some of those already mentioned and ranged from documentary – such as *Framed Youth: Revenge of the Teenage Perverts* (1982) (co-funded with the Greater London Council), *Veronica 4 Rose* (1983), *Breaking the Silence* (1984) and *Bright Eyes* (1984) – to feature films like *My Beautiful Laundrette* (1985) and *Maurice* (1987). They also part-funded other films including Derek Jarman's *Angelic Conversation* (1985), *Caravaggio* (1986) and *The Last of England* (1987)

In addition to their own films, Channel 4 regularly screened other movies of interest to queer people and – unsurprisingly given the political environment at the time – this usually generated some degree of political outcry. One of these was Derek Jarman's unambiguously homoerotic movie *Sebastiane*, which included a shot of a man getting an erection. This was cut from the movie prior to its screening but accidentally played in the background during an interview about the shot in a programme called *Sex and the Censors!*

The conservative press were constantly up in arms about the station, with the tabloids nicknaming it 'Channel Porn'. When the station introduced the practice of displaying a red triangle in the corner of movies it thought might be contentious this simply led to further criticism, not least from serial complainer Mary Whitehouse who had long established herself as an enemy of queer people.

In spite of the regular press criticism and the questions in Parliament, Channel 4 management generally held its nerve and continued to screen programmes that it was created to screen – including queer-themed films. One exception to this was in 1986, in the course of *In the Pink*, an eight-week series of queer films that began in September of that year. Films included *Buddies, Breaking the Silence* and *What Can I Do With a Male Nude?* but the station backed away from screening Caroline Sheldon's *17 Rooms; or, What Do Lesbians Do In Bed?* due to anticipated objections because of its title. [4]

That retreat notwithstanding, Channel 4 ran a second series of *In the Pink* at the end of the following year.

Television

The emergence of AIDS undoubtedly influenced the perception and portrayal of queer people on television; significantly more so than on film, not least because of the greater volume and immediacy of television. In 1985, for example, the UK's Gays and Broadcasting Project monitored one week's television and radio output to look at the treatment of lesbianism and male homosexuality. Out of a total output of 688 hours, only 10 hours made any reference to gay men. Of these 10 hours references were predominantly about AIDS or throwaway jokes in comedy sketch programmes. All references in news programmes were about AIDS [5].

It has also been argued [6] that, in the US at least, the emergence of HIV/AIDS, along with the ultra-conservativism of the Reagan administration, led network executives to avoid depicting queer issues and characters on-screen. My own perception – based on quite a broad overview of programming during the 80s – is that there was a temporary drop in queer characters in mainstream programmes between 1983 and 1986 while television, along with the rest of the world, struggled to understand the new phenomenon of AIDS. Queer people did feature in a number of AIDS-themed programmes – both drama and documentary – during that period but it wasn't until 1986 that there was a noticeable increase in the coverage of other 'non-AIDS' queer issues.

Pre-AIDS and Non-AIDS-Related Programming
Documentaries

A cluster of documentaries screened in the early years of the decade acknowledged an increasing queer profile in the UK, Australia and the USA but also demonstrated the different national responses to this.

In 1980 in the UK, for example, the BBC screened *Coming Out*, which looked at the lives of five lesbians and gay men who had taken part in the 1979 Gay Pride March in London. The documentary was 'very BBC' in its tone, warning viewers that *"frank language will be used throughout"* (one instance of a man saying he enjoyed sodomy) and explaining that *"today they're called 'gays'"* (then referring to them as homosexuals for the duration of the programme). To explain just how far queers had progressed in their 'Coming Out' we were told that the march itself was *"the largest assembly of homosexual men and women Europe had ever seen"* (there were fewer than 3000 participants). And as a further indicator of how brazen they'd become, we're also advised of *"the participation in this programme – full face – of five of the homosexual marchers."*

60

Its cautious 'grab the smelling salts' approach is hilarious in retrospect but at the time it reflected the perception of queer people in the UK. In the USA, on the other hand, the word 'gay' didn't need to be explained to viewers nor, indeed, did their increased organisation. In fact, the same year that the BBC was still struggling with the word 'gay', CBS felt it necessary to screen a documentary about *"... the troubling questions [the birth of the gay movement] raises for the 80s, not only for San Francisco, but for other cities throughout the country."*

Gay Power, Gay Politics, according to the initial voiceover, was *"... not a story about lifestyles or the average gay experience."* It then went on to focus predominantly on the practice of BDSM and suggest that it was normal sexual behaviour for the majority of gay men. Not only was it the sexual norm but, according to the producers, it was an immensely dangerous activity; responsible for one in every ten deaths in San Francisco, to the point that the Emergency Department:

"... had a gynaecological table there with a doctor and nurse on hand to sew people up."

Having thus declared that this apparently deadly sexual activity was routine gay sexual behaviour, it then implied that it was the promotion of such risky behaviour that lay at the heart of the 'gay agenda'. In case the producers' own political agenda wasn't already abundantly clear then a question to San Francisco Mayor Dianne Feinstein left no doubt: *"How does it feel to be Mayor of Sodom and Gomorrah?"* She threw them out of her office.

Two years later, the Australian Broadcasting Corporation (ABC) screened *Sydney, the Golden City for Gays.* It was far less reticent than the BBC's approach but completely devoid of the sensationalism and conspiracy of the CBS documentary. Indeed, the warning in its preamble very much laid any potential problem with the viewer rather than the subject:

"... this may be a subject that you feel you or your children would be best to avoid. If so, please switch off now. If not, here is our report ..."

While it too documented the increasing profile and visibility of queer communities (listing, for example, Sydney's 61 gay groups and social clubs, three gay newspapers, nine gay hotels, eight gay discos and 14 gay restaurants) its key theme was revealed in the statement that:

"about 145 homosexuals are prosecuted in NSW each year and 20 go to prison: the majority of them for between two and five years."

Its focus, therefore, was not to 'explain' or warn but rather to acknowledge an extraordinary anachronism in the law: homosexuals were clearly a significant and established part of society but were arbitrarily incarcerated for no other reason than the existence of an outdated law. Unlike the BBC documentary, the approach was informed and mature; and unlike the CBS programme, the tone was supportive rather than alarmist.

'Golden City' was screened one month before Australia's first diagnosis of AIDS and it is interesting to speculate if or how this might have skewed the approach had the programme been aired just a few weeks later. Certainly those opponents of gay rights already included in the programme would undoubtedly have exploited it to support their arguments. Interestingly, a 1984 Australian documentary – *We'll Dance If We Want To* – made no mention of AIDS either, despite being produced by gay filmmaker Richard Turner and narrated by prominent gay activist Dennis Altman. Screened on Channel 0/28 (later to become the Special Broadcasting Service (SBS)) it used the development of the annual Sydney Gay Mardi Gras to highlight the situation of LGBT people in New South Wales. In some ways reiterating the message of the earlier ABC documentary, it too noted the high visibility of LGBT people within the state, while simultaneously pointing out that male homosexuality was still a crime. As one of the parade participants says: *"20–30 000 people can come out in solidarity and flout the laws of the state, which make us all criminals still."*

Talk Shows

As late as 1987, the UK's Gays and Broadcasting Project found that:

"Lesbians and gay men generally tend to be involved in audience participation programmes when the subject under discussion involves homosexuality. But they are seldom central … Lesbians and gays are seldom represented on the panel of 'experts', who are given standing and authority by their professional authority … 'self-confessed' questions whether we are ordinary people." [7]

While this might have been the case in the UK, it was different in the USA and Australia, where queer people were generally appearing on their own terms. Perhaps this was down to national differences; for example, the UK talk show format was still more focused around either celebrities or 'experts' discussing particular issues. Additionally, with the exception of the AIDS charity, the Terrence Higgins Trust, the UK did not have high-profile organisations from which producers could seek a spokesperson until the late 80s with the formation of both Peter Tatchell's 'Outrage' and actor Ian McEwan's 'Stonewall'.

In the USA, on the other hand, talk shows such as Phil Donahue's were well entrenched and the existence of national organisations facilitated the presence of queer issues and guests such as Aaron Fricke and Larry Kramer. In Australia, television tended to mirror the USA rather than the UK so the talk show format was long-established and there is some evidence that chat shows were more accommodating of queer guests. For example, in 1987 TV presenter Ray Martin interviewed transsexual Trixie Laumont on his *Midday Show* – albeit in a state of obvious discomfort throughout.

Light Entertainment

By the end of the 80s the portrayal of queer people had increased significantly – particularly in US programmes (many of which were, happily, broadcast in the UK and Australia too). Not all of these could be described as positive: for example, the US comedy *Soap*, which ran from 1977, claimed to have one of the first upfront gay characters in a television series; a gay man named Jodie Dallas. And yet, by the time it came to a rather abrupt end in 1981, Jodie had been in only one relationship with a man (in the very first series) and a string of relationships with women thereafter.

Similarly, the NBC series *Love Sidney*, which began in 1981, had a gay man – Sidney Shorr – as its central character, but his homosexuality is rarely evidenced. Like Jodie Dallas, far more effort is put into creating a heterosexual 'ambience' as Sidney contrives a family by inviting a single mother and her daughter to live with him and agrees to go out on a series of fruitless dates with a female co-worker. Indeed, it seems that Sidney's homosexuality is merely a plot device to 'neuter' him so that he can interact in an intimate but non-sexual way with various female characters.

When *Love Sidney* ended – after only two series – everyone must have breathed a sigh of relief: the network executives who had worried constantly about losing sponsors; the show's critics who had objected to the notion of a homosexual as the lead character (no matter how desexualised); and queer activists, who had criticised the 'de-homosexualisation' of this supposedly homosexual man.

The hugely successful series *Dynasty*, which began in 1981, did offer the 'gay' character of Steven Carrington. However, much like *Soap*'s Jodie Dallas, Steven seemed to have a lot of relationships with women and, also like Jodie Dallas, managed to father a child with one of them. He did differ from Jodie Dallas in one significant way by managing to have male lovers – even though many of them seemed to end up dead! Perhaps unsurprisingly, the actor who played Steven initially – Al Corley – left at the end of the second series, citing Steven's *"ever-shifting sexual preferences"* as one of the reasons.

But some television producers were beginning to take notice of complaints made by queer activists. *Barney Miller,* for example, had generated protests in 1975 when it portrayed its only gay character as a stereotyped, swishy queen (and criminal, to boot). By 1980 new and more realistic gay characters were introduced, including a closeted gay cop whose coming out story formed a major part of the storyline over one season.

In 1982 PBS broadcast *Fifth of July*, a play about a gay paraplegic Vietnam veteran, living with his lover in his family home. Lesbian, gay and transgender characters and issues featured in a wide range of TV series, including *WKRP in Cincinnati, Trapper John MD, Magnum P.I., Diff'rent Strokes, Hotel, The Love Boat, Night Court, Murder She Wrote* and *Miami Vice. The Golden Girls* (which dropped the live-in gay cook after the pilot episode) went on to explore a number of issues including Dorothy's lesbian friend who has an interest in Rose, Blanche's involvement with a politician who used to be a woman and Blanche's younger brother coming out.

Nonetheless, queer characters in a leading role were thin on the ground in free-to-air US TV for the majority of the 80s (possibly due to the sponsorship difficulties experienced by both *Soap* and *Love Sidney*). The majority of programmes would occasionally (and briefly) explore an 'issue' – often using the long-standing practice of temporarily introducing a queer character to make a particular point, then writing them out immediately afterwards. Thus, a 1983 episode of *Cheers* introduces an old teammate of bar owner and retired baseball player Sam Malone, who comes out during his visit to the bar. Cue panic among the regulars who fear that Cheers will become a gay bar, barmaid Diane reeling out the arguments against their homophobia and, finally, Sam doing the right thing by publicly supporting his old teammate. Once the episode ends the teammate never reappears and is not mentioned again.

A slightly more prolonged version of this occurs in 1982, when a child psychologist – Lynn Carson – is introduced to *All My Children*. Lynn is openly lesbian and manages to last for two months while one of the main characters – a recently divorced woman – questions her own sexuality and wonders if she is falling in love with the psychologist. Once it's established that she isn't the psychologist is quickly despatched from the cast.

In 1986, Cagney in *Cagney and Lacey* got a gay neighbour who managed to remain for the rest of the series. Similarly, dress designer Hank Williams managed to hang on from 1988 to 1989 in the soap opera *As the World Turns*. Despite the stereotypical job, Hank was far from stereotypical in presentation; he was a handsome, masculine man, leading to one of the female characters misreading the signals and anticipating a romance. There was also the homophobic response of two of the young male characters when Hank came out but attitudes were changed and all was resolved by the time Hank left following the AIDS death of his lover Charles (who never actually appeared on screen).

The first permanent queer character in a US free-to-air soap didn't arrive until 1988 when *HeartBeat*, a series set in a women's health centre, began. The founding partners of the centre included lesbian nurse practitioner Marilyn McGrath. Unfortunately *HeartBeat* was cancelled after two series due to poor ratings.

The expansion of cable TV helped to lift the profile of queer people – gay men in particular – in television series. In 1982, for example, a series called *Brothers* was produced in the hope that it would be taken up by a national network such as ABC or NBC. However, its central theme, the relationship between three brothers when one of them comes out, proved to be too unpalatable for these networks and it looked like the series might not make it to air. However, it was picked up by the Showtime pay-cable TV network in 1984 and aired in the summer of that year. It ran until 1989 and was syndicated to a number of countries including free-to-air stations in the UK and Australia.

Somewhat ironically, it was Rupert Murdoch's Fox cable network that introduced two more gay male characters to US television in 1987. While Murdoch's newspapers have been at the forefront of homophobic journalism for decades, his television network had no problem in including two gay men parenting a 14-year-old girl in the *Tracey Ullman Show*. (The timing was particularly interesting: in that same year Murdoch's UK newspaper the *Sun* was deriding the first British onscreen gay kiss in the soap EastEnders as *'EastBenders'*.)

By 1986 the mainstream networks seem to have become sufficiently confident to chance their arms with one-off telemovies around homosexuality. Thus CBS produced *Welcome Home Bobby*, about a young man who is thrown out of home by his father and also put under pressure to quit school after admitting to a sexual encounter with an older man. It's never established whether the eponymous young man is, in fact, gay but there's a relatively happy ending when Dad sees the error of his ways and Bobby comes home. That same year, HBO's *The Truth About Alex* tells the story of a young American football player who comes out and the reactions of his friends and teammates. But there's still a happy ending as everyone realises that, even though Alex is gay, he's still a regular guy. School-aged gay jocks seem to be the vehicle of choice for television producers during this period because CBS's *What If I'm Gay?* (1987) explores the experience of the captain of a school football team who is outed after the discovery of a gay porn magazine in his room. Admittedly, this latter one is a 'School Break Special'.

1986 also saw the exploration of lesbianism in *My Two Loves* (ABC), in which a recently bereaved woman finds a shoulder to cry on – and a lot more – in the form of her work colleague. As if reflecting the absence of lesbians on television, one of the characters actually says that lesbians are America's *"largest invisible minority"*. Then *HeartBeat* came along two years later and, in 1989, the ABC ran a two-part mini-series *The Women of Brewster Place*. Set in a tenement block, the tenants included a lesbian couple who experience various levels of acceptance and prejudice. When one of them is raped this acts as a trigger for the tenants to finally put their differences aside and come together.

In Australia, where gay and lesbian characters had featured prominently and unapologetically throughout the 70s (for example, *Number 96*, *The Box and Prisoner*), there was a surprising dearth of them in the 80s. Apart from Prisoner, which ran until 1987, the only other programming seems to be a 1980 miniseries *Players in the Gallery* from the Australian Broadcasting Corporation (ABC). This featured a gay character who is drawn into a child custody battle between his landlady and her husband when his

66

possible 'influence' over the child is raised to support the husband's case. Throughout it all his presence is portrayed as being entirely beneficial for the child.

Apart from those two exceptions, it seemed like Australia had to rely on imported programmes to see queer characters in mainstream storylines. In 1982 the usual supply of imported soap operas was supplemented with *Brideshead Revisited*, a lavish British adaptation of Evelyn Waugh's novel. Pivotal to the storyline was the relationship between two men which, in its early stages was portrayed very much as a romance (albeit non-sexual). While one of the men quickly 'grew out of it', it was clear that the other – Lord Sebastian Flyte – was to remain ensconced for life. Despite the complete absence of sex (or even the slightest hint of it), *Brideshead's* screening in Australia gave serial bigot the Reverend Fred Nile the opportunity to declare his self-promoting outrage. *Brideshead* went on to be a ratings winner in Australia.

The UK had a more consistent run of queer characters throughout the 80s, starting with the non-stereotypical gay neighbours in the sitcom *Agony*, which ran until 1981. A gay son appeared in the BBC sitcom *Time of My Life* (1980) and a gay psychoanalyst in ITV's *It Takes a Worried Man* (1981–83). 1983 saw the British fascination with cross-dressing sustained in the sitcom *Dear Ladies*: George Logan and Patrick Fyffe as two genteel spinsters Dr Evadne Hinge and Dame Hilda Bracket. The dear ladies engaged in a constant stream of double entendres, many with a decidedly gay spin (for example, the nephew dismissed from the Army after being found playing cards with his privates).

The birth of Channel 4 in 1982 brought a new stream of queer characters as well as attempts to portray them more creatively. On Channel 4's opening night, for example, the Comic Strip presented a satire on the works of children's author Enid Blyton. In *Five Go Mad in Dorset* the 'crime' that the children enthusiastically uncover is Uncle Quentin's homosexuality and his relationship with a young American man. They gleefully hand them both over to the police.

Some of Channel 4's other attempts at 'alternative' comedy didn't fare quite so well. *Dream Stuffing* (1984) was a series about two unemployed women and their gay neighbour. *The Guardian's* television critic described it as *"heroically bad"* [8]. Similarly, *The Corner House* (1987) was a sitcom set in a 'right-on' gay-run cafe: even one of the writers – Robert Llewellyn – remembers it as *"a true disaster that wasn't*

67

particularly funny". Indeed, even the television critic for *Marxism Today* struggled to find kind words for it:

"It is not a glossy product; beside its nearest stablemate Cheers it looks positively downmarket. But it does have an enthusiasm and commitment to tackling issues that TV usually ignores. That is a bit hard to adjust to when you're used to re-digested paper – the shiny, high-finance moralistic packages that require no chewing." [9]

But there was no denying Channel 4's commitment to queer issues: in 1985 its soap, *Brookside*, featured the first long-term gay character in a British soap when 18-year-old Gordon Collins came out. He and his family remained in Brookside until 1990 when they were written out following the death of the actress that played his mother. In the interim Gordon and his family faced various issues around his sexuality, including a homophobic attack on their house. There was even discussion of Gordon's lovers – although none of them actually appeared on the show.

Brookside's reluctance to show two homosexual lovers together was symptomatic of the 'No sex please, I'm homosexual' culture that was pervasive across the globe at that time. While Australia had challenged this taboo with the first homosexual on-screen kiss in the 1970s, this didn't happen on US television until 1991. In the UK the BBC pushed the boundaries by introducing a gay character into their soap *EastEnders* in 1986 then causing uproar the following year by having that character – Colin Russell – kiss another gay man. Despite the fact that this was merely a kiss on the forehead, the Murdoch media led the homophobic outcry, labelling the show *EastBenders*.

Happily, the BBC was not discouraged by the hysteria and, in January 1989, reignited it when Colin had a 'full' mouth-to-mouth kiss with another gay man, Guido. Once again, it was Murdoch's newspaper The Sun that was at the forefront of the uproar, describing the scene as *"a homosexual love scene between yuppie poofs"* and claiming that MPs wanted a ban on *EastEnders* as a result of the kissing scene. The BBC continued to stick to its guns, using *EastEnders* to introduce the first person with AIDS to a soap opera in 1990.

But one rule remained constant for queer representation in soaps and other dramas around the globe – no sex! Homosexuals existed, they looked just like other people, they weren't paedophiles but their sex lives – a pretty important element in defining someone as homosexual – weren't to be depicted. For example, in 1989, when *Thirtysomething*

featured two gay men in bed they were under very strict instructions that there had to be no physical contact whatsoever. It was left to the viewer to conclude that they had just had sex but the network (ABC) made it clear that **any** touching would result in the episode being pulled. And once the episode was shown (with a loss of $1.5 million in revenue after some advertisers withdrew) it was withdrawn from the rebroadcast rotation.

The Importance of Channel 4

From 1982, Britain's Channel 4 pursued its mission to better serve queer people on television, introducing a range of programming to achieve this. In 1983 it created the 'lifestyle' series *One in Five*, which, from memory, ran for one season and was greeted with outrage from Conservative MPs. A second attempt at a lifestyle programme, *Out on Tuesday*, was launched in 1989. The producer told *The Guardian* newspaper that *"this series will challenge the idea that there's one kind of gay person, politics or sensibility"* [10]. Despite the positive sentiments, the programme was initially broadcast at the less than appealing hour of 11 p.m. Somewhat ironically, a move to a 9 p.m. slot for the second series saw a ratings slump, so it was re-named *Out* and moved to Wednesday evenings where it increased its ratings but was ultimately dropped after the fourth series.

1986 was a particularly notable year in terms of Channel 4's queer programming. In September it ran an eight week season of LGBT films under the banner *In the Pink*. In November it then ran a six-week series of documentaries and dramas *Six of Hearts*, looking at specific queer individuals and aspects of queer life. The individuals featured included a gay furniture maker, a lesbian holiday representative and a lesbian stand-up comedian.

As if to end the year off, Channel 4 broadcast *Framed Youth: Revenge of the Teenage Perverts* – a video made by the London Lesbian and Gay Youth Video Group – as the first episode of its *Eleventh Hour* youth season.

In contrast to Channel 4, the other three television stations – BBC1, BBC2 and the Independent Television network (ITV) – were well behind in the field: indeed, it seemed that they weren't particularly interested in being players. London Weekend Television

69

– a regional member of the ITV network – did produce a lifestyle series *Gay Life* in 1980. Developed by its Minorities Unit, it was the UK's first queer-specific television series (although it didn't go out nationally; transmission being limited to the London Weekend Television region). Running for 11 episodes, it covered a wide range of issues, including gays in the civil service, child custody and adoption, and gays in the armed forces. Unsurprisingly, it was screened in the late night slot of 11:30 p.m. on Sundays.

Despite its status as the first queer-specific television series, it wasn't welcomed by all sections of our communities. Reviewing the programme in *Gay News*, John Russell Taylor said he was amazed at the number of hostile comments he had heard, including the suggestion that *"it would be better not to have such a programme if it's going to show men in drag and men in leather."* [11] Some people, it seemed, would prefer invisibility rather than risk the 'wrong' type of representation.

AIDS on Television
Drama and Light Entertainment

AIDS inevitably crept into the news headlines as it emerged but it seems 1983 was the year when television coverage diversified into dramas and documentary. The US hospital drama *St Elsewhere* was the first to feature an AIDS-related storyline with its *AIDS and Comfort* episode, the tale of an ostensibly heterosexual politician who is admitted to the hospital with a mysterious condition. Needless to say, it turns out to be AIDS, the skeletons come flying out of the closet and he finally admits to a recent sexual relationship with another man.

St Elsewhere went on to run other AIDS-related storylines, as did a number of other television series including *Trapper John MD*, *Hill Street Blues*, *The Young and the Restless* and even *The Golden Girls*. Unsurprisingly, some of them opted for sensationalism over sensitivity. Such was the case with the episode 'After it Happened' on NBC's *Midnight Caller* in 1988, wherein a bisexual man deliberately infects a woman with HIV. In spite of protests during and after the filming, NBC still ran the episode, albeit with NBC's San Francisco affiliate running a disclaimer before the episode and following it with a half hour programme in which activists and public health officials presented their concerns and criticisms.

70

At the other end of the scale was *Designing Women's* 1987 episode 'Killing All the Right People', in which prejudice against people with AIDS is wholeheartedly attacked. When a gay man with AIDS asks the Sugarbaker company to design his funeral it triggers a number of prejudicial outbursts from customers and staff alike – as well as some heated responses by one of the 'designing women'. The episode was triggered after the mother of the series creator Linda Bloodworth-Thomason died of AIDS. While Bloodworth-Thomason was in the hospital she overheard a comment that *"the good thing about AIDS is that it's killing all the right people."*

It was fortunate that so many US serials ran AIDS storylines, since there were none in the UK until the introduction of a character with AIDS in EastEnders in 1990. Australia did little better, with a 1986 episode of the *Flying Doctors* in which a war hero with HIV returns to a country town, a 1988 episode of *A Country Practice* where an injecting drug user contracts AIDS and a 1989 episode of GP, which deals with a case where an HIV test has been undertaken without the patient's consent.

One-off dramas did slightly better in the UK, with Central Television producing *Intimate Contact* in 1987 in which a married businessman contracts HIV after having sex with a prostitute in New York. He remains unaware of this until he develops AIDS 18 months later. The drama – broadcast as three one-hour episodes – then explores the health and personal implications for his wife and himself as well as the wider social consequences for his whole family. *Intimate Contact* was also shown in the US on HBO.

A year later the BBC produced *Sweet As You Are*, with a similar storyline to *Intimate Contact*; that is, a husband's lack of fidelity and the consequences for his wife as well as him. In this case the husband is a college lecturer who has a (heterosexual) one night stand that results in HIV infection. One can only speculate as to why both Central Television and the BBC chose heterosexual sex as the route of HIV transmission when gay and bisexual transmission were much more common. Were they trying to avoid reinforcing the stereotype? Did they feel that viewers would be less engaged with a story about gay men? Or were they trying to point out that everyone should be concerned about AIDS?

Once again, the US was far more prolific, with NBC producing the first telemovie on the subject *An Early Frost* in 1985. This was the story of a gay man returning to his parents' home to break the news that, not only is he homosexual, he also has AIDS. The

71

film depicted the prejudices and misconceptions that existed at that time but despite being nominated for 14 Emmy Awards and winning three, NBC lost half a million dollars in sponsorship because advertisers were reluctant to support such a movie. The film was also criticised for its focus on the impact on the family rather than on the son and his lover.

The following year the Showtime cable network screened *As Is*, another story about a gay man with AIDS but this time with the focus primarily on his relationship with his ex-lover who comes back to care for him. If advertisers had been reluctant to sponsor *An Early Frost*, they would have run a mile from *As Is*, since it included scenes shot in gay bars as well as discussions about gay sex!

In 1988 the focus moved a little wider. *Go Toward the Light* (CBS) was a film about a family dealing with their haemophiliac son's demise and ultimate death from AIDS. Because it involved the death of a child it was, inevitably, a tearjerker although it managed to avoid overplaying the 'innocent victim' theme. *Tidy Endings* (HBO) originated from a stage play by Harvey Fierstein and explored the issues that arose when the surviving male partner of a man with AIDS meets up with his lover's ex-wife to divide up his belongings.

1989 brought *The Littlest Victims* (CBS) and the *Ryan White Story* (ABC). *The Littlest Victims'* working title was *The Innocent Victims*, which, thankfully, was changed prior to broadcast. It focused on the work of real-life doctor James Oleske, who was one of the first doctors to work with HIV-infected children. Despite its working title it sought to bring a political message – that of the government's slow response to the AIDS crisis – to a mainstream audience. That message included the fact that AIDS perception as a 'gay disease' had meant it was a low priority for the Reagan administration. However, the film itself was criticised for its own failure to include any gay characters. Having accused the government of ignoring gays, the critics said it was guilty of doing exactly the same thing itself.

The Ryan White Story told the story of Ryan White, a child who – along with his family – faced immense discrimination and hostility after contracting HIV through a blood transfusion shortly after birth. Ryan White was still alive at the time of the filming and played a cameo role in the movie.

Documentaries

Ryan White's story was, undoubtedly, something that had to be told since, among other things, it demonstrated just how brutal AIDS hysteria could be. But it is interesting to note that out of eight AIDS telemovies or miniseries produced in the US and UK (Australia doesn't seem to have produced any) during the 80s, only two – *As Is* and *Tidy Endings* – really seem to have acknowledged and explored the impact on gay men. It was almost as if the producers hadn't seen any of the many and varied AIDS documentaries that were aired during the 80s. The vast majority of these focused on gay men.

Once again, 1983 was the year that saw the first AIDS documentaries. In San Francisco KPIX-TV, a CBS affiliate, presented a four-part series on AIDS and went on to develop a comprehensive range of programmes thereafter. In 1985, and in consultation with AIDS organisations, it produced a one-hour programme, *Our Worst Fears*, that sought to present the facts about HIV/AIDS in a way that was both interesting to and accessible by the general population. Later that same year it launched its AIDS Lifeline programme, a series of regular but brief updates. Both of these initiatives had an influence on other CBS affiliates, with *Our Worst Fears* being syndicated in 1985 and the AIDS Lifeline programme being syndicated in 1988.

In Australia, Channel Nine's *Sixty Minutes* programme featured a 15 minute report on AIDS on 28 May 1983, a month after the first Australian was diagnosed with AIDS. Despite the initial use of some rather dramatic language (*"Australia could be next on the death list"*, *"... more contagious than hepatitis, deadlier than leukaemia"*, *"It's called the wrath of God syndrome"*) the overall approach was quite measured. Interviewees included staff and patients at New York's Mount Sinai hospital, Larry Kramer and a doctor destined to play a central role in Australia's response, Professor Ron Penny. Unfortunately they also included one Paul Dexter, whom they described as *"a Sydney businessman and gay community leader"*. He may have been the former but he certainly was not the latter. He claimed to be the leader of 'the Gay Army' – an entirely fictitious organisation – and under that guise made a number of seriously damaging claims over the years, including one that gay men with AIDS were deliberately infecting blood supplies to 'get revenge' and provoke a more urgent response from the government.

73

Two 1983 documentaries from the BBC – Panorama's *Love's Pestilence* and Horizon's *Killer in the Village*, both broadcast in April of that year – certainly provoked a response from the British media. In the three months up to March 1983 there were few references to AIDS in the British press, with a combined total of less than 200 column centimetres; from April to June there were more than 75 references and more than 1900 column centimetres [12]. 1983 was the year that AIDS made the front pages for the first time – although with headlines like the *Daily Mail*'s *'Hospitals Using Killer Blood'* (a report for which they were subsequently censured by the Press Council) it was clear that hysteria was going to be the hallmark of press coverage of AIDS.

And it was the media's representations of AIDS that formed the basis of Stuart Marshall's documentary *Bright Eyes*, broadcast by Channel 4 in 1984. The programme drew its title from 19th century criminologists' attempts to classify certain physical characteristics as indicators of abnormality. Criminologist Cesar Lomboros, for example, had declared that homosexuals' eyes are 'nearly always bright'. Marshall then goes on to demonstrate how much of the media's reporting of AIDS echoes historical representations of homosexuality as illness, using examples such as the common use of the term 'gay plague' through to a *Sunday People* reference to the once bright eyes of a gay man with AIDS.

Bright Eyes, along with Marshall's other work *Journal of the Plague Year* (1984) were rare examples of documentaries that sought to explore representations and perceptions of AIDS: the majority looked at the history and impact of the disease itself. One other significant exception was *AIDS: The Unheard Voices* (1987), also broadcast on Channel 4, in which Professor Pete Duesberg and others argued that HIV was not the cause of AIDS.

The bulk of AIDS documentaries also focused largely or exclusively on gay men, for example the Australian Special Broadcasting Service's (SBS) *Close Up: After the Shouting Dies Down* (1984), *AIDS: Chapter One* on the USA's PBS (1985), the Australian Broadcasting Corporation's (ABC) *AIDS* (also 1985) and *The Paul Cronan Story*, syndicated by Boston's WBZ-TV in 1987. There were one or two notable exceptions, one of which was the Australian documentary *Suzi's Story*, broadcast on Australia's Network 10 in 1987 and subsequently screened on HBO in the US the following year. Made at the request of Suzi Lovegrove following her diagnosis with

AIDS in 1986 it followed her both at home and in hospital as the disease progressed and ultimately brought about her death. Suzi had contracted HIV through a heterosexual sexual encounter prior to meeting and marrying her husband Vince. By the time she received her diagnosis she had given birth to a son Troy, who had become infected in the womb. Troy's own battle with and subsequent death from AIDS was the subject of a 1993 documentary *A Kid Called Troy.*

In 1988 PBS broadcast *SIDA is AIDS* about the impact of the disease on the Latino community in America. Despite constituting 9 per cent of the American population they accounted for 14 per cent of all US AIDS cases. The documentary, which was broadcast simultaneously on Spanish- and English-speaking networks, included cases of heterosexual and bisexual transmission as well as injecting drug use.

In 1987 the Australian Broadcasting Commission tried a new approach to the coverage of AIDS when it broadcast what was essentially a panel discussion with the title *Does Dracula Have AIDS?* Hosted by QC and broadcaster Geoffrey Robertson the programme was one of a series of so-called 'hypotheticals' that explored issues of the day. The panel was comprised of a series of eminent 'experts' in the field of AIDS including leading researcher Professor Luc Montagnier and Australian Federal Health Minister Neil Blewett. More controversially it also included the Reverend Fred Nile, leader of the Festival of Light, a move that was questioned by a number of activists since Nile had no authority other than his own self-proclaimed (and much disputed) moral authority. Needless to say, he came off second best but his participation again highlighted the tendency for television producers to include a morality figure during any discussion of AIDS. The same was true in the US, where Jerry Falwell was drafted in to the ABC's *AIDS: Anatomy of a Crisis* on 17 July 1983 for a discussion on what was, in reality, a medical issue. No other medical issue has been discussed with anything like the amount of moralistic – and judgmental – input as AIDS.

Music
Pop

The 80s saw an increasing visibility of queer musical performers helped, in part, by the continuing growth of gay clubs. Some artists had begun their careers performing in gay clubs in order to build a core of followers and were now beginning to build a greater presence in the mainstream music scene. Hazell Dean, for example, had her first UK Top Ten hit in 1984 (*Searchin'*) after performing in gay clubs since the mid-70s. Another memorable breakthrough was Divine – the star of many of John Waters' 'bad taste' movies – snarling out *You Think You're a Man* on the UK's staid music show *Top of the Pops* in 1984. Admittedly, Sylvester had been leading the charge since the late 70s with songs like *You Make Me Feel (Mighty Real)* (1978) and *Do Ya Wanna Funk* (1981). Then Boy George appeared in 1982 with *Do You Really Want to Hurt Me*, allowing the media to create the concept of 'gender benders'.

For a brief period gender fluidity was fashionable – in as much as 'gender benders' were the people the media loved to hate. (*The Sun*, for example, had screamed 'EECHHH!!!' in response to Divine's 1984 appearance on *Top of the Pops*). Marilyn (real name Pete Robinson) first came to fame after an androgynous appearance in the Eurythmics pop video *Who's That Girl?*, then had a hit of his own in 1983 with *Calling Your Name*. In 1985 the world made its first acquaintance with the increasingly androgynous singer Pete Burns when his band Dead or Alive had a hit with *You Spin Me Round*.

But it wasn't just the so-called gender benders who were raising their profile on the mainstream music scene. In 1983 Tom Robinson, forever associated with the 70s song (and gay anthem) *(Sing If You're) Glad to be Gay* returned to the charts with *War Baby*, which reached Number 6 in the UK. In that same year Frankie Goes to Hollywood ruffled establishment feathers with their single *Relax*. The record didn't fare particularly well on its initial release in October 1983 but then the band appeared on *Top of the Pops* on 5 January 1984 and the record rose to the Number 6 position. But what pushed it to the Number 1 spot – where it remained for a further five weeks – was a BBC ban on the grounds of its 'sexual content'.

As is often the case when the BBC bans something, the band's profile rocketed due to their new-found notoriety. And part of that profile was the upfront sexuality of the two leading band members, Holly Johnson and Paul Rutherford, while the other, straight, band members weren't afraid to don the trademark leather man uniform of white T-shirt and black leathers either. Meanwhile, the marketing ramped up the sexuality even further with fetish and S&M imagery. If people hadn't noticed the sexual overtones in *Relax* before, they did now!

76

A few weeks later, the BBC lifted the ban, which had become far more embarrassing than the record itself could ever be. But while the ban on the song was lifted, the promotional video was less fortunate. With its upfront portrayal of leather queens, S&M, simulated sex and various other types of fetishism, the BBC would have none of it. Nor, indeed, would MTV, so the band was forced to shoot another, more restrained video. Yet, significantly, in the debate around the record and video bans, the issue at stake always seemed to be sexual explicitness rather than the overt homosexuality. Despite its very obvious presence in both the video and the band itself, it didn't seem to be contentious. Or if it was, the BBC weren't game enough to point it out.

Perhaps there was a more relaxed attitude to upfront queerness – or maybe they just stopped listening to the lyrics. Either way, 1984 also saw the upfront gay band Bronski Beat enter the charts around the world with their debut single *Smalltown Boy* – without even the merest hint of a BBC ban. The lyrics told the tale of a young gay man who packs his bags and heads for London in response to homophobic violence in his home town. In case anyone didn't get the lyrics, the accompanying video put the same message across, unambiguously showing boys lusting after other boys as well as an episode of homophobic violence and the family tensions that arise from that. Even during 'live' television performances, the band's logo – incorporating a large pink triangle – was hard to miss.

In 1985 Bronski Beat teamed up with Marc Almond, formerly of Soft Cell, and released a version of Donna Summer's *I Feel Love*. While the original intention may have been quite radical – that is, openly gay men singing what *The Advocate* magazine described as *"let's fuck anthems"* – the decision was criticised by some queer activists. The reason for this lay in pronouncements Summer had allegedly made at one of her concerts two years earlier. As well as telling the crowd that *"God made Adam and Eve, not Adam and Steve"*, it has also been claimed that she declared that AIDS was God's punishment on gay men. When Bronski Beat were informed of this they had, apparently, responded *"Donna Summer is dead"* [13] but continued to perform the song. This displeased a number of people, including *Advocate* journalist John Bryant who argued that the royalties Summer received from Bronski Beat went to the right-wing Christian Hale Campaign [14].

Elsewhere, Summer's alleged comments triggered calls for a ban on her music in gay clubs. Ian Levine, from London's *Heaven* nightclub, was one of many DJs to ban her records and ACT UP picketed her shows. However, the 'Trash Donna' campaign was far from universal: some clubs continued to play her records, leading to one particular incident where ACT UP members jumped up on stage at an AIDS benefit when the DJ played one of her songs. In 1989 Summer told *The Advocate, "What I supposedly said, I did not say, and my reference to AIDS was really an innocent reference."* [(15)] *She also sent a letter to ACT UP, which was heavily laced with biblical quotations but included the statement, "If I have caused you pain, forgive me. It was never my intention to reject you but to extend myself in love."*

For some it was a case of 'too little, too late'; for others it was the opportunity to forgive and forget. But there were others still for whom it was a case of 'carry on as usual', since they hadn't bothered to do anything in the first place!

Meanwhile, Jimmy Somerville left Bronski Beat in 1985 due to 'personal and political differences' and formed The Communards with Richard Cole – another openly gay man. In 1985 they had the first of a number of hits, which included *Don't Leave Me This Way*, which spent four weeks at the Number 1 slot in the UK charts. Bronski Beat – without Jimmy Somerville – also had a hit in 1985 with *Hit That Perfect Beat* and another in 1986 (*C'Mon, C'Mon*). Indeed, chart-wise, 1985 proved to be a very high-profile year for out queer artists, gay men in particular. As well as The Communards and Bronski Beat, there was also Divine (*Walk Like a Man*), Marc Almond with Bronski Beat (*I Feel Love*), Frankie Goes to Hollywood (*Welcome to the Pleasuredome*) and Pete Burns/Dead or Alive with *You Spin Me Round*. Even Marilyn made it to the outskirts of the charts (Number 70) with *Baby U Left Me* and crooner Johnny Mathis – who had come out in 1982 – had a record in the US 'Adult Contemporary' charts with *Right From the Heart*.

Then there were the ambiguous Pet Shop Boys (*West End Girls*) who chose not to declare their sexuality throughout the 80s but produced singles such as *Rent* (for which Derek Jarman directed the video) and worked with a host of lesbian and gay icons including Dusty Springfield (*What Have I Done to Deserve This?* 1987).

The pairing of the Pet Shops Boys with Dusty Springfield didn't exactly represent a high watermark in queer openness since Springfield had also remained relatively guarded about her sexuality in public, despite a string of lesbian relationships throughout her life. However, this was about as good as it got for lesbian visibility in the music charts during the 80s. kd lang didn't come out until 1992 (albeit having put in a pretty queer performance in her 1990 movie *Salmonberries*), Melissa Etheridge until 1993 and Tracy Chapman hasn't publicly declared her sexuality, despite once dating writer Alice Walker. Those female performers who were out in the 80s – such as Phranc and the Violent Femmes – tended to remain on the periphery of the mainstream music charts. Even in *Sisters Are Doin' It For Themselves* – a 1985 song that was understandably popular with lesbians – Annie Lennox and Aretha Franklin felt it necessary to include the line, *"Don't you know that a man still loves a woman, and a woman still loves a man."*

As we now know, there were also gay male artists who chose not to come out during the 80s: for example George Michael, who chose to promote his song *I Want Your Sex* with a video depicting an unambiguously heterosexual encounter between himself and an unnamed female. Then there was Elton John's 1984 wedding to his recording engineer Renate Blauel in Sydney, Australia: described by Australia's Channel Nine News as *"the most unexpected wedding of the year"*.

Two years later this title could easily have been applied to another wedding – that of Tom Robinson and Sue Brearley. Very much a queer icon up to that point because of his song *Glad to be Gay* and his high profile queer activism, Robinson's marriage led to negative responses from some sections of the queer community as well as the predictable gloating from the tabloids. He was booed when he appeared at London Pride in 1987, for example, while the *Sunday People* declared, *"Britain's Number One Gay in Love with Girl Biker!"* Even *The Independent* newspaper had published an article headlined *"Glad Not to Be Gay"* [16].

In some ways the queer community reaction was understandable: people felt betrayed – in their eyes he'd signed up for the other team; bailed out when we were increasingly under siege. It was a case of our own insecurities being inflamed by media misreporting. Robinson spent a number of years trying to put the true picture across, blogging, giving interviews and even writing songs to tell people that there's more to sexuality than a simple heterosexual/homosexual divide. In the end he got sick of explaining and got angry instead. In 1996 he added a new verse to *Glad to be Gay*: *"Well if gay liberation means no freedom for all, a label is no liberation at all. I'm here and I'm queer and I do what I do. I'm not going to wear a straightjacket for you."*

Robinson still identifies as queer – and, indeed, remains determined to be seen as such – as opposed to David Bowie, who made it clear in 1983 that he'd changed his mind. He'd never been gay after all.

The Rise of the Choirs

While lesbian and gay choirs had begun to emerge in the late 70s, 1981 is generally seen as a landmark year in their development. In North America this has been attributed largely to the 1981 national tour of the San Francisco Gay Men's Chorus, which is said to have inspired others to form their own choirs. For example, the Vancouver Men's Choir was formed by a group of Canadian gay men after seeing the SFGMC perform in Seattle and the Gay Men's Chorus of Washington D.C. after a SFGMC performance at the Kennedy Center Performance Hall. Such was the interest in queer choruses by 1981 that the Sister Singers Network was established for women's and lesbian choruses. In June of that same year a meeting of 12 queer choirs was held in Chicago with participants coming from as far afield as New York, Los Angeles, Seattle and San Francisco. It was at this meeting that a framework was established for a network of choirs under the banner of Gay and Lesbian Association (GALA) Performing Arts.

1981 also saw the birth of Australia's first queer choir with the formation of the Gay Liberation Quire in Sydney, a group of 16 men who came together to promote gay liberation through music. Despite being considerably smaller than most of their counterparts in other countries, the Quire was probably one of the first to release a record – an EP called *Hormones or Jeans: The Gay Liberation Quire Goes Down on Vinyl* (1983).

Meanwhile, back in the USA, the 1982 Gay Games in San Francisco afforded the opportunity for the organisation of the First West Coast Choral Festival, attended by 14 choirs. This, in turn, led to the establishment of the Gay and Lesbian Association Choruses Network and the appointment of its first President. That same year also saw the establishment of Europe's first gay men's chorus – Gaykor – in Stockholm, Sweden.

The Pink Singers – an 80-strong group – was established in London in 1983, becoming Europe's first lesbian and gay choir. In New York, GALA presented the first national queer choral festival under the banner COAST – Come Out and Sing Together –

80

an event that marked the beginning of a three-year cycle of national queer choir festivals in various cities around the country. Thirty years on, the number of queer choirs is still growing.

Literature

The 1984/85 trial of Gay's the Word bookshop in London (covered in the chapter *Under Attack*) highlighted a major issue in accessing queer literature in Britain: the limited amount of locally produced literature meant a certain dependence on imports. This put the importers at the mercy of HM Customs and their bigoted and arbitrary nature of determining what was and was not obscene. Australia had faced the same situation up until the early 1970s, when the Whitlam government scrapped Customs' power of censorship. In America, the government was more concerned with incoming homosexuals than incoming literature, although the reality for much of the 80s was that America was producing far more queer books than it was importing anyway.

The stream of publications in the UK gradually grew during the 80s for three main reasons. The first was a 1986 decision by the European Court of Justice that effectively took away HM Customs' power to seize books that would not have been declared obscene under the British Obscene Publications Act. The second was the growth of queer publishing houses in the UK and the third was a significant increase in the publication of queer publications by mainstream publishing houses (so much so that *The Bookseller* magazine called the 80s *"the decade of the gay novel"*).

The European Court of Justice decision meant not only that books could be imported but they could be imported without risk of seizure, which, in practice, took away a considerable financial risk from the importers. Not only did detained books represent a loss of income but even those that were eventually returned by Customs were often too damaged to be sold at normal price. The removal of this risk benefited not only Gay's the Word but the many other bookshops up and down the UK that sought to increase their range of queer literature.

Certain books led the charge into the book chains: Armistead Maupin's *Tales of the City* series was especially popular because its diversity and inclusivity gave it a broad appeal. But the book chains also took titles like *Boy's Own Story* (Picador), *Oranges Are Not the Only Fruit* (Pandora) and *The Penguin Book of Homosexual Verse*. They

81

may have been reassured by the fact that these books came from mainstream publishing houses but some also began stocking titles from emerging queer publishers like Gay Men's Press, which started at the end of 1979, and Brilliance Books, which began in 1982.

However, not all titles were met with universal enthusiasm. *Jenny Lives with Eric and Martin*, published in the UK by Gay Men's Press in 1983 was decried by Conservative MPs and the British tabloid press as nothing more than gay propaganda. Created by Danish author Susanne Bosche to facilitate discussion with children about homosexuality it took the form of a black and white photo book depicting six-year-old Jenny, her father and his male partner going about their day-to-day business together. However, it was taken up by Conservative MP Dame Jill Knight as another weapon in her campaign for the introduction of Section 28 of the Local Government Act, prohibiting Local Authorities from 'promoting' homosexuality.

Knight's campaign of misinformation included the claim that the book was available in schools. Despite the fact that she was unable to name a single school using it – unsurprising, since none were – her campaign was backed to the hilt by *The Sun* newspaper, which was bent on discrediting any progressive Labour-controlled local authority. They ran a front page headline that screeched *"Vile Book in School: Pupils See Pictures of Gay Lovers"* and claimed that the book was available in school libraries in Labour-controlled areas. Given the reference to *"pictures of gay lovers"*, readers would have been forgiven for thinking that the book was a queer *Karma Sutra*. It wasn't – nor had it ever been available in school libraries. Nonetheless, Jill Knight would continue to refer to it – and the press would continue to report her claims without question – until the passage of Section 28.

References

1. Bell, Arthur. Bell Tells. *The Village Voice*, New York. 16 July 1979.

2. Review by Rex Reed of the *New York Times*, quoted in *Statemaster Online Encyclopedia*. [Online] Available at http://www.statemaster.com/encyclopedia/Partners-%281982-film%29 Accessed May 2014.

3. Interviewed in the film *The Celluloid Closet*, Sony Pictures. 1995.

4. Gever, M., Parmar, P. and Greyson, J. 2013. *Queer Looks*. London: Routledge, p202.

5. The Gays and Broadcasting Project. 1987. *Are We Being Served: Lesbians, Gays and Broadcasting*. London.

6. For example, Capsuto, Steven. 2000. *Alternate Channels: The Uncensored Story of Gay and Lesbian Images on Radio and Television*. New York: Ballantine Books.

7. *Are We Being Served: Lesbians, Gays and Broadcasting*, p3.

8. Walker, Martin. Slice of Life. *The Guardian*, London. 7 January 1984.

9. Landreth, Jenny. *Right On and On Your Screen*. Marxism Today. May 1987.

10. Beavan, Clare. *The Guardian*, London. 6 February 1989. Quoted in Burston, P. and Richardson, C. (eds). 2005. *A Queer Romance: Lesbians, Gay Men and Popular Culture*. London: Routledge, p233.

11. Taylor, John Russell. Making a start. *Gay News*. Issue 185, 21 February 1980.

12. Meldrum, Julian. 1984. *AIDS Through the British Media*. London: AIDS Action Group.

13. Block, Adam. Summer and Smoke. *The Advocate*. 23 July 1985.

14. Block, Adam. Summer and Smoke.

15. Koffler, Kevin. Not the Last Dance. *The Advocate*. 4 July 1989.

16. Thorpe, Vanessa. Glad not to be gay. *The Independent*, London. 3 March 1998.

Chapter Two

The Growth of Queer Communities

The queer social and commercial scene also began to undergo changes in the 80s. These were driven by a number of factors that included politics, economics (the increasing recognition of the 'Pink Pound/Dollar'), the increasing visibility of queer communities and, of course, HIV/AIDS.

Keeping it Queer

By the beginning of the 80s, the queer social scene was moving well out of the shadows. Major cities offered all manner of clubs such as the Mineshaft (New York), Heaven (London) and the Midnight Shift (Sydney). But even in more provincial towns, entrepreneurs were beginning to recognise the value of the pink pound or dollar, leading to increasing numbers of exclusively queer venues as well as other establishments that allocated specific areas or evenings for queer customers.

In mid-80s Nottingham, for example, 'Part Two' was our full-time gay club and the Foresters Arms our full-time, predominantly lesbian, pub. The downstairs lounge at the Hearty Goodfellow pub was for gay men (complete with a 'Private Party' sign posted halfway down the staircase, ostensibly to deter any stray heterosexuals). The upstairs bar was for lesbians (I don't know if there was a sign as I never went there). The back bar of The Dog and Partridge and the lounge of Gatsby's pub were largely for gay men, with the landlady of the latter warning a gay friend of mine that we should do nothing to offend her *"normal customers"*. The Astoria nightclub offered 'Gay Night' on the first Monday of the month and the Bridge pub hosted a lesbian disco on the first Wednesday of every month. Meanwhile, a few miles out of town was the Pavilion club, a men-only member-run establishment that operated once a week from a former lawn bowls pavilion tucked away down a little lane. Provision was certainly diverse – even if you did feel like you needed a spreadsheet, a compass and an Ordnance Survey map to access it!

But increased visibility also brought with it the issue of 'intrusion' – increasing numbers of non-queer people attracted by the creative hedonism of the queer scene. And intrusion brought with it a range of problems. The mildest were the staring, sniggering and general voyeurism but the more serious was the sexual harassment of lesbians by straight men and physical and verbal abuse of gay men and lesbians by both straight men and women.

Entrepreneur Jeremy Norman had come up against this when he opened his Embassy Club in London in 1978 as an attempt to offer a more spacious, upmarket alternative to the smaller London gay clubs of that time. Within a short space of time non-queer people were outnumbering queer customers so Norman sought out premises for another gay club that, he determined, would remain gay. He found them in a disused roller-skating rink under a railway arch on the Thames Embankment. After spending £300,000 transforming it into the ultimate, multi-level, hi-tech venue, he opened it in December 1979 as 'Heaven'. In its early years it enforced a 'gay men only' door policy [1] but this too was soon eased as Heaven became the place to be seen. Madonna, Donna Summer, Sheena Easton, Divine, Sylvester and Cher were but a few of the names to grace its stage.

Meanwhile, in Australia, Sydney was witnessing the birth of an event that would come to dominate the queer social calendar and, consequently, become victim to 'intrusion' too – the Gay Mardi Gras party.

The early years of Sydney's annual Gay Mardi Gras parades had been marked by hostility from and conflict with the police; in particular, the arrests of 53 people at the first Mardi Gras parade in 1978. And despite the fact that there had been no further arrests at subsequent parades, tensions were still so high that organisers of the 1980 parade felt it wise to organise a post-parade party – and a bail fund – just in case. This would get people off the streets as quickly as possible but also maintain the sense of celebration and excitement that had been generated during the parade. The parade passed off without major incident then some 700 people enjoyed the first ever Mardi Gras party – a fancy dress ball organised by the Gay Solidarity Group at Paddington Town Hall.

But the timing of the parade – in the middle of Australia's winter – proved to be a point of some considerable debate for organisers. Some felt that it should be moved to the summer to attract a larger number of supporters and, in so doing, demonstrate the size and diversity of the queer communities. Others felt that this would de-politicise the event by breaking the important historical connection with the Stonewall riots of June 1969 [2].

The advocates of a summer time parade won the day and Sydney saw its first summertime Mardi Gras parade in February 1981. By 1982 a new party venue had been found – the Sydney Showgrounds (now part of a broader entertainment complex that includes Fox film studios) – where it has remained more or less ever since. Four thousand people attended that year but, as the party established a reputation for creativity and unabashed hedonism, the numbers rose quickly in subsequent years: by 1989, for example, 15,000 tickets were sold.

Parallel to the development of a summer Mardi Gras party was the creation of the Sleaze Ball, primarily a Mardi Gras fundraiser but also a celebration of 'sleaze as a style invented by the gay sub-culture' [3]. As the Sydney Star defined it, *"Everything from high camp drag to full S&M leather can have an element of sleaze in it."* Like the first Mardi Gras party, Sleaze also made its debut at Paddington Town Hall – on 18 September 1982 – and was so popular that 500 people had to be turned away. The following year it too moved to the Sydney Showgrounds and sold 2000 tickets. By 1990, 12,000 tickets were sold. But as the number of participants increased, so did the issue of intrusion.

One alleged source of this problem was gay men bringing their straight female friends who, in turn, began to bring their boyfriends along and so the issue – and the tension – began to escalate. Central to the debate on this was the view that non-queer people were importing active homophobia into those few spaces queers could call their own.

There has been much anecdotal evidence of homophobic behaviour within queer venues. In Sydney it finally came to a head in 1996: in response to increasing complaints about straight men sexually harassing lesbians and verbally and physically abusing gay men at the Mardi Gras parties, organisers banned non-queer people from becoming members [4]. The decision was not taken without some considerable debate (and was eventually rescinded) but the fact that it happened at all is an indication of the extent of the problem of homophobia in queer venues.

Thirteen years later a study by the Australian Institute of Criminology [5] found that 40 per cent of queer participants at events like Mardi Gras had witnessed some form of hostile activity, but very few had reported it to the police. More than 65 per cent said they avoided certain events because of safety and comfort issues and more than 30 per cent specified Mardi Gras parties as an event at which they felt unsafe or uncomfortable.

The increased visibility of queer events and venues clearly served as a beacon for those homophobes keen to translate their hate into direct action. In queer venues non-queer people can become hostile and abusive as any repressed discomfort with seeing demonstrations of same sex affection surfaces in the course of intoxication with alcohol or other drugs. Unsurprisingly then, the report found that queer people were becoming increasingly uncomfortable about 'being themselves' at queer venues, especially where drugs and alcohol were also in use. As one respondent declared: *"I have to live in a heterosexual world 24/7. I wish they would respect our space and show that respect by not attending."* [6]

The Politics of the Scene
Separatism

Lesbians and gay men socialising in separate spaces is a long established and (generally) accepted practice. Historically, many lesbians have felt that they have more in common with women in general than they have with gay men. This was highlighted during the debate on moving Sydney's Mardi Gras to the summer months, which resulted in decreased participation by lesbians.

"The decision to move from winter to summer escalated involvement and a more celebratory atmosphere. But there was a loss. It caused a few of the 'protest' hardliners to pull away, especially almost all the lesbians who re-hitched their wagon to the burgeoning Women's Liberation movement." [7]

Lesbians identified with the wider feminist agenda around women's unequal position in a patriarchal society, which they felt was lost by moving towards a more 'carnival' atmosphere. Gay men, on the other hand, felt that the focus should be the demand for urgent law reform to decriminalise male homosexual acts. In consequence:

"Mardi Gras, including management and Parade participants remained almost exclusively male until the late 1980s." [8]

It would not be until 1988, when an Extraordinary General Meeting voted to change the name from the Sydney Gay Mardi Gras to the Sydney Gay and Lesbian Mardi Gras, that the first lesbian – Cath Phillips – joined the Mardi Gras Management Board.

There were other reasons for separate socialising of course; these included the simple desire to be in a women-only space and to escape the misogyny that some gay men manifest.

87

But establishing a women-only space in a 'mixed' venue is not always easy, as the proprietors of the Fallen Angel pub in Islington, London, discovered in 1984. They had gone to great efforts to develop the pub into an accessible queer community resource. For example, in those days of restricted licensing hours, they ran the premises as a cafe during the hours that they weren't allowed to serve alcohol. Vegan and vegetarian food was available, regular exhibitions of art work were held, poetry and other literary events were held and the upstairs meeting room hosted a range of groups such as Lesbians and Gays Support the Miners and queer youth groups.

And then they introduced a 'women-only' night.

From memory, I think the night in question was a Tuesday: it certainly wasn't one of their busiest nights. Sadly, this didn't stop a small group of gay men from being outraged at their perceived 'exclusion'. Such was the apparent degree of distress at this exclusion that they took the proprietors to court, alleging a breach of Equal Opportunities legislation. Very sadly, they won and the Fallen Angel was forced to abandon its women's night.

Not all gay men supported the legal action and, for a while at least, some stood outside the pub on what had been women's night and tried to dissuade other men from going in. I'm afraid I have no idea as to the success of this strategy as I left London shortly thereafter.

Drag

"I have spoken to drag performers who have been genuinely hurt at the suggestion that they are satirising women because they feel – however mistakenly – that they are paying homage to their female idols; and while there are Diana Rosses and Shirley Basseys in this world I cannot see how they will ever be dissuaded of this … There are also drag acts like Dave Dale who consider themselves to be character actors who do caricatures of both men and women. There are acts who are still doing the pregnant bride routine which they were doing 20 years ago. And there are acts which prey on the basest instincts of their audience, perpetuating the notion that women smell like fish and that black men swing from trees. What the latter acts do is unforgivable and I prefer to reserve my venom for them and those unthinking audiences of gay men who appear to share their brute misogyny and racism." [9]

88

This quote, from the 1984 book *Men in Frocks*, effectively summarises the perceptions of and debate around drag within the queer scene during the 80s. Certainly, my first experiences of the British and Australian drag scenes left me with a very strong impression of misogyny and racism. My first ever drag show was at London's Vauxhall Tavern, where the performer not only presented as a large-breasted Vera Lynn but ended the show with a mass waving of the Union Jack. It wouldn't have been out of place at a rally of the far-right National Front.

Two years later, during my first visit to Australia, I witnessed the casual racism that seemed to be the stock-in-trade of some drag artists. In this case it was the aforementioned 'pregnant bride' routine, with one of the performers 'giving birth' on stage by dropping a baby doll from under her skirt. The 'joke' was that the baby was black, as if to suggest that this 'woman' was so desperate she'd stoop to having sex with a black man.

But, as *Men in Frocks* amply demonstrated, there were other perspectives on gay men in drag. One of these stems from the so-called birth of Gay Liberation – the Stonewall Riots – and recognises that it was the transgenders and drag queens who led the fightback against the police harassment. Someone in Sydney once told me that this was why the Mardi Gras parade had such a high prevalence of men in drag.

Intertwined with this historical perspective was the concept of 'gender-fuck', which challenges notions of gender identity based on factors like dress and behaviour. Put simply: why shouldn't a man wear a dress and make-up if he wants to? This view of drag was certainly far more palatable to hardened lefties like me, not least because it was based on the subversion of patriarchal tradition, not the oppression of women.

That's certainly what I told myself when I lost my drag virginity in West Hollywood, Los Angeles, in 1986. It was completely spontaneous: had it been at all pre-meditated I would have spent weeks analysing myself into a stupor over the politics and appropriateness of it all. Instead it came down to my arriving in that fair city to discover that my host and his friends were intending to drag up to attend a Halloween street party. Call it peer pressure, fear of being a wallflower or just temporary insanity; whatever it was, I found myself one day in a second-hand clothing store in West Hollywood eyeing up a stunning, full-length, scarlet satin evening dress.

I was too embarrassed to try it on in the store but, thankfully, it turned out to be a perfect fit for my then skinny frame. Accessorised with a white plastic 'pearl' necklace, matching bracelet and droplet earrings as well as vivid red lipstick and nail varnish, the whole scheme went perfectly with my beard and long brown curly hair – especially when topped off with a faded denim jacket and white trainers!

My drag enlightenment continued when I returned home to England. In London, the Terrence Higgins Trust had held a hugely successful 'Night of a Thousand Frocks' fundraiser at the Hippodrome Club in 1986.The sight of some of England's leading AIDS activists in ball gowns is certainly a strong incentive to rethink your political stance on drag!

Settling in Sydney in 1987 I soon learned that there was a lot more to the drag scene than racist 'female impersonators'. Drag in Sydney had a much higher profile and a much more diverse manifestation than I had experienced elsewhere. For example, real-life 'drag racing' (as well as other events such as handbag tossing) was an event at the 'Pollympics', an annual fundraising sports day attended by a wide range of queer people. And as the AIDS crisis unfolded, many drag performers and events were at the forefront of fundraising efforts.

The London Lesbian and Gay Centre

Perhaps it was the growing pains of the burgeoning queer communities or the political legacy of the early gay liberation movement but it seemed like it was necessary to have 'positions' on just about everything in the 80s – even disco [10]. Disco notwithstanding, two rather more contentious issues were bondage/sado-masochism and bisexuality. In 1985, practitioners of both were banned from the London Lesbian and Gay Centre – a project that had been established in recognition of the diverse needs of an even more diverse community.

The London Lesbian and Gay Centre (LLGC) had been funded by the Greater London Council (GLC) as part of the London Labour Party's pre-election commitment to support queer communities. After its successful re-election it had expanded on the need for such a centre in its 1985 report *Changing the World: A Charter for Gay and Lesbian Rights*:

"Community and leisure provisions for lesbians and gays are severely limited. The commercial social scene comprises pubs and clubs, usually catering for men who

enjoy disco music. There are very few commercial clubs or pubs which cater for either lesbians, older lesbians and gays or people with disabilities. Young people who are not old enough to go to clubs, or who find them too expensive, have no alternative way of socialising with lesbian or gay people of their own age. Most commercial establishments are situated in the centre of London and high admission and drink prices put them out of reach of many lesbians and gays; many present physical problems of access for lesbians and gay men with disabilities." [11]

In fact, by the time the report was published, the GLC had already allocated £750,000 to acquire a centre in 1984. (Indeed, such was the GLC's enthusiasm to carry through on its commitment, it took everyone by surprise. I had just moved to London at that time and I remember a friend describing the rush to set up an organising committee to turn this unexpected windfall into a reality.)

But a committee was established, premises were acquired and the Centre opened ('unofficially' because some building work was still incomplete) in December 1984. A range of activities and events not usually offered on the commercial scene were provided; for example, in addition to the 'staples' of a bar and cafe, there were art exhibitions, cabaret and theatre, discos (including a Tuesday night 'Body Positive' disco for HIV+ people and their friends), support and interest groups and special events such as beer festivals and stand-up comedy.

But shortly after its opening it was, apparently, 'agreed' that BD/SM and bisexual groups would be banned for five years. The reasons, as I understand them, were because of the violence implicit in BD/SM practices (and particularly the use of Nazi regalia) and because lesbians would feel sexually threatened by bisexual men.

In fairness, it should be said that there was not universal support for these bans and such support as there was came under further question when it was revealed that the centre was to host the Second National Bisexual Conference in April 1985. This, apparently, was because the booking had been taken 'in error'! Further pressure was added by the fact that both the National Lesbian Strength and the National Lesbian and Gay Pride marches – scheduled for June and including bisexuals and BD/SM practitioners – were due to culminate at the centre.

On 9 June 1985 an Extraordinary Meeting of LLGC members overturned both bans.

Marginalisation and Diversity

The LLGC was now open to bisexuals and BD/SM practitioners – albeit after a bit of a struggle. But there were others who still did not feel welcome.

One such group was black and Asian lesbians and gay men. Like many of the groups who used the LLGC, they too felt alienated from the commercial scene, not least because of the racism they experienced there. As one black gay man told *The Voice* magazine in 1988, *"It's a majority white middle class scene … Black people feel more vulnerable."* [12] *As far as the LLGC was concerned they too felt that it was "predominantly male, predominantly white"* [13].

Such was the sense of alienation among black lesbians and gays that a group of them established the London Black Lesbian and Gay Centre Project in 1985. Initially operating as a 'virtual' centre – organising a range of social and support activities from various local authority-owned premises across London – the project finally managed to raise the funds necessary to open its own premises in Peckham, South London. From there it ran a variety of events and activities including support groups and social events; much like the London Lesbian and Gay Centre but targeting those who, by virtue of their ethnicity, did not feel comfortable in either commercial venues or the LLGC. Its promotional brochure declared:

"BLGC welcomes lesbians and gays of First Nation/Third World descent, i.e. lesbians and gays descended from Africa, Asia (i.e. the Middle East to China, including the Pacific nations) and Latin America (Third World peoples); and lesbians and gays descended from the original inhabitants of Australasia and North America (First Nation peoples)."

Of course it wasn't just in the UK that people of colour were feeling marginalised within the queer scene. In Australia, for example, the first Aboriginal Australian float did not appear in the Sydney Gay and Lesbian Mardi Gras until 1988 (the Bicentennial of white settlement in Australia). The *Sydney Morning Herald* reported the comments of the float's organiser, Malcolm Cole:

"Gay Aborigines have had to battle prejudice from within their own community, which traditionally does not recognise homosexuality as a lifestyle, as well as fight for acceptance from the largely middle class gay culture. Many of them can relate to experiences of being refused entrance to gay clubs, ostensibly for being drunk, though no more so than their white companions." [14]

It would be a further three years before the first Asian gay men's float, Asians and Friends, appeared and another four before the first Sydney Asian Lesbian Network float.

With the advent of HIV/AIDS, queer social venues took on a crucial role in getting out information about things like safer sex, treatment options and support services. Queer publications such as *Capital Gay* and the *Sydney Star Observer* carrying up-to-date news were most readily available in queer venues. At the same time, AIDS prevention projects would often distribute resources such as condoms, lubricant and explicit safe sex information (such as the AIDS Council of New South Wales' *Six Tips for Hard Cocks* photo leaflet).

Thus those who were unable to access these venues and resources were at a distinct disadvantage and this became increasingly obvious in the infection rates. Membership of ethnic or linguistic minorities – from Latino and African American gay men to Asians and Australian Aborigines – was found to be a factor in increased exposure to HIV [15].

So, too, was disability as people with disability were found to be excluded from mainstream queer culture due to a number of factors. These ranged from lack of wheelchair access to the attitudes of others – including HIV/AIDS educators.

For example, one service reported the experience of 'James' – a man with cerebral palsy:

"... James had to cope with some carers' negative reaction towards his sexual orientation ... Once he was even prevented by a driver of a disability transport service from entering a gay club ... And another time inside a gay bar [his companion] heard someone mutter, "Why on earth would he even bring him here?" [16]

A joint United Nations/World Health Organisation policy brief identified how such attitudes influence access to HIV prevention and support services:

"... persons with disabilities may also be turned away from HIV education forums or not be invited by outreach workers because of assumptions they are not sexually active or do not engage in other risk behaviours such as injecting drugs." [17]

Queer Community Periodicals

In the pre-internet 80s, a key element in the development of strong queer communities was a network of community periodicals. These ranged from newsletters of queer organisations to a variety of local and national newspapers and magazines.

93

Survival depended on successfully anticipating the personal and political tastes of a post-Liberation queer market, navigating a minefield of legal constraints, such as decency and obscenity laws, and attracting sufficient advertising to cover production costs. Practical considerations like finding a printer and distribution networks also played a part (for example, the printers of Canada's *Body Politic* magazine ended their contract after the magazine won an anti-discrimination case against their parent company). Unsurprisingly, therefore, there was some degree of volatility in the queer publication market, with some publications folding after failing to tick all the necessary boxes.

One publication that appeared to survive this was the UK's *Gay News*. Since its inception in 1972, it had been prosecuted (unsuccessfully) for obscenity when its cover photo featured two men kissing, then subsequently – and successfully – for 'blasphemous libel' after it published a poem *The Love that Dares to Speak its Name*. And for much of the 70s, the UK's largest newspaper distributor, WH Smith had refused to stock or distribute it.

It had survived all of these challenges, not least because it had immense support from the UK's queer communities and was, consequently, seen as well worth defending.

One of a number of initiatives that had grown out of the early gay liberation movement (others included London Gay Switchboard), it was produced by and for both lesbians and gay men. In keeping with the egalitarian politics of Gay Liberation, it was generally regarded as a collective enterprise where the division between managers and mainstream staff was virtually non-existent. Its unapologetically queer politics regularly brought it into conflict with the law: for example, editor Denis Lemon was prosecuted for 'obstructing police in the course of their duties' in 1972 after he photographed them harassing gay men outside a London gay pub. And as stated earlier, the newspaper was successfully prosecuted for the ridiculous offence of 'blasphemous libel'.

But, despite being found guilty, both Lemon and *Gay News* endured – until 1982 that is, when Lemon sold his shares in the paper and triggered a crisis that saw the paper cease publication and the title incorporated into a gay men's glossy magazine, *Gay Times*.

The seeds for its demise – and the collectivist politics on which it had been established – were set as early as 1973 when Lemon was allocated 46 out of 100 shares during a cash crisis. Thirty-three of these shares were, allegedly, to be held only while he remained in post as editor. But six years later he was allowed to buy a further 49 of the 100 shares and the *Gay News* directors also waived the requirement for Lemon to hand back the 33 shares if he left the post of editor.

In February 1982, Lemon announced that he had sold all of his shares to a new player, Robert Palmer. The announcement effectively declared an end to the era of collective decision-making and shared ownership at the paper.

But the agreement ran into difficulties when Robert Palmer failed to pay a £10,000 instalment on the deal by 31 December 1982, throwing the future of *Gay News* open to speculation again. Undaunted, Lemon announced that he and Palmer had come to a new arrangement, part of which involved Lemon being kept on as editor-in-chief.

In response to vigorous protests from staff and other *Gay News* supporters, Palmer denied that Lemon was to be given the editorial role, and that he was actually to be appointed as a consultant to Palmer's marketing company. But even this offer was quickly withdrawn and it seemed that everything was up in the air again.

In consequence, agents acting on behalf of the staff of *Gay News* wrote to Lemon and Palmer in February 1983, requesting that negotiations begin on taking the newspaper into some form of community ownership. The following week *Gay News* itself carried a statement from the staff explaining their actions. This included the declaration that:

"We on the staff are NOT seeking to buy the paper for profit, other than our own wages. We plan simply to organise the means by which Gay News can truly be regarded as the communal possession of gay people – who, we hope, will entrust us, as paid staff, to bring it out so that it will amuse, inform and campaign."

The request fell on deaf ears: while Palmer ultimately dropped out of negotiations, Lemon sold the paper to Nigel Ostrer, heir to the British Gaumont movie empire, instead. Ostrer's lack of experience in both publishing and queer politics quickly showed: after a short-lived attempt to publish as *The New Gay News* he sold the title to Millivres Ltd, publishers of gay soft-porn magazine *HIM*. Millivres had attempted to launch their own version of *Gay News* – *Gay Reporter* – early in 1983. This had been widely criticised for its perceived anti-lesbian stance and managed only four issues before being incorporated into *HIM* as a news supplement.

In 1984, Millivres combined *HIM* magazine and the *Gay News* title and launched *Gay Times* (with the words *"incorporating Gay News"* in small print below the title). It explicitly and unapologetically targeted gay men; lesbians would have to wait for a further decade before Millivres produced their sister magazine, *Diva*.

In the meantime, a group of activists attempted to produce a new national periodical for both lesbians and gay men. *Outrage!* was launched in the summer of 1983 as a *"radical (inter)national monthly magazine covering a multitude of issues that matter to lesbians and gay men"* [18]. Sadly, despite a determined effort to sustain both the political astuteness and collectivist spirit of *Gay News, Outrage!* failed to raise the necessary financial resources and was gone by the end of the year.

References:

1. Howard, Luke. 2013. Luke Howard's Brief History of London's Gay Clubs: From Bang to
    Heaven. *Faith Fanzine*. 25 July.
    [Online]. Available at
    http://sabotagetimes.com/music/luke-howards-brief-history-of-londons-gay-clubs-pt-1-from-bang-to-heaven/
    Accessed August 2014.

2. Harris, G., White, J. and Davis, K. 2008. *New Day Dawning: The Early Years of Sydney's
    Gay and Lesbian Mardi Gras*. Sydney Pride History Group. Quoted in Walford, Megan.
    2010. Protest & Memory. University of New South Wales.
    [Online]. Available at
    http://www.phansw.org.au/wp-content/uploads/2012/09/MeganWalford2010.pdf
    Accessed August 2014.

3. Sleaze for Sydney. *Sydney Star*. 28 August 1982.

4. Sydney Gay and Lesbian and Mardi Gras membership controversy. *Green Left*. 22 May 1996.

5. Tomsen, S. and Markwell, K. 2009. *When the glitter settles: safety and hostility at and
    around gay and lesbian public events*. Canberra, Australia: Australian Institute of
    Criminology.

6. *When the glitter settles: safety and hostility at and around gay and lesbian
    public events*, p14.

7. Waites, James. 2013. G&L Mardi Gras – 2013. [Online] Personal blog available at http://
    jameswaites.ilatech.org/?p=8054. Accessed August 2014.

8. *G&L Mardi Gras – 2013*.

9. Kirk, Kris and Heath, Ed. 1984. *Men in Frocks*. London: Gay Men's Press. Quoted in
    A Gender Variance Who's Who.
    [Online] Personal blog available at
    http://zagria.blogspot.co.uk/2013/04/a-review-of-kris-kirk-ed-heath-men-in.html#.VDJsghbQoSk
    Accessed August 2014.

10. Dyer, Richard. In Defence of Disco. *Gay Left*. Issue 8, Summer 1979.

11. Greater London Council and GLC Gay Working Party. 1985. *Changing the World: A Charter
    for Lesbian and Gay Rights*. London.

12. Burgess, Mike. Why We're Proud to be Gay. *The Voice*, London. 19 January 1988.

13. Un-named participant's comment in *Under Your Nose*, documentary in production. 2013. Twice As Proud Productions, London.

14. Stapleton, John. It's the black and white Mardi Gras. *Sydney Morning Herald*. 27 February 1988.

15. See, for example, *Black Americans and HIV/AIDS*. [Online] Website of the Henry Kaiser Family Foundation.
    Available at
    http://kff.org/hivaids/fact-sheet/black-americans-and-hiv-aids/#footnote-110986-6
    Accessed March 2015.

16. Benedetti, Michael. 2011. *The second closet: LGBTs with disabilities*. {Online]. Website of MyHandicap International.
    Available at
    http://www.myhandicap.com/gay-lesbian-disability.html?PHPSESSID=550fad963f37c100795abe40434ce9a9
    Accessed March 2015.

17. United Nations High Commission for Human Rights and the World Health Organisation. 2009. *Disability and HIV: Policy Brief*.

18. As described in an advert for the magazine that appeared in *Gay East Midlands*, Issue No 5, October 1983, p5.

Mainstream Politics

While activists had pushed for the inclusion of queer rights on the platforms of political parties for many years, the 80s finally began to see these campaigns bear fruit. There were essentially two main areas in which activists sought change: decriminalisation of homosexuality and effective anti-discrimination measures. The advent of HIV/AIDS made these measures even more important for a number of reasons. For example, discrimination and violence against queer people increased enormously as a consequence of the fear and alarmism with which media reported the disease. And in terms of preventing the spread of the disease, the sustained criminalisation of gay men fuelled furtive and anonymous behaviour, which meant the people who needed prevention information the most were also the hardest to access.

For queer political opponents, however, homosexuality and HIV/AIDS were simply evidence of immorality. In their eyes, decriminalisation and 'equal rights' were nothing more than measures to expedite the spread of HIV/AIDS to 'innocent' people and facilitate the mythical 'gay agenda' of turning everyone into homosexuals. Thus the battle lines were drawn.

Australia
States of Confusion

Australian politicians had been calling for, and Australian political parties had been voting in favour of, decriminalisation of homosexuality from as early as 1968. Even the Australian Federal Parliament voted in favour in 1973. And yet, at the beginning of 1980, homosexuality had been decriminalised in only one state (South Australia) and one territory (the Australian Capital Territory (ACT)). States such as Queensland and Tasmania would hold out until 1990 and 1997 respectively and, somewhat confusingly, the state of New South Wales included sexuality in its Anti-Discrimination Act in 1982 – two years before it decriminalised homosexuality.

In Western Australia, the state's Labor government held intensely homophobic views throughout the 80s. At the end of that decade, when it finally accepted that decriminalisation of homosexuality was a key measure in the fight against HIV/AIDS, it did so with astonishing animosity.

When it presented its Criminal Code Amendment (Decriminalisation of Homosexuality) Bill to State Parliament on 16 November 1989, the debate appears to have been between those who were completely opposed to decriminalisation and those who felt it to be a necessary evil. Those who were completely opposed called for a public referendum on the issue; those who saw it as a necessary evil inserted an extraordinary preamble to the bill just to ensure that everyone knew just how reluctant they were to take this step. It included the statements:

- *"Parliament disapproves of sexual relations between persons of the same sex ..."*
- *"Parliament disapproves of the promotion or encouragement of homosexual behaviour ..."*
- *"Parliament does not by its actions in removing any criminal penalty in private between persons of the same sex wish to create a change in community attitude to homosexual behaviour ..."*

In case that wasn't explicit enough, a new offence was also created under the Act that made it a crime to *"... promote or encourage homosexual behaviour as part of the teaching in any primary or secondary educational institutions ..."* or to create public policy *"... to encourage or promote homosexual behaviour and the encouragement or promotion of homosexual behaviour shall not be capable of being a public purpose."* [1] It was Western Australia's own version of the UK's more infamous Section 28 – although on this occasion under a Labor government.

The USA
The Homophobia of Michael Dukakis

Australia wasn't the only place where political parties voted in favour of decriminalisation at party conference then failed to put their policies into practice when they came to power. In the USA, for example, Democrat Michael Dukakis consistently ignored his own party's policy – even when he was running for president.

The Democrats had finally included queer rights in their political platform in 1980. In practice this meant little more than adding sexual orientation to their anti-discrimination statement but even this measure had required years of concerted effort by activists. But when Dukakis was chosen as Democratic presidential candidate in 1988 queers only had to look at his appalling track record to see that they could expect no support from him. And he made no effort to rectify that perception.

He already brought with him the legacy of both his views and his behaviour around queer adoption when he was Governor of Massachusetts (as detailed in Chapter One).

And from the beginning of his candidacy for the US Presidency, he continued to antagonise the queer community with his repeated assertions that the heterosexual nuclear family was *"ideal"*.

Undoubtedly driven by a desperate need to find an alternative to Republican candidate George Bush, queer community leaders tried to find ways by which Dukakis could redeem himself. Dukakis, on the other hand, behaved as if he wanted none of it. At a May 1988 public forum organised by the Western States Political Action Committees – a coalition of queer rights organisations – Dukakis repeatedly antagonised his audience. As the *Los Angeles Times* reported:

"An attempt by Massachusetts Governor Michael S. Dukakis to mend troubled relations with the gay community was met Saturday with occasional hisses and boos at a public meeting that turned into a critique of the candidate's gay rights positions.

Dukakis stuck tenaciously to his views during the tense half-hour session, finally defending the Massachusetts policy that gives homosexual couples less chance of becoming foster parents than heterosexuals by declaring: 'There is no civil right to be a foster parent.'

Many in the crowd at Los Angeles Four Seasons Hotel then hissed with displeasure, and some responded with applause when a heckler called the presidential candidate a 'bigot' and 'anti-gay'." [2]

In spite of this performance, queer community leaders maintained their support for him – only to have it wholeheartedly rejected. Millions of dollars were raised within the community to support his campaign – but Dukakis refused to accept it, on the grounds that this would damage his image in the view of 'mainstream' voters.

To no one's surprise, he was soundly thrashed in the presidential elections, with polls suggesting that some 35-40 per cent of gay and lesbian voters chose Bush – hardly a champion of queer rights himself – instead of him.

The United Kingdom
The Labour Party's Discomfort with Queer Rights

In the UK, moves to have the Labour Party incorporate queer rights into its manifesto also required many years of work across both trades unions and the Labour Party itself. Within the party members and supporters of the Labour Campaign for Lesbian and Gay Rights (previously the Gay Labour Group) undertook a concerted operation of education and lobbying at both local and national level.

At the same time, activists ran similar awareness-raising campaigns within their trades unions; partly to ensure that unions addressed the needs of their many queer members but also because the unions had input to the Labour Party's policy-making process.

A breakthrough of sorts was achieved in 1981 when Labour's National Executive published a discussion paper, *The Rights of Gay Men and Women*: the first official party publication to raise the issue, let alone actually call for equality for homosexuals. It began with a statement from Ron Hayward, the party's General Secretary, which read:

"As socialists we cannot be concerned about inequalities of class, wealth and privilege and ignore the inequalities experienced by minorities such as homosexuals. The elimination of prejudice and injustice in our society is fundamental to the fight for socialism." [3]

It was immediately attacked by a rabidly homophobic and pro-Thatcher press as evidence of the influence of the 'loony left' on the Labour Party. This panicked the Labour leadership – who saw 'contentious' issues such as queer rights as vote losers – and also Labour traditionalists, who believed the issue to be a middle class irrelevance. In consequence *The Rights of Gay Men and Women* was quickly buried, never to be seen again.

The Bermondsey By-Election

Two years later, in February 1983, a similar dynamic was played out during a by-election for the South London seat of Bermondsey; a seat that had been held by Labour for decades.

The by-election had been triggered by the retirement of long-serving Labour MP Bob Mellish. The subsequent histrionics were triggered by the alleged politics and sexual orientation of the official Labour candidate Peter Tatchell.

The tabloid press and Tatchell's political opponents had made much of his sexuality as well as his alleged links with the Labour left faction, the Militant tendency.

Party leader Michael Foot was so unnerved by the press hostility he felt compelled to declare that: *"Peter Tatchell would never be accepted as a [Labour] Parliamentary candidate."* [(4)] The party's National Executive Committee formally ratified Foot's statement the following week.

Sadly for Michael Foot, Bermondsey Labour Party members were not prepared to buy into the hysteria: they held a second vote on their next Labour candidate – and Tatchell was selected again. Not only did this displease the tabloids (and, therefore, the national Labour Party) but it also put the nose of sitting MP Bob Mellish firmly out of joint. His preferred candidate – Southwark Council leader John O'Grady – had been snubbed.

Thus the stage was set for what *Gay News* subsequently declared *"the most homophobic by-election of our times"*, characterised by what *The Guardian* described as a *"high and insistent level of vilification."*

Michael Foot, having soundly dismissed Tatchell's candidacy, now found himself in the uncomfortable position of having to publicly endorse it. John O'Grady, with the backing of outgoing MP Bob Mellish, decided to stand as 'The Real Bermondsey Labour' candidate. And Tatchell refused to confirm or deny suggestions that he was gay – a position that brought some considerable criticism from queer media and activists [(5)].

Unsurprisingly, the tabloids had a field day. For example, *The Sun's* reference to Tatchell as *"Red Pete, the gay rights campaigner"* encouraged the homophobia as well as linking him with a broader media obsession – the notion that the Labour Party was being taken over by 'the loony left'. And with Foot publicly humiliated by Bermondsey Labour's decision to retain Tatchell, the press weren't slow in conflating this into a challenge to Foot's leadership. For example, on 20 February 1983, the *Sunday Express* ran a cartoon of Tatchell hammering a nail into a coffin marked *"RIP Foot's Leadership"*, while the ghost of Foot moans *"I always said Peter Tatchell would only become a Labour candidate over my dead body ..."*

Meanwhile, within Bermondsey itself, Tatchell's political opponents made much of his alleged sexual orientation. It is claimed, for example, that John O'Grady toured the constituency sitting alongside Bob Mellish on a horse-drawn cart (presumably to emphasise his working class credentials). As they went around the streets he sang, to the tune of *My Old Man's a Dustman:*

Tatchell is a poppet, as pretty as can be,

But he must be slow if he don't know that he won't be your MP.

Tatchell is an Aussie, he lives in a council flat.

He wears his trousers back to front because he doesn't know this from that. [(6)]

It has also been alleged that O'Grady's supporters were responsible for a leaflet that was distributed during the final week of the campaign. It included a photograph of Tatchell – re-touched to make it look like he was wearing lipstick and eyeliner – and another of the Queen, with the message *"Which queen will you vote for?"* [(7)] More disturbingly, the leaflet also called Tatchell a traitor, gave his phone number and invited people to *"let him know what you think of him"*.

But it wasn't just Labour supporters who were putting the boot in. It's also alleged that the local Liberal Democrats also exploited the homophobia to their advantage. Their choice of campaign slogan, *"It's a straight choice"*, is one example quoted by critics. It's further alleged that a slogan in the closing stages of the campaign was *"Vote for Simon Hughes: A Real Man"*. In March 1983, the Chair of Libgay – the Liberal's own gay group – admitted that their male canvassers had worn badges declaring *"I've not been kissed by Peter Tatchell yet"*. [(8)]

The heady mix of homophobia and alarmism both inside and outside the Labour Party led to the Labour vote dropping from 63.6 per cent at the previous election to 26.1 per cent in 1983. The Liberal Democrat candidate Simon Hughes won the election by a landslide, acknowledging on election night that he had *"benefited"* from *"the allegations"* made against Tatchell. Twenty-three years later he apologised for his party's role in the homophobia – when he came out as bisexual.

Success in the Face of Scaremongering

Tatchell's defeat was used by many people – both outside and within the Labour Party – as evidence that queer candidates or policies were vote losers and should be avoided at all costs. Such was the case in my local Labour Party in Nottingham – so we knew we had a bit of a challenge on our hands when, less than a week after Tatchell's defeat, a long-time gay activist was chosen as one of the candidates in our local council elections.

Richard McCance had been invited to stand largely because Labour wanted to field a full slate of candidates in the elections – and his seat was perceived to be an unwinnable, safe Tory seat. Those considerations notwithstanding, Tatchell's defeat still panicked some of the party faithful: when McCance made it clear that he was going to be completely upfront about his sexuality, his election agent immediately resigned.

The agent was eventually persuaded to return, although McCance remained steadfast in his view on how to avoid his sexuality becoming an issue. It was, quite simply, a question of being *"... out from the start, rather than 'found out' ... There were no smear campaigns or exposes ..."* [9] His election material included the fact that he was gay, he made no secret of the fact that he was gay when he was canvassing and, of course, he was a strong advocate of the City Council taking firm measures in support of queer rights.

Unsurprisingly, the local Labour leadership was far from comfortable. But what was more disturbing was the ease with which many of those that supported queer rights 'in principle' fell to arguing that it probably wasn't the right time to be pursuing them now. Quite when 'the right time' was wasn't ever specified. The Bermondsey affair had clearly unnerved a lot of people.

McCance, to his credit, stuck to his guns and was more than vindicated by the election results. In the May election, his was the only Labour victory, turning a Conservative majority of 400 into a Labour victory of 470. Elsewhere across the city the electoral pendulum swung in the opposite direction: the Labour Party lost five seats and were left with a majority of only one – Richard McCance!

Four months later the Labour Party elected Neil Kinnock to replace Michael Foot as leader. When asked his opinion on the homophobic witch hunt that had been conducted against Peter Tatchell, Kinnock had replied, *"I'm not in favour of witch hunts but I do not mistake bloody witches for fairies!"* [10]

Despite Kinnock's casual homophobia, Labour saw its first MP come out a year later. In September 1983 Chris Smith was speaking at a rally against Rugby Council's homophobic policies. He began his speech with the words, *"My name is Chris Smith. I am Labour MP for Islington South and Finsbury, and I am gay."* He received a five-minute standing ovation. Smith went on to contest – and win – subsequent elections as an openly gay man, with no discernible impact on the size of his vote.

105

Labour in Local Government

As the 80s moved on, the tensions around queer rights continued to grow within the Labour Party. While the leadership and a majority of Labour MPs resisted its inclusion in the Labour manifesto, a number of local Labour councils actively developed and implemented pro-queer policies and programmes. These included funding lesbian and gay men's workers in equal opportunities units (Nottingham), youth workers (Haringey) and, in Manchester, the establishment of one of the country's first gay centres.

Much to the chagrin of the Labour leadership, the high-profile Greater London Council (GLC) went even further. It created a Gay Working Party that undertook an extensive needs assessment of queer people around a range of issues including employment, housing, social services, health and aged care. The findings were used to inform a detailed policy document – *Changing the World: A London Charter for Lesbians and Gay Men* – in 1985. This, as well as other work by the Gay Working Party, triggered a whole raft of measures, including the development of inclusion and anti-discrimination policies, financial support to community organisations such as London Lesbian and Gay Switchboard and the Black Lesbian and Gay Centre, and the allocation of £750,000 to fund the establishment and operation of a London Lesbian and Gay Centre.

Predictably, the tabloid press attacked GLC leader Ken Livingstone – whom they demonised as 'Red Ken' – for wasting ratepayers money on 'trivial' issues. The Labour leadership watched on in horror; partly because of the bad press but partly because Livingstone and his so-called 'radical' policies proved to be highly popular with the local electorate.

A National Policy Breakthrough

1985 turned out to be a challenging year for the Labour leadership on another front too: a party conference vote in support of queer rights.

In fact the ball had started rolling much earlier. By 1984, the efforts of the Labour Campaign for Lesbian and Gay Rights (LCLGR) – who had been campaigning for several years – were supplemented by a new queer group that was winning crucial support from some of the most unlikely unions. Lesbians and Gays Support the Miners (LGSM) had been established to support striking coal miners during the 1984-85 national miners' strike. (See separate section on LGSM.)

By the end of the dispute LGSM had not only raised tens of thousands of pounds but had also generated a real commitment to queer rights from the National Union of Mineworkers (NUM). For example, at the 1984 *Pits and Perverts* London fundraiser concert, Dai Donovan from the NUM told the 1500 strong audience:

"You have worn our badge, 'Coal not Dole', and you know what harassment means, as we do. Now we will pin your badge on us; we will support you."

And they were true to their word. Not only did the miners and their families bring their trade union banners to the 1985 Gay and Lesbian Pride rally in London, they were crucial in pushing through a queer rights policy at the 1985 Trades Union Congress (TUC) conference and, subsequently, the 1985 Labour Party conference.

As the peak body for British trades unions, the TUC had considerable sway within the Labour Party at that time. In consequence, it was difficult for the Labour leadership to ignore issues that were being supported at the TUC conference. In this case it was a motion supporting equal rights in the workplace for lesbians and gay men and calling on all member unions to campaign for legislation outlawing homophobic discrimination.

The National Union of Mineworkers not only voted in favour of the motion but also lobbied other unions to support it too. In consequence, it was passed with only one speech against. With the TUC effectively setting a precedent, a motion was put before the Labour Party's national conference a month later on 4 October 1985. Its demands included an equal age of consent, outlawing discrimination against lesbians and gay men wherever it occurred and the establishment of a working party to produce a fully developed policy. The party's National Executive Committee recommended that the motion be remitted – in other words, passed over. This left the motion's backers only one option – to call for a card vote of delegates present at the conference. Once again, due to the combined efforts of LCLGR lobbying and NUM support, the motion was passed with a majority of more than 600,000. Sadly, this constituted only 58 per cent of the vote, which, in procedural terms, meant that it was not large enough to require inclusion in the party's election manifesto.

Nonetheless an important victory had been won and a clear message had been sent to the Labour Party's leadership. The following year, after further lobbying on the part of LCLGR, a similar motion was presented at annual conference, this time specifically calling for a commitment in the party's manifesto to equality for lesbians and gay men. And on this occasion it received 79 per cent of the vote: well over the two thirds majority required to get the policy into the party manifesto.

You Win Some ...

But even this large majority was insufficient to protect it from internal party manoeuvrings: the Labour leadership decided to ignore the conference resolutions. For the 1987 general election they opted instead for a one line pledge to outlaw discrimination against lesbians and gay men. It was a far cry from MP Jo Richardson's conference pledge that *"there is no socialism without lesbian and gay liberation"*; a confidential memorandum from the party's Home Policy Directorate spelled out the process by which the conference resolution had been so effectively undermined:

"We were pressed hard by the Labour Campaign for Lesbian and Gay Rights to fulfil our commitment to a clear party statement on lesbian and gay rights. But election preparations – and the desire not to divert attention from our central message during the campaign – prevented the NEC from setting up the agreed working party and producing the statement we promised. We did, however, commit ourselves in Labour's manifesto to take steps to ensure that lesbians and gay men were not discriminated against." [11]

Clearly the era of political spin was already well underway within the Labour Party: the *"desire not to divert attention from our central message"* being proffered to explain the failure to commit.

The Labour Party lost the general election again.

Disappointed but undaunted, activists submitted a new lesbian and gay rights policy to National Conference in 1988, this time with an additional clause pledging to oppose Section 28. It was passed with 84% in favour and Jo Richardson, MP, felt sufficiently moved by the size of the vote to declare that it:

"...made it absolutely clear that there will never again be any suggestion of the Labour Party backing off from its support for lesbian and gay rights." [12]

108

She spoke too soon. At a meeting of the National Executive committee in May 1989, Deputy Leader Roy Hattersley proposed that the party's commitment to an equal age of consent and the repeal of all discriminatory laws be removed from Party policy. A majority voted in favour of Hattersley's proposal and the commitments came off the Party's agenda again.

Until October of the same year, when another vote at National Conference reinstated them. On this occasion it was followed up with sustained campaigning by the Labour Campaign for Lesbian and Gay Rights, sympathetic MPs and the newly-established queer rights organisation Stonewall. The pressure worked: Labour's 1991 election manifesto included a full paragraph outlining the Party's policy – although committing only to a free vote when it came to the age of consent.

The Conservatives and Queer Rights

While the 1987 election result was a disappointment for queer Labour Party supporters there were a number of queer people within the Conservative Party who saw it as a reason for optimism.

The Conservative Group for Homosexual Equality (CGHE) was established in 1976 *"to encourage support within the Conservative Party for ending of laws and practices that discriminate against homosexuals and to ensure support for the Conservative philosophy and a free society within the homosexual community"*.

In 1983 it produced a brochure, *Homosexuality in Britain: A Conservative Perspective*, setting out its goals. These included:

- *"Sexual conduct between men should be lawful in circumstances in which it would be lawful between men and women.*
- *... a reduction in the age of consent for homosexual relationships between males from 21 to 16. However, as history has so often shown, British legislators have tended to adopt a gradualist approach to reform and CGHE recognises that the next feasible step may be the reduction of the age of consent to 18 ...*
- *... it should not be an offence to assist, promote or induce behaviour which is itself lawful.*
- *... the amendment of the 1975 Sex Discrimination Act and of the Employment*

109

Protection (Consolidation) Act so that discrimination on grounds of sexual orientation would be illegal.

- *... police resources and the time of the courts would be better used in dealing with real crime than in being diverted to the consensual behaviour of adults or to minor infringements of the law involving adults."* [13]

The brochure also included the results of a 1981 readership survey by Gay News that found:

"Labour and Conservatives are running neck and neck in the gay electorate; more Gay News readers favoured Labour than any other single party (25%) but 23% favoured the Conservatives."

It also acknowledged that support for queer rights was far from unanimous within the Conservative Party:

"Nonetheless, it cannot be said that our party had acted with vigour in these matters. Most of the opponents of the bills which ultimately resulted in the 1967 Act were Conservatives; in 1980 the Conservative government, in debate, and a majority of those Conservative MPs who voted in the crucial divisions, opposed the amendment to the Scottish bill; in 1982 the government acted in Northern Ireland primarily because of a decision in the European Court of Human Rights ... The government even introduced a fresh inequality when, after an amendment to abolish imprisonment as a penalty for women convicted of soliciting men it rejected an amendment abolishing imprisonment as a penalty for men convicted of soliciting men ..." [14]

However, they optimistically declared:

"Increasingly, from MPs and from the constituencies come signs that attitudes are changing and that a climate of opinion in which important changes in the law can be effected is rapidly materialising." [15]

A year after the brochure's publication, the Conservative-led Rugby council declared that they would specifically exclude queer people from their Equal Opportunities policies. Comments from Tory councillors included the declaration that all homosexuals were *"vile and perverted people"* and the statement that *"...by including these words [sexual orientation] we shall give the people of Rugby the idea that this Council welcomes all queers and perverts ..."*

This all fed into the predominant media portrayal of LGBT issues as nothing more than an irrelevant preoccupation of Labour's 'loony left'. The Conservative Party most certainly benefited from this and there is some evidence that they actively bought into it. In the run-up to the 1987 general election, for example, Conservative Party billboards showed young men carrying gay rights banners and asked, *"Labour camp: do you want to live in it?"*

In that same year, at the first post-election Conservative Party conference, Prime Minister Margaret Thatcher denounced local authorities who taught children that *"they had an inalienable right to be gay."* It was the first hint of what was to come – Section 28 of the Local Government Act, which required that local authorities *"shall not intentionally promote homosexuality or publish material with the intention of promoting homosexuality"* or *"promote the teaching in any maintained school of the acceptability of homosexuality as a pretended family relationship"*

This was a long way from CGHE's goal that *"it should not be an offence to assist, promote or induce behaviour which is itself lawful."*

But it wasn't only queer Tories that would be dismayed by the support expressed for Section 28: Labour's senior representative on the Parliamentary Committee examining the legislation was keen to add his party's support too:

"I speak on behalf of the Labour Party when I say that it is not, and has never been, the duty or responsibility of either a local or education authority to promote homosexuality ... I hope that no one in the Committee had any doubt about that." [16]

While the position was changed shortly thereafter, Labour's failure to mount any serious opposition to Section 28 left activists questioning the party's understanding and commitment to queer rights.

A European Approach

While reform efforts in Australia and the USA were slowed by the federal structure of those countries, a different type of federation was facilitating reform in the UK: specifically, the European Economic Community (now the European Union).

Even though it has existed since 1957 it was only in 1979 that representatives were democratically elected instead of appointed by each country's MPs. One of the consequences of direct elections was that an element of politics was introduced into the process. And one area of politics that soon raised its head was queer rights.

In 1981 the European Court of Human Rights heard the case of Dudgeon v UK. This led to the ruling that Northern Ireland's sustained criminalising of homosexuality was in breach of Section 8 of the European Convention on Human Rights. In consequence, Britain's 1967 Sexual Offences Act was finally implemented in Northern Ireland.

But this case was only an indication of bigger things to come. In that same year a sustained lobby of the Council of Europe's Assembly by the International Gay and Lesbian Association also began to produce results. Swayed, perhaps, by the European Court taking the lead in discrimination in criminal law, European Parliamentarians tried to tackle discrimination in employment.

Their first attempt, in the form of a detailed gay rights resolution in 1981, was passed by the members of the Assembly. Then it was passed up to the Assembly's Council of Ministers – and never heard of again.

The next attempt involved a more considered and detailed response: the Committee on Social Affairs for the European Parliament began an investigation into *'Sexual Discrimination in the Workplace'*. This culminated in the Squarcialupi Report, a detailed report and set of recommendations on establishing equal rights for homosexuals in all member states.

It called for the abolition of all legal restrictions against adult homosexual relationships; the introduction of equal ages of consent for homosexuals and heterosexuals; the outlawing of workplace discrimination on the grounds of sexual orientation; and an end to the classification of homosexuality as a mental illness.

The proposals were incorporated into a resolution and put to the vote in the Assembly. The resolution was not without its opponents: the UK Conservatives voted against the measure and the Irish Christian Democrats abstained on the grounds that *"the EEC has no competence to decide the moral patterns of society or the pattern of criminal laws in the member states"*.

Conservatives and Christian Democrats notwithstanding, the resolution was carried overwhelmingly – then again faced passage up to the Council of Ministers.

Social Affairs Commissioner Iver Richard initially made positive noises about it, arguing that there was no doubt that such measures were needed. Then he said that there were *"significant practical, legal and political problems"* to consider and that there was no specific European Treaty agreement authorising action on behalf of homosexuals. Then he acknowledged that Article 235 of the Treaty could be used for this purpose, since it had already been used as the basis for the 1976 Equal Treatment Directive.

But his final word, to no one's great surprise by this stage, was that he *"could not see the matter being acceptable to the Council of Ministers – at least in the immediate future"*. He didn't even bother to prepare draft legislation to support the proposal. The issue was lost and the same pattern was played out repeatedly over the next decade or so: legislation, resolutions and proposals were approved by the Assembly – then lost when they entered the void that was the Council of Ministers.

No Homosex Please, We're Amnesty International!

While politicians of various hues had shown greater or lesser degrees of support for queer rights, there was one global organisation that one might have imagined would be 100 per cent behind queer rights – the human rights organisation, Amnesty International.

Sadly, this was not the case: Amnesty didn't include homosexuality in its definition of 'prisoners of conscience' until 1991 and was still refusing to include 'sexual orientation' in its mission statement as late as 1997 [17]. In consequence it effectively turned a blind eye to the persecution of queers.

Even in countries that persecuted a broad range of its citizens, Amnesty almost seemed to be making a point of excluding queer people in its reports. A particular case in point was Iran, where the country's hard line Islamic regime wasted no time in implementing a programme of barbaric punishments in the name of moral righteousness when they came to power in the late 70s. Floggings, beheadings, stonings and being buried alive were (and still are) but a few of the punishments meted out.

The exiled Iranian LGBT group Homan reported that, in the early 80s, an attempt to set up a queer organisation resulted in 70 executions. The Abdorrahman Boroumand Foundation [18] has documented the cases of many people murdered by the regime for committing *"a homosexual act"*, including 15 men executed on 12 September 1982 in Sanandaj for being gay.

Most organisations acknowledge that these figures are likely to be only the tip of the iceberg: the secrecy under which executions occur means that the details are rarely made public and the stigma associated with homosexuality means that victims' families rarely raise the issue. Not that Iran has ever made a secret of its treatment of homosexuals: its Penal Code explicitly states that homosexuals can be executed by lashing, hanging, stoning, cutting in half by sword, dropping from a tall building or cliff, beheading or burning alive.

The evidence has been around since 1979, yet Amnesty avoided the issue until 1991.

For example, in its report *Human Rights Violations in Iran* of 7 September 1982, it railed against abuses carried out against *"persons imprisoned because of their political or religious beliefs or by reason of their ethnic origin, sex, colour or language, who have not used or advocated violence."* Despite the evidence already available, they chose not to include sexual orientation.

In July 1985, Amnesty issued a report expressing concern over the execution of drug offenders: its Iran Briefing of 1987 makes reference to *"offences against the sexual and moral code"* then refers only to adultery and prostitution. In June 1989, a media release – *Over 900 Executions Announced in 5 Months* – refers to those charged with drug offences, rape, murder and armed robbery. Even a retrospective report issued in December 1990 – *Report of Human Rights Violation 1978-1990: The Massacre of 1988* – refers solely to political prisoners.

During my research on this issue I was unable to find a single Amnesty document from the 1980s that even mentions queer Iranians, let alone any report or media release that specifically addresses their plight. I don't think I'm missing anything: as I have recorded earlier, Amnesty only agreed to include homosexuality in its definition of 'prisoners of conscience' in 1991: as late as 1997 its International Council Meeting was still refusing to add 'sexual orientation' to its mission statement. [19]

References:

1. Parliament of Western Australia. Law Reform *(Decriminalisation of Sodomy) Act 1989*.

2. Jehl, Douglas. *Dukakis Seeks Gays' Support, Draws Occasional Hisses. Los Angeles Times*, Los Angeles. 15 May 1988.

3. Quoted in Purdon, Peter. 2006. *Sodom, Gomorrah and the New Jerusalem*. London: Labour Campaign for Lesbian and Gay Rights, p42.

4. Tatchell, Peter. 1983. *The Battle for Bermondsey*. Heretic Books: London, p132.

5. See, for example, Lumsden, Andrew. The most homophobic by-election of our times. *Gay News*, London. Number 260, 3-16 March 1983.

6. See, for example, Derbyshire, Jonathan. Peter Tatchell and the 1983 Bermondsey by-election. *Time Out*, London. 5 February 2008.

7. Tatchell, Peter. Votes, smears and homophobia. *Capital Gay*, London. 26 February 1993.

8. Anon. *Libgay's error of judgement*. In *Gay News*. London. Number 260, 3-16 March 1983.

9. Anon. Gay Activist Elected to City Council. *Gay East Midlands*, Nottingham, England. Issue 1, June 1983 p3.

10. Quoted in Rayside, Morton David. 1998. *On the Fringe: Gays and Lesbians in Politics*. New York: Cornell University Press, p28 (among others).

11. *On the Fringe: Gays and Lesbians in Politics*, p29.

12. Quoted in Tatchell, Peter. Labour Party: Blackpool and After. *Lesbian and Gay Socialist*, London. Winter 88/89, p8.

13. Conservative Group for Homosexual Equality (CGHE). 1983. *Homosexuality in Britain: A Conservative Perspective*.

14. *Homosexuality in Britain: A Conservative Perspective*.

15. *Homosexuality in Britain: A Conservative Perspective*.

16. *On the Fringe: Gays and Lesbians in Politics*, p30.

17. International Gay and Lesbian Human Rights Commission. Undated. *International Jurisprudence and Policy Precedents Regarding Sexual Orientation*.

18. Abdorrahman Boroumand Foundation. [Online]. Available at www.iranrights.org

19. *International Jurisprudence and Policy Precedents Regarding Sexual Orientation*.

115

Lesbians and Gays Support the Miners

LGSM members at a picket of Neasden Power Station in London, 11 February 1985. (I'm second from right). Photo: Copyright LGSM 2014

In March 1984 the UK's National Union of Mineworkers (NUM) began a nation-wide strike in protest at the proposed closure of 75 coal mines around the country. The Thatcher government responded with measures that were not only tough but frequently brutal and often illegal. The government justified its response by stating that the strike had been called without a ballot of the membership and was, therefore, illegal. The dispute polarised public opinion including that within queer communities.

Many queer people gave practical support to the miners from the outset, for example by donating through their trades unions, working at local strike centres or helping with street collections. The queer caucuses of left political parties – such as the Labour Campaign for Lesbian and Gay Rights (LCLGR) – offered immediate support

116

to the striking miners. And many lesbians were active through various women's support groups that were established around the country.

Three months into the strike, in June 1984, a queer organisation was established with the sole purpose of raising funds for the miners: this was Lesbians and Gays Support the Miners. It came out of two specific events on the day of Lesbian and Gay Pride celebrations in London: a collection organised by two gay men – Mike Jackson and Mark Ashton – during the Pride march itself and a meeting organised by LCLGR after the march. For Jackson and Ashton, the positive response they had received from the marchers had convinced them of the need to better tap into this support. The LCLGR meeting essentially brought together likeminded people and quickly led to a group meeting on a weekly basis as Lesbians and Gays Support the Miners.

LGSM began with a small group of people collecting money for the miners at the 1984 Lesbian and Gay Pride march in London. A year later, so many people had assembled behind the LGSM banner that they were asked to lead the march. Photo: Copyright *Colin Clews 1985.*

117

Membership was broad-reaching: some came from specific political groups like the Communist Party, the International Marxist Group, the Labour Party, the Socialist Workers Party and even, apparently, the Liberals. Others – myself included – were aligned to none of those but simply supported the miners cause for their own reasons. I had grown up in a mining community so was more than aware of the dangers and hardships endured by miners, as well as the heavy social and economic impact wrought on those communities by the closure of their collieries. And as a gay man I could readily identify with the sustained media vilification and government and police attacks that mining communities were now experiencing.

Police abuse and entrapment were common experiences for queer people (see, for example, the earlier section *'Constructing a Clearer Picture of Queer Reality'*) but so too were other forms of attack. In April 1984, for example, only a month after the miners' strike began, HM Customs and Excise resurrected a piece of Victorian legislation to mount a sustained assault on one of the key community resources, Gay's the Word bookshop (this is covered in more detail in the chapter *'Under Attack'*). So, even in the days before the passage of Section 28, many queer people were already feeling up against it and very much in sympathy with other communities who were experiencing the same thing.

Three months after the London LGSM group was formed, it was joined by a second, this time in Lothian in Scotland. By the end of the year there were 11 such groups around the country. This period also saw the establishment of Lesbians Against Pit Closures (LAPC), which, it has been suggested, arose from lesbians' frustration at male domination of LGSM as well as the belief that sexism within mining communities should also be addressed. [1] Whatever the origins of LAPC, relations between the two groups were always amicable and supportive, and joint activities were quite common, for example a benefit evening at The Bell pub in London's Kings Cross.

Of course, not all sections of the queer community supported the miners. A number of queers felt that a working class, blue collar group such as coal miners were the very epitome of homophobia – and there was certainly some evidence to support that view. The Conservative Group for Homosexual Equality even went so far as to donate £25 to the non-striking miners because they felt support for the miners was likely to damage support for the gay cause.

For my own part, I was acutely aware of the homophobia in mining communities but didn't feel it was relevant to my decision to support them during the strike – and I certainly didn't believe that supporting them would be counter-productive to the queer rights movement. I began my involvement more or less from the outset of the strike, while I was still living in Nottingham – the centre of the anti-strike miners and, consequently, something of a miniature police state.

Nottinghamshire mineworkers had held their own ballot on the strike and a majority had voted not to support it. Despite this vote, a number of Nottinghamshire miners did actually join the strike -although not in sufficient numbers to shut down any of the local pits. Both sides in the dispute were well aware of the significance of the continuing output from these pits: had they been shut down they would have greatly strengthened the hand of the National Union of Mineworkers. As long as they remained open, they were not only a source of coal but also a useful propaganda tool for the Government. In consequence, Nottinghamshire become a battleground.

Striking miners came from around the country to support those local miners who were on strike and lobby those who were still working. They were billeted at the homes of supporters across the area, with many staying in Nottingham itself then being shipped out to the various local picket lines.

Meanwhile, Nottinghamshire took on more and more characteristics of a police state. Police roadblocks were set up (illegally) on roads in the vicinity of local coal mines. Vehicles were stopped, occupants questioned as to their destinations, vehicles were searched, paperwork of all descriptions – from newspapers to leaflets – examined and confiscated, and occupants were even questioned about which political party they voted for. On one occasion a friend of mine was ordered to open the boot of her Mini car (about three feet wide and nine inches deep) on the grounds that she might be concealing pickets in there!

It was well-known that army personnel were drafted in – in police uniforms – to bolster police lines, and their brutal treatment of striking miners and their supporters was common and quite blatant. This was all illegal but such activity was par for the course by then with the conservative media unequivocally blaming striking miners for any violence, despite clear evidence to the contrary. Margaret Thatcher had made it clear that political opposition was to be put down at any cost, labelling those who opposed her as *"the enemy within"*.

My first contribution to the cause was volunteering at the local strike headquarters – as a typist. This in itself had required a bit of explanation when I first turned up on the doorstep, electric typewriter in hand. A couple of days earlier, the local strike committee had realised they needed a typist and, in a wonderful display of sexist logic, had asked the Women's Support Group if they could provide one. A friend who was involved with the Women's Group passed the request on to me and I duly turned up for duty the next morning.

Such was the confusion and consternation at my arrival that I was subjected to some detailed interrogation to confirm that I was indeed there for the typist role. This was not motivated by any sense of suspicion but rather the fear of some terrible misunderstanding that would have resulted in my being given the demeaning and unmanly role of typist. Even after we had fully and exhaustively explored that possibility and I was finally allocated a desk, it took a couple of days for them to get over their embarrassment and actually give me some typing work to do. To this day I remain convinced that there were probably reams of documents that remained in their handwritten form because it was too uncomfortable to ask a man to type them up.

Nonetheless I remained at my typewriter until I subsequently moved to London. I sat in my corner and watched the comings and goings: full collection buckets brought in to be emptied and counted, empty buckets sent out to be filled, all of which was punctuated with visits from 'flying pickets' on their way through to the next line of battle with the police.

In September 1984 I left my 'frontline' post and applied my energies through the London Lesbians and Gays Support the Miners Group. The group, like every other miners support group, had 'twinned' with a particular community – in this case Dulais in South Wales. This strategy had been adopted because the government had frozen the bank accounts of the National Union of Mineworkers, thus preventing funds going in or out. The net effect was to bring supporters and mining communities directly into contact with each other – something that served to strengthen rather than weaken support. Indeed, it's interesting to speculate whether mining and queer communities would have come together – with the subsequent impact on progressing queer rights in the UK – had it not been for that freeze.

Certainly, strong bonds were formed between London LGSM and the community in Dulais. In November 1984, for example, London's *City Limits* magazine described an LGSM visit to Dulais:

"Welcomed into the miners' homes for the weekend, whole families apparently started discussing gay rights and human sexuality over the tea table." [2]

I arrived in London shortly before this visit but, coming from a mining community myself, felt there was little to be gained from my attending. I did, however, attend the weekly LGSM meetings at the Fallen Angel pub in Islington where activities were organised for the following week. Occasionally we joined picket lines but our main activity was rattling a collection bucket in queer pubs or on the pavement outside Gay's the Word bookshop in Bloomsbury. The latter usually involved playing cat-and-mouse with the police.

The bookshop manager, Paud Hegarty, was quite insistent that we had the right to stand on the footpath immediately in front of the shop window – but the police had other ideas. Clearly unimpressed by a bunch of leftie poofs collecting for those subversive miners, they regularly threatened us with arrest if we didn't stop collecting. We all knew they had no legal right to do so but we also knew that that wouldn't stop them: they would simply make up some charge by the time we got to the police station. And so we stepped inside the shop until they had moved on, then we returned to our place on the pavement. Such was the pattern of the police power play for the duration of the strike.

Collections in queer venues provided variable results, the most supportive being The Bell pub in Kings Cross (£1500 raised by December 1984 – twice as much as any other venue). It is, perhaps, no surprise that The Bell's customers were predominantly young, working class people, suggesting a greater sense of identification with the miners than their counterparts in the more well-heeled queer establishments. In the Royal Vauxhall Tavern takings would increase significantly on those nights when Lily Savage (a.k.a. Paul O'Grady) was performing as she would often stand with collectors beside the exit and refuse to let people leave until they had donated!

'Pits and Perverts', at London's Electric Ballroom, 10th December 1984.

Design and copyright Kevin Franklin 1984.

In December 1984 London LGSM supplemented its regular fundraising activities with a benefit concert at the Electric Ballroom in Camden. Headlined by Bronski Beat, the 'Pits and Perverts' gig raised £5650 (equivalent to around £20,000 today). The Manchester LGSM group also organised a benefit concert at the Hacienda Club, featuring Pete Shelley from the Buzzcocks and raised some £3,500

South Wales miners and their families line up behind the LGSM banner prior to the 1985 Lesbian and Gay Pride parade in London. Photo: Copyright Colin Clews 1985.

The miners' strike was eventually called off in March 1985 following a relentless government and media campaign against them. Nonetheless, three months later a large contingent of miners and their families led the Lesbian and Gay Pride march in London. And three months after that the National Union of Mineworkers played a pivotal role in the passage of queer rights motions at both the British Trades Union Congress (TUC) conference and the Labour Party conference – the latter in the face of opposition from the party's leadership.

Their support continues to this day.

123

References:

1. See, for example, the film *Dancing in Dulais*, produced by LGSM in 1985, or Kelliher, Diarmaid. 2014. Solidarity and Sexuality: Lesbians and Gays Support the Miners 1984-85. *History Workshop Journal*. January 2014, p7.

2. Anon. Out in the City. *City Limits,* London. Circa November 1984.
    Quoted in Solidarity and Sexuality: Lesbians and Gays Support the Miners 1984-85.

Under Attack

Any perceived advancement of queer people has generally been met with some form of opposition. In the 80s this took three broad forms:

1) Direct attacks from governments and politicians or a deliberate failure to act in queer interests.
2) The lobbying of governments and politicians.
3) In the USA, the use of ballots to overturn rights ordinances or actively impose constraints on queer people.

The United Kingdom

Attacks from Governments and Politicians

The Trials of Gay's the Word Bookshop

On 10 April 1984 UK Customs and Excise officers raided Gay's the Word bookshop in London and seized all of their imported books. This was the start of 'Operation Tiger', which also included raids on the homes of the shop's directors and the detention of thousands of pounds worth of imported books at their UK ports of entry. These detained books had a retail value of some £12,000 – around 85 per cent of the shop's usual stock at that time – and had been imported because Britain's own queer publishing industry was still very much in its infancy and therefore incapable of offering a sufficiently large range of titles.

Six months after the first raid the bookshop received a further 20 seizure notices detailing 144 titles, many of which were standard academic texts. All of the impounded items had been seized under the Customs Consolidation Act of 1876, which applied to the importation of 'obscene' literature. In reality this was an antiquated law that allowed HM Customs to sidestep the more contemporary legal perspective on 'obscenity' defined in the Obscene Publications Act of 1959.

For example, the 1876 Act defined 'obscene' in subjective terms such as filthy, loathsome, repulsive or lewd [1]. The Obscene Publications Act, on the other hand, defined obscenity as something that would *"tend to deprave and corrupt persons who are likely, having regard to all relevant circumstances, to read, see or hear the matter contained or embodied in it"* [2]. However, the latter act applied only to material published in the UK, thus giving HM Customs and Excise the power to decide what

125

imported material was and was not obscene unless and until this was overruled in court. For Gay's the Word this meant that, even if the decision was ultimately overruled, this process would be a protracted one during which the bookshop would be without a substantial amount of the stock that was its lifeblood.

Furthermore, this arbitrary act of censorship meant that Gay's the Word had no guidelines as to what could and could not be imported. There was no requirement that the Obscene Publications Act definition be taken into account, nor could it be raised as a defence. Even more confusingly, it wasn't even a question of 'if we've seized it, it's obscene': Paud Hegarty, the shop's manager at that time, told me that books were occasionally released after Customs scrutiny. However, when they arrived at the bookshop they were generally damaged as a result of their poor treatment 'in custody' making it impossible to sell them at their full market price, thus incurring another financial loss.

In reality, the bulk of the seized literature was the work of authors such as Gore Vidal, Tennessee Williams, Jane Rule, Kate Millett, Jean-Paul Sartre and Jean Genet. Even Armistead Maupin's innocuous *Tales of the City* books had been seized. Some works – such as *The Joy of Gay Sex and The Joy of Lesbian Sex* – were sexually explicit, but their heterosexual equivalent, *The Joy of Sex*, was never subjected to such measures.

For Britain's queer communities the raid on its largest community bookshop was seen as nothing more than an attack on queer people themselves. The use of an antiquated piece of legislation to do this simply echoed Mary Whitehouse's use of archaic blasphemy laws to attack *Gay News* in 1977. But on this occasion it was the state that was undertaking the attack.

Despite the huge outcry, the shop's eight volunteer directors and the shop's manager were charged with *"conspiracy to import indecent or obscene material"* in December 1984. HM Customs were clearly determined to keep up the assault.

In response, support for Gay's the Word grew ever larger. Queer communities were already rallying round but many other people now saw the prosecutions for what they really were – a serious assault on civil rights and freedom of expression – and joined the defence campaign. Authors, the book industry, MPs, civil rights groups, trade unions and many others added their voices and their support to the defence fund which, by the time of the committal hearing in June 1985, had reached £50,000 [3].

The Gay's the Word defendants remained defiant throughout; one example of this being their decision to go to a committal hearing in order to highlight the absurdity of the case and the waste of resources that the government had poured into it (for example, 36 customs officers had been involved in Operation Tiger). Somewhat ironically, the committal hearing was held during Gay Pride Week in 1985. Renowned barrister Geoffrey Robertson – who had previously been involved with the defence of *Gay News* – led the defence. One of his first acts was to ask Customs to produce the guidelines they used for such cases – a request that was rejected by the presiding magistrate. In the week prior to the hearing, the London newspaper *Capital Gay* had published a list of what they claimed were secret guidelines for customs officers on how to spot 'indecency'. When Robertson presented these to Colin Woodgate, a senior customs officer, Woodgate refused to confirm that they were authentic guidelines but acknowledged a close similarity [4]. He also confirmed that all customs officers were given a photocopied sheet of guidelines telling them to look out for 'masturbation, homosexuality, lesbianism and group sex'. Another customs officer admitted they had seized novels by Tennessee Williams and Gore Vidal 'because they had the name of a homosexual author on the cover'. A top secret blacklist of homosexual publishers was subsequently obtained by the defence [5].

But, as Robertson later explained in his autobiography, *The Justice Game*:

"*The case against Gay's the Word collapsed ... through the agency of a life-size love-doll.*" [6]

More specifically, the trial of Gay's the Word came to an end largely as the result of a judgement in another case – *Conegate Ltd v Customs and Excise Commissioners* (1986). This involved a British businessman who had attempted to import inflatable sex dolls from Germany. When these were seized then subsequently destroyed by HM Customs after a magistrate had declared them 'indecent', the businessman took the case to the European Court of Justice.

The court ruled that the actions of HM Customs were unlawful on the grounds that they constituted a 'quantitative restriction' on imports between member states of the European Union. What was of particular relevance to the Gay's the Word trial was the court's determination that the Customs Consolidation Act was valid only where it applied to publications that would also have been declared obscene under the Obscene Publications Act.

127

But I have subsequently discovered that this case did not, in itself, fully resolve the Gay's the Word case. In a response to a post I wrote on my blog about the trial, Jonathan Cutbill, a former GTW director commented:

"The case was not ended by a judge but followed a government shake-up. We got supporting MPs to see the new [Home Secretary] ... he was a book collector. He took one look and ordered customs to get them out. We negotiated an agreement in which they saved face by retaining about 15 titles that they claimed were obscene under the Obscene Publications Act." [7]

Operation Spanner

In 1987, during a raid on the homes of gay men, police in Manchester, England, obtained a video showing men perpetrating acts of torture on other men. These acts included beatings, genital abrasions and lacerations.

All the men had consented to the acts undertaken as they were members of a gay men's BDSM (Bondage, Discipline, Sadism and Masochism) group. To further reassure the police they also reported that none of the injuries inflicted had required medical attention.

The police responded by charging 16 of them with a range of offences that included 'assault occasioning actual bodily harm'. And, despite all participants engaging in the acts consensually and in private, they were all found guilty and given a range of punishments that included fines, suspended sentences and jail sentences of up to four and a half years.

The majority of the sentences were subsequently reduced on appeal on the grounds that the men were unaware that their actions were illegal. But none of them were completely quashed – even when the appeals went as high as the European Court of Human Rights.

The House of Lords, for example, ruled against the appellants in a three-to-two judgement. One of the judges, Lord Templeman had declared:

"In principle there is a difference between violence which is incidental and violence which is inflicted for the indulgence of cruelty. The violence of sadomasochistic encounters involves the indulgence of cruelty by sadists and the degradation of victims. Such violence is injurious to the participants and unpredictably dangerous.

I am not prepared to invent a defence of consent for sadomasochistic encounters which breed and glorify cruelty [...]. Society is entitled and bound to protect itself against a cult of violence. Pleasure derived from the infliction of pain is an evil thing. Cruelty is uncivilised." [8]

And yet a different logic appears to have been applied for heterosexuals. The same – or even worse – acts have been deemed to be lawful when conducted within the context of heterosexual marriage. For example, in the case of *DPP v Morgan* (1976) – where a man convinced three of his friends to rape his wife – the House of Lords declared that even a mistaken belief that the victim consented was enough 'to rebut a charge of rape' [9]. In 1996, in the case of *R. v Wilson* [10], a man used a hot knife to brand his initials on his wife's buttocks with her consent: this was decreed to be a lawful act.

Clearly, none of the gay men caught up in Operation Spanner had the defence of being married. Their only defence was that they had all genuinely consented and acted in private.

Section 28 of the Local Government Act

Section 28 had its origins in the media-generated hysteria around the so-called 'loony left' local councils. In essence these were any Labour-run local authority that sought to implement policies disliked by Conservatives and the conservative media. Particular venom was reserved for policies that sought to offer equality to queer people. *The Sun* newspaper, for example, labelled these as *"sick nonsense"* [11].

Once again, a central tenet of the homophobic vitriol was the myth of homosexuals as paedophiles, allowing opponents to argue that any local authority support for queer people put 'innocent' young people at risk. Thus, support for lesbian or gay youth groups was portrayed as the corruption of young minds while any proposals to bring resources on homosexuality into schools were deemed tantamount to child abuse. Underpinning this – and despite the complete absence of supporting evidence – was the view that merely discussing homosexuality with young people would inevitably lead them to adopt it.

From this the argument extended into the 'threat' to the family: queer people were perceived as incapable of procreation and same sex relationships undermined traditional gender roles. Conservative MP Dame Jill Knight was a particularly rabid exponent of this:

129

"Millions outside Parliament object to little children being perverted, diverted or converted from normal family life to a lifestyle which is desperately dangerous for society and extremely dangerous for them." [12]

A particular focus for criticism was Haringey Council in London, which came to national attention in 1983 when the *Daily Mail* reported that one of its libraries stocked *Jenny Lives with Eric and Martin*, a picture book about a young girl living with her father and his male partner. Three years later the hysteria intensified when the controlling Labour Group included in their local election manifesto the intention to include *"positive images of homosexuality in local schools"* [13].

In response, the local Conservatives produced a leaflet that declared:

"You do not want your child to be educated a homosexual or lesbian." [14]

On the 9 May 1986 the local newspaper, the *Hornsey Journal* ran a front page headline that read:

"Lesbians to adopt kids. Schools to get lessons about homosexuals. HarinGAY!"

Yet in spite of this hysteria and the declaration of a local Tory councillor that *"We are on the edge of an abyss. We call on all decent, ordinary people to have an 'uprising' of their own – at the ballot box"*, Labour actually gained six seats at the election and the Conservatives lost seven.

When the new council established a Lesbian and Gay Unit that wrote to all local head teachers to advise them of the new policy, opponents formed the Campaign for Normal Family Life. This was changed shortly thereafter to the Parents' Rights Group (PRG). What followed was a coordinated attack on Haringey's queer-positive policies: it was carried out locally, in the national media and in Parliament and it fed the campaign for Section 28.

On 7 July 1986, *The Sun* newspaper made the unsubstantiated claim that:

"Courses to teach children about homosexuality and lesbianism are to be started in schools run by Barmy Bernie Grant's left-wing council. And Haringey council may even extend the scheme to nursery and primary schools."

On 1 October, the *Daily Mail* reported a meeting of the council's Education Committee:

"As parents burned a copy [of Jenny Lives with Eric and Martin] they were jeered by homosexuals and lesbians entering the building. Inside, parents were bombarded

with missiles and spat on from the public gallery as they spoke against the Labour council's 'anti-heterosexist' policy."

At a local level, the Parents' Rights Group did everything they could to misrepresent the reality of the queer policies and ensured that every last bit of information – accurate or otherwise – was fed up to Conservative peers and MPs in Parliament.

Such was the case when local queer youth workers showed *How to Become a Lesbian in 35 Minutes* – a short film documenting the experiences of young lesbians. The film was screened at an evening support group for young lesbians at the Blanche Neville School in Tottenham. During the day the school catered for children with learning disabilities; in the evening rooms were let out for use by local community groups.

Kyriacos Spyrou, a gay youth worker for Haringey Council at that time, subsequently described the events of that evening in the Hall Carpenter Archive publication, *Walking After Midnight: Gay Men's Life Stories* [15].

He said that a woman from the Parents' Rights Group arrived and asked to be admitted. She was refused on the grounds that she was neither lesbian nor under 25. However, she was offered a viewing at a more appropriate time in the future. Seemingly accepting this suggestion, she left without further incident. But a few days later she rang and asked Kyriacos for his full name, claiming that he had punched and kicked her at the time of her visit. She subsequently took out a summons and claimed in court that she had been pregnant at the time of the alleged assault and had miscarried as a consequence.

In court, accompanied by the Reverend Rushworth Smith – a man who had gone on hunger strike in protest against Haringey Council's Positive Images [of gays and lesbians] campaign – she was unable to produce any evidence of either pregnancy, miscarriage or the assault. The case was, consequently, thrown out – although the local press made little effort to remedy the hurt already inflicted on Kyriacos: he continued to receive death threats and hate mail.

Unbowed by the outcome of their vengeful fiasco, the Parents' Rights Group simply told a different set of lies to some sympathetic Conservative MPs. In consequence, on 23 April 1987, Michael McNair-Wilson stood up in Parliament and proposed an early-day motion:

"That this House expresses its abhorrence at the showing of a video entitled 'How to Become a Lesbian in 35 Minutes' shown at a Haringey Council

community centre recently to an audience, including young people, and calls upon the government to require local authorities to submit sexually explicit videos and literature to the Department of Education before such material can be shown to the public." [16]

It wasn't sexually explicit, but that didn't stop him continuing on his rant with the claim that the video was *"shown recently at the Labour-controlled Haringey Council community centre when disabled teenagers were present."*

That claim was groundless too but it was all that was needed for Dame Jill Knight to add her own vivid fabrications. On 8 May 8 1987 she told Parliament that:

"Recently the lesbian and gay development unit of Haringey Council made a video called 'How to Become a Lesbian in 35 Minutes'. Under the aegis of the council, it was shown to mentally handicapped girls, of whom one was aged 18, one was aged 16 and the others were much younger." [17]

Knight's ill-informed and alarmist speech of May 1987 wasn't made as an isolated remark: by this time the rabid homophobia of the media and the uninformed rantings of Conservative politicians had generated the first manifestation of what would become Section 28. This was the Earl of Halsbury's 1986 Private Member's Bill – an amendment to the Local Government Bill that sought *"to restrain local authorities from promoting homosexuality"*. It was Knight who introduced the bill into the House of Commons.

In the House of Lords one of the bill's supporters, Lord Campbell of Alloway, left no one in any doubt as to the motivations of its sponsors:

"One of the characteristics of our time is that we have for several decades been emancipating minorities who claimed they were disadvantaged. Are they grateful? Not a bit. We emancipated races and got inverted racism. We emancipate homosexuals and they condemn heterosexism as chauvinist sexism, male oppression and so on. They will push us off the pavement if we give them a chance." [18]

Yet the government seemed reluctant to support it at that time: for example, Conservative peer Lord Skelmersdale advised the House of Lords that his government supported the aims of the bill in seeking to put an end to 'irresponsible and inappropriate teaching in this field' but:

"... the distinction between this and ... proper teaching about homosexuality cannot be drawn sufficiently clearly in legislation to avoid harmful misinterpretation. That is a risk we cannot take." [19]

This argument was conveniently forgotten when the government introduced Section 28 – with virtually identical wording – a year later.

Halsbury's Bill failed due to lack of time because of an impending general election but Jill Knight remained determined to keep it on the agenda. During Prime Minister's Question Time before the dissolution of Parliament she reminded Margaret Thatcher that the initiative had been lost and sought her reassurance that it would be revived post-election. Thatcher assured Knight of her full support for the measure and confirmed that it would be reintroduced in the next session of Parliament.

The build-up to the 1987 general election gave queer people little to be optimistic about. For one thing it became increasingly clear that the Labour Party saw queer rights as an electoral liability. Party press secretary Patricia Hewitt had made this absolutely clear in a letter she sent to right-wing Labour MP Frank Dobson following the party's loss of the seat in Greenwich in a February by-election. She wrote:

"The 'Loony Labour Left' is now taking its toll; the gays and lesbians issue is costing us dear amongst pensioners ..."

This explanation had been published in *The Sun* newspaper, following the leaking of the letter to a number of newspapers. For queer activists the claim was doubly disappointing, not just because it confirmed Labour's lack of commitment to queer rights but also because Hewitt had been General Secretary of the National Council for Civil Liberties for several years prior to election to Parliament.

Whether the Conservatives knew that Labour would not defend the issue is not known; however, they – and their supporters – ramped it up during the election campaign. One Conservative election poster featured three books in red covers – *Police: Out of Schools, Young, Gay and Proud* and *The Playbook for Kids about Sex* – with the message: *"Is this Labour's idea of comprehensive education? Take the politics out of education. Vote Conservative."*

At the same time, the Committee for a Free Britain, a group with ties to the Conservative Party, launched a series of advertisements featuring Betty Sheridan from the Parents' Rights Group in Haringey. In these, Sheridan stated:

"I live in Haringey. I'm married with two children. And I'm scared. If you vote Labour they'll go on teaching my kids about GAYS and LESBIANS, instead of giving them proper lessons." [20]

The Sun's gleeful leaking of Patricia Hewitt's letter indicated exactly where the press stood on the issue. With the continuing media hysteria about 'the AIDS threat' (which will be covered elsewhere in this book) the ingredients combined to give Thatcher her third general election victory.

On 9 October 9, she delivered her famous speech to the Conservative Party Conference wherein she declared:

"Children who need to be taught to respect traditional moral values are being taught that they have an inalienable right to be gay."

Any reluctance to support the measures in the Halsbury Bill had clearly vanished now. On 8 December 1987 a new clause – on the *"prohibition on promoting homosexuality by teaching or by publishing material"* was inserted into the Local Government Bill. Inserted initially as Clause 14 before finally ending up as Section 28 it stated that a local authority:

"... shall not intentionally promote homosexuality or publish material with the intention of promoting homosexuality"

or *"promote the teaching in any maintained school of the acceptability of homosexuality as a pretended family relationship."*

Despite expressions of concern from a number of mainstream organisations, such as the Library Association, the Council for Voluntary Organisations, the Family Planning Association and the Arts Council, Labour's opposition was generally lukewarm. Indeed, Labour's initial preoccupation appears to have been to show support for it. For example, on 2 December 1987 in the committee stage of the bill:

"Dr Jack Cunningham also expressed his support for the new clause, stating that the Labour party did not believe that councils or schools should promote homosexuality." [21]

Labour's continuing perception of queer rights as a vote loser was again demonstrated by its frontbench spokesperson Jeff Rooker. When questioned about his party's failure to defend what was, in reality, its own policy, he replied:

"If anyone comes to me quoting Labour conference resolutions I shall point out to them that between those resolutions and now Labour has lost a general election." [22]

Meanwhile queer people were feeling the impact of the intensified homophobia generated by the bill. In December, the offices of *Capital Gay* in London were firebombed.

When this was mentioned in Parliament Conservative MP Elaine Kellett-Bowman had shouted out *"Quite right"*. When challenged to clarify her position she expressed no remorse:

"I am quite prepared to affirm that it is quite right that there should be an intolerance of evil."

Margaret Thatcher made her a Dame the following year.

Other attacks during this period included the placing of a bomb outside a disco hosting a 'Stop the Clause' benefit in Manchester and the throwing of tear gas canisters into a crowded gay pub in Rochester.

On 15 December the bill was debated for the second time in Parliament. Even at this stage it was reported that Labour's frontbench were undecided as to whether they should call for the deletion of Section 28 [56]. In the end they opted to seek amendments – none of which were successful.

On that same day openly gay Labour MP Chris Smith was reported as saying that Labour had made *"a tactical error"* by not opposing Section 28 from the outset [23].

But it wasn't just the timing of Labour's opposition that was a cause for concern; it was also the weakness of that opposition. Many queer activists felt that the Labour leadership remained pre-occupied with the media's perceptions of its actions (as demonstrated, for example, by Patricia Hewitt's letter). In practice this meant that, rather than challenge the many factual inaccuracies that informed much of the press coverage and Parliamentary debate, Labour used it as an opportunity to try and distance itself from the so-called 'loony left' [24].

When the bill was debated in the House of Lords on 11 January 1988, Social Democrat peer Lord Falkland tabled an amendment seeking to address alleged concerns by making it illegal for local authorities to publish material that presented homosexuality as more acceptable than heterosexuality. This amendment also failed, a result that has been attributed in part to:

"... the refusal of the opposition parties to match the whip imposed by the Conservatives with a whip of its own members ... the Labour leadership were quite evidently scared stiff by the prospect of negative publicity." [25]

On 2 February 1988, and despite Labour leader Neil Kinnock's belated declaration of opposition to Section 28, an attempt by Labour peer Lord Willis to have the clause deleted failed.

135

"These fears [of negative publicity] were very clearly revealed in their failure to support an attempt by a Labour peer, Lord Willis, to have the clause deleted. Indeed, it was rumoured among activists in London that strenuous efforts were made by the party leadership to persuade him to abandon his stand." [(26)]

But even if Labour was still ambiguous about its approach to Section 28, queer activists certainly were not: as the 2 February debate ended, four lesbians abseiled into the chamber of the House of Lords.

This action was only one of a series that took place around the country during Section 28's journey through Parliament. A number of marches took place; for example 10,000 people in London on 9 January (with 32 being arrested); 15,000 in Manchester in February then a further 20,000 in London in April. And on 23 May, the day before the bill's enactment, two lesbians invaded the studio of the BBC's *Six O'Clock News* programme just as it was going to air.

Despite the sustained campaigning of queer communities, Section 28 passed into law. No prosecutions were ever brought under it, not least because, as its critics had repeatedly pointed out, the wording was so vague as to make it unworkable. But given the history behind its creation, it is arguable that its purpose had always been political rather than legal or fiscal. As the media demonised queer people the government saw the opportunity to make political capital at the expense of both the Labour Party and queers.

And despite the absence of prosecutions, the threat of Section 28 still led to some local authorities resorting to ridiculous measures. For example, East Sussex County Council banned a National Youth Bureau resource pack on voluntary organisations from its schools and colleges on the grounds that it included a reference to the London Lesbian and Gay Centre; Leeds College of Music and Essex County Councils banned lesbian and gay organisations from meeting on their premises; Strathclyde Regional Council instructed further education colleges to withhold money from student unions that funded lesbian and gay societies; and the London Borough Grants Committee included a new clause in its funding agreement that forbade 'the intentional promotion of homosexuality'.

Even when action was finally taken to repeal it in 2003 there was still strong opposition from the Conservatives. David Cameron, for example, had described its repeal as *"deeply unpopular"* and *"a fringe issue"*. Meanwhile, the increasingly rabid

Jill Knight was still so caught up in her campaign of misinformation that she re-wrote history even further when she claimed in 1999:

"Haringey Council made a video 'How to Become a Lesbian in 35 Minutes'. It was intended to be shown in a school for mentally handicapped girls, some of whom were extremely young ... From my experience of those children it is difficult enough for them to understand normal sexual relations without having homosexuality foisted upon them. I find it horrifying that anyone would support that." [27]

Government Failure to Act

While both the USA and Australia have state and federal governments that somewhat fragment the fight for queer rights, the UK system was, prior to limited devolution to regional assemblies in the late 90s, generally perceived as far more centralised.

However, there were still some regional issues that affected the progress of queer rights; in particular the differing application of certain laws in Scotland and Northern Ireland.

The 1967 Sexual Offences Act

'Different legal systems' was cited as the reason for the failure to apply the 1967 Sexual Offences Act beyond England and Wales. In fact there was plenty of scope for the British government to implement the 1967 Act elsewhere; indeed, that is what they ended up doing in Scotland anyway. The real obstacle to reform was the perceived strength of conservative forces, as well as the government's continued failure to see homosexual law reform as a priority, which, in practice meant they were unwilling to commit to a political battle in order to drive it through.

In Scotland the battles lines had been established as early as 1957 when the Church of Scotland and the Catholic Church rejected the findings of the 1957 *Wolfenden Report on Homosexual Offences* and opposed any legislative changes that arose from that. The government was finally forced to act when three Scottish gay activists took their case to the European Court of Human Rights in 1979. At this point the Thatcher government decided that driving through law reform would be slightly less onerous than fighting a protracted (and unwinnable) legal battle in Europe. In consequence, measures to reform the law in Scotland were launched with such a serious lack of commitment that they almost failed to get through.

137

The chosen strategy was an amendment to the 1979 Criminal Justice Bill. It was submitted during the latter stages of the bill's progress through Parliament and late at night, in the hope that most MPs would have gone home by then [28]. In spite of this, the amendment was still opposed by a number of government backbench MPs, the government's own Secretary of State for Scotland and every Scottish Conservative MP. Somewhat remarkably, therefore, the amendment (which *The Sun*, unsurprisingly, called *"The McGay's Charter"*) was still voted through.

However, opponents determined to fight on and lobbyists began to pressure members of the House of Lords – and Scotland's Lord Advocate in particular – to reject the amendment. The debate was as misinformed and bigoted as ever: for example, Raymond Johnston, the Director of the Nationwide Festival of Light wrote to all Scottish newspapers arguing that bringing Scottish law in line with England meant:

"... to lose sight of a much graver issue, namely the extraordinary and dangerous spate of homosexual propaganda which has arisen in England since the law was changed in 1967.

There has now emerged a vast sub-culture of homosexuals militantly organised to convert society to their own doctrine that there is nothing intrinsically harmful or immoral in homosexual practices ... In effect these practices are being publicly commended with the inevitable corruption of the young." [29]

The familiar conflation of homosexuality with paedophilia and the corruption of young people reached such a level that it triggered the formation of the pressure group Parents Concern. This group lobbied to have the amendment scrapped, using language that echoed that of Anita Bryant a few years earlier in Dade County, Florida:

"Since they cannot multiply by natural procreation, are they therefore to be permitted to do so by public display, advertising, soliciting (at least in private) and other forms of proselytising?" [30]

Yet, despite the pressure, the scaremongering and the government's own immense ambiguity over the measure, the amendment was finally passed in the House of Lords on 21 October 1980, albeit with a majority of only 11 votes.

There was an even greater reluctance to address the issue in Northern Ireland where reform was opposed by an unholy alliance of the Catholic Church and notorious anti-Papist, the self-styled 'Reverend' Ian Paisley, leader of the Democratic Unionist Party (DUP).

138

In the face of government inaction and an active campaign of harassment and intimidation of gay men, gay activists established the Campaign for Homosexual Law Reform in 1974. A year later they changed the name to the Northern Ireland Gay Rights Association (NIGRA) and focused on achieving the implementation of the 1967 Sexual Offences Act in Northern Ireland. In 1976 Jeffrey Dudgeon, acting on behalf of NIGRA, submitted a complaint against the British government to the European Court of Human Rights in relation to the sustained harassment of gay men in Northern Ireland. These actions prompted Ian Paisley to launch the 'Save Ulster from Sodomy' campaign in 1977 and raise a petition of 70,000 signatures, which he presented to the government buildings in Stormont in 1978.

The NIGRA campaign had also prompted the then Labour British government to consider implementing homosexual law reform and it issued draft legislation to that effect in 1978. However, this quickly stalled: whether this was in response to perceived opposition or, as some have suggested, the result of a political trade-off with Unionists in Parliament, is not known. But in practice it meant that the only remaining hope for law reform lay with the appeal to the European Court of Human Rights.

In October 1981 the court found in favour of Jeffrey Dudgeon, declaring the British government to be in breach of Article 8 of the European Convention on Human Rights due to their failure to extend the provisions of the 1967 Sexual Offences Act to Northern Ireland. In light of this judgement the government declared that they would extend the act to Northern Ireland by October the following year, 1982. In response, Ian Paisley's Democratic Unionist Party presented a submission opposing decriminalisation to the British government on 30 April 1982. Their arguments included:

- *"The effect of the law as a restraint on bestiality, incest and rape will be further reduced."*
- Establishing an age of consent of 21 will lead to *"inevitable demands for a further lowering"* giving *"impetus to the paedophile movement which is rampant within the homosexual movement today."*
- Decriminalising homosexuality would be *"a scandalous surrender to a tiny minority campaign for homosexuality to be treated as a normal way of life, instead of a harmful deviance."* (31)

On 25 October 1982 the provisions of the 1967 Sexual Offences Act were extended to Northern Ireland.

The USA
Reagan's Failure to Act

Ronald Reagan's intransigence and hostility towards the queer community is legendary and he established his position very early on. For example, during his 1980 presidential campaign he stated:

"My criticism is that [the gay movement] isn't just asking for civil rights; it's asking for recognition and acceptance of an alternative lifestyle which I do not believe society can condone, nor can I." [32]

Four years later, the 'Presidential Biblical Scorecard' – a 'how-to-vote' publication produced by the right-wing National Citizens Action Network – is reported to have quoted Reagan as saying:

"Society has always regarded marital love as a sacred expression of the bond between a man and a woman. It is the means by which families are created and society itself is extended into the future ... We will resist the efforts of some to obtain government endorsement of homosexuality."

In recent years some of Reagan's supporters have questioned this, some arguing that neither the quote nor the publication ever happened, others arguing that it came from someone in his administration but he never knew about it. But there are others who use this quote – with full attribution to Reagan – to sing his praises.

Reagan was certainly not slow in appointing to his administration those who saw women's rights and gay rights as counter to 'traditional family values'. For example, shortly after his election he established the Family Policy Advisory Board, a 25-person body drawn from Christian, pro-life and 'pro-family' organisations. The common philosophy for the constituent organisations was that 'liberal' ideas such as women's rights and queer rights were leading to the breakdown of the American family. This was reflected in the working of the board, with a particularly notable example being the Family Protection Act, which was presented to Congress in 1981.

Proposed provisions of the act included a ban on federal funds to *"any organisation that suggests that homosexualty can be an acceptable alternative lifestyle."* [33] The act failed to pass through a Democrat-dominated Congress but five years later Reagan established his 'Special Working Group on the Family', headed up by right-wing activist Gary Bauer, whom Reagan had appointed to his administration in 1982.

Bauer had connections with a number of homophobic organisations including Focus on Family and the Family Research Council (which the Southern Poverty Law Center has designated a hate group). Unsurprisingly, the Working Group's subsequent report, '*The Family: Preserving America's Future*', merely reiterated the New Right's position that the traditional family was under threat as a consequence of decades of 'liberal' policies.

To demonstrate the 'threat' to the American family, it quoted *"distinguished social scientist"* Amitai Etzioni:

"If we continue to dismantle our American family at the accelerating pace we have been doing since 1965, there will not be a single American family left by the year 2008." (34)

As for sex and sex education, morality replaced reality as it railed against the cost of 'promiscuity' and 'the sexual revolution':

"We must either make a massive and open-ended commitment of public resources to deal with the consequences of promiscuity (including illegitimacy, abortion, venereal diseases, AIDS, teen suicide) or we must explain to the young, for their own good, one clear standard of conduct which tells them how we expect them to grow up." (35)

Thus the report linked a broad range of social issues to one moralistic and undefined common cause – 'promiscuity'. This is simplistic nonsense: even if 'promiscuity' refers to high frequency of sexual behaviour it fails to take into account the nature of that sexual behaviour (for example, the availability and use of condoms or various other types of safer sex). But the practice of safer sex comes down to the knowledge levels of the participants, which should, therefore, support the argument for comprehensive sex education. But that would be contrary to 'traditional family values' so the report makes the extraordinary (and unsupported) claim that:

"There is little in the record to suggest that value-free sex education courses or the availability of contraceptives to minors has helped – in fact the evidence is quite to the contrary." (36)

Furthermore, the inclusion of teen suicide as a consequence of 'promiscuity' is even more dubious as it again flies in the face of the evidence (which, for example, identifies

141

access to guns as an important factor). The disproportionately high incidence of suicide and attempted suicide amongst queer teens (which is due largely to hostility at home or in school) is not mentioned. Indeed, there is a complete absence of references to queer people in the report (unless one takes the word 'AIDS' as a veiled allusion) and that, essentially, summarises its entire focus. The 'solution' is the monogamous, heterosexual family unit: evidence or problems that don't easily fit into this simplistic solution are merely ignored.

Ironically, this report is one of the few official publications that talks about the President and AIDS in the same document (although, in this case, purely to make moral capital). Reagan was renowned for his failure to acknowledge the issue, mentioning it for the first time when asked about AIDS funding at a press conference in 1985. This was four years after it had first been identified in the USA, the same year that his friend Rock Hudson had died from it, and the year in which American cases of AIDS had reached 15,948 [37]. It would be a further two years before he established the Presidential Commission on HIV in 1987. By that point the number of US AIDS diagnoses had reached 47,022. [38]

Even in his 1985 comments, he managed to offend those with the most basic knowledge of AIDS by suggesting – in the face of overwhelming evidence to the contrary – that HIV could be transmitted by casual contact. Asked what he thought about children with AIDS being allowed to attend school he replied:

"I can well understand the plight of the parents and how they feel about it. I also have compassion, as I think we all do, for the child that has this and doesn't know and can't have it explained to him why somehow he is now an outcast and can no longer associate with his playmates and schoolmates. On the other hand, I can understand the problem with the parents. It is true that some medical sources had said that this cannot be communicated in any way other than the ones we already know and which would not involve a child being in the school. And yet medicine has not come forth unequivocally and said, 'This we know for a fact', that it is safe. And until they do, I think we just have to do the best we can with this problem. I can understand both sides of it." [39]

Such a statement demonstrates not only his obsession with sticking to his 'family values' agenda regardless of the evidence but also the lack of leadership on the AIDS issue that characterised his entire presidential incumbency. To assert that there was a possibility that HIV was spread by casual contact merely fed the fears of the general public and played into the hands of the conservative bigots such as Jesse Helms who demanded compulsory testing and quarantining of 'high risk groups' [40]. It also deliberately ignored the Center for Disease Control's 1983 categorical statement that casual contact does not transmit HIV/AIDS [41].

AIDS was an inconvenient political fact for Reagan: objective social and scientific research clearly demonstrated the need for public discussion around the key routes of transmission – sex and intravenous drug use. However, this conflicted with the conservative view that these sorts of things simply didn't happen or, as demonstrated by the report on The Family, that talking about it encouraged people to go out and do it. Such was Reagan's obsession with maintaining his political line he actively prohibited his own Surgeon General from talking to the media about AIDS until 1985. (Indeed, he failed to include him in the 1987 Presidential Commission on HIV, which he had stacked with those who supported his pro-family, anti-condom line, such as Catholic Cardinal John O'Connor.)

This prohibition gives a very clear indication of the lengths to which Reagan was prepared to go to shore up his flawed political agenda. In 1981 Reagan had fought long and hard to have Koop appointed to the role of Surgeon General. The confirmation process had taken eight months, which was unusually long for that time but no real surprise given Koop's outspoken views on abortion, women's rights, gay rights and welfare provision (which he regarded as akin to fascism). As well as writing a number of books opposing abortion he had also made five films on the subject, with which he toured the country on an anti-abortion crusade. He couldn't have been a more perfect representative of Reagan's values.

But, unlike Reagan, Koop then listened to the facts about AIDS and, much to everyone's surprise (and Reagan's great discomfort) came to an objective decision about what needed to be done. And, to the fury of the conservatives, this included an end to the scapegoating of those most affected by the disease, dismissing compulsory testing and quarantining as effective prevention policy and providing detailed sex education to school children.

These issues were spelled out very clearly in the Surgeon General's 1986 report on

143

AIDS – but even this only came about after some considerable manoeuvring on Koop's part. In a speech on 'The Early Days of AIDS as I Remember Them', Koop seemed to suggest that Reagan put very little thought into the idea of a report and, indeed, may have just come up with it to give the impression that his administration was actually doing something about it:

"... [in 1986] the President made an unprecedented trip across town to the Humphrey Building and addressed in the Great Hall as many people as could crowd in there from the Department of Health and Human Services. And he said all the right things, you know, and thanked them all for their great and faithful work and, in the course of his remarks, he said that AIDS was a top priority for the Department and he looked forward to the day when there would be a vaccine. And he announced that he was asking the Surgeon General to prepare a special report on AIDS. That was it. There was never a formal request. And I've often thought it's a good thing I went and it was a good thing that I was paying attention." (42)

Koop then went on to speculate as to whether Reagan had really thought through how his conservative supporters would react to the contents of such a report; further fuelling speculation that the commitment to a report was made purely for the sake of short-term political expediency. Certainly Reagan had shown little interest in the matter up to that date:

"The major problem was that the President was reluctant to go out front offering the leadership that only he could provide. At least a dozen times I pleaded with my critics in the White House to let me have a meeting with the President so that he could hear from me my concerns about America and the AIDS epidemic and what his role should be in it. And for months I had been trying to cover the rather embarrassing silence of the Oval Office on the scourge of AIDS." (43)

Koop further acknowledged the hurdles to having any sort of meaningful report endorsed by the White House and undertook a number of strategies to minimise this. These included writing the report from his home to minimise potential 'interruptions' and collecting all copies of the final draft after it was discussed at White House's Domestic Policy Council on the pretext that he didn't want it leaked to the media. He even had the documents printed on high-quality expensive paper so that he could resist any proposed amendments by pointing to the high costs of a reprint!

As a result of this remarkably adept political manoeuvring his report survived – and was published – intact. A shorter version, complete with unambiguous references to sexual and drug using practices, was distributed to 107 million households across the country, much to the chagrin of the ultra-conservatives. And the media subsequently came directly to Koop for comment on AIDS, rather than trying to battle their way through a wall of censorious, conservative political henchmen.

Unsurprisingly, AIDS activists were delighted: at the 1987 International AIDS Conference in Washington D.C. he was given a rapturous welcome by delegates. The following day, delegates booed and turned their backs as Vice President George Bush gave his speech arguing for compulsory testing. Clearly the White House still wasn't listening to its own AIDS expert: Koop himself recalled an episode where Reagan *"briefly and superficially"* touched on AIDS during a speech to the Philadelphia College of Physicians in April 1987. As Reagan arrived at Philadelphia Airport for his flight back to Washington:

"... he was crowded by reporters who kept asking him question after question [about AIDS] to which he replied nothing at all until he got to the top step, just about to enter Air Force One, and he turned and said, "Just say no". And that night Tom Brokaw reported in his evening news hour that the President had never read The Surgeon General's Report on AIDS." (44)

Given the nature of the speech he had given a few hours earlier, it isn't surprising that he was bombarded with questions – and also so reluctant to answer them. With more than 47,000 AIDS diagnoses in the USA at that time, most of which were gay or bisexual men, Reagan had explained his determination to find a cure for the disease with the following anecdote:

"Some time ago I heard the story of a man who received what turned out to be a transfusion of blood contaminated with the AIDS virus. He was infected, and in turn his wife was infected. And within two years they had both died. Well, I'm determined that we'll find a cure for AIDS." (45)

Gay and bisexual men were obviously of no concern for Reagan.

But Reagan's speech was criticised for other reasons too – including criticism from members of his own Republican Party. Whereas the President had stated that *"we want to spend 28 per cent more on research and education"*, Senator Lowell Weicker, ranking

Republican on the Senate appropriations subcommittee that oversaw AIDS research, pointed out that:

"The most damaging piece of deception as far as the president is concerned is that he says, 'I'm asking for $100 million more in AIDS research'. That sounds very good until you hear that he is asking for a $600 million cut in the funds to go to the National Institutes of Health for basic biomedical research. The net of all that is he has cut $500 million for AIDS." [46]

This was not the first time Reagan had been criticised for making misleading statements about his administration's commitment to AIDS funding – nor would it be the last. In 1985 a report by the congressional agency the Office of Technology Assessment had declared that *"increases in funding specially for AIDS have come at the initiative of Congress, not the Administration"*. They had further pointed out that *"PHS [Public Health Service] agencies have had difficulties in planning their AIDS-related activities because of uncertainties over budget and personnel allocations"*.

In essence, Reagan was reluctant to commit significant funds to AIDS research because of his political beliefs on 'family values' and also those on minimising the role of federal government. And where the evidence failed to support his views – including the Surgeon General's call for a nationwide, federally-driven AIDS education initiative – he simply ignored it. Increasingly aware of growing concern at and potential electoral impact of his perceived inaction in the face of the growing AIDS crisis, he simply 'talked the talk' but remained reluctant to put real resources into 'walking the walk'. For example, in 1988, Professor Daniel M. Fox had this to say:

"In January 1986 President Reagan called AIDS "one of the highest public health priorities" but at the same time proposed to reduce spending in AIDS research by considerably more than the amount mandated in the Gramm-Rudman-Hollings Act. In 1986 and 1987 Congress continued to appropriate more funds for research than the administration requested – in the last days of the 1987 session, for instance, increasing the AIDS budget of the National Institutes of Health (NIH) to $448 million from $253 million the previous year. Throughout the Reagan administration, budget officials had deliberately understated the NIH budget request, knowing that Congress would add to it." [47]

Reagan's Right-wing Administration

Reagan also packed his administration with exponents of extreme right-wing views. As mentioned previously, he brought Gary Bauer from the Family Research Council into his administration in 1982. The Family Research Council is a rabidly homophobic organisation that promotes and perpetuates ridiculous stereotypes about queer people. These include the view that a disproportionately high percentage of murderers are gay, homosexuals have far shorter life spans than heterosexuals and:

"One of the primary goals of the homosexual rights movement is to abolish all age of consent laws and to eventually recognise pedophiles as the 'prophets' of a new sexual order." [48]

In addition to his ongoing presence as a 'domestic policy advisor', Bauer was also the chair of the White House Special Working Group on the Family.

From 1985 until 1987 Reagan's Director of Communications was Patrick J. Buchanan. Buchanan was yet another man who wasn't prepared to let the evidence get in the way of a full-blown prejudice. He called AIDS *"nature's revenge on gay men"* because *"runaway promiscuity"* was *"the essence"* of homosexual life. He believed that HIV positive gay men should be quarantined because HIV could be transmitted through casual contact and, on that basis, demanded that the 1983 New York City Gay Pride Parade be cancelled *"because of the risk of AIDS transmission"* [49].

William Bennett, Reagan's Education Secretary, was also cast from the same mould, advocating the compulsory testing of marriage licence applicants, all hospital patients, prison inmates and foreigners applying for immigration visas [50]. He vigorously and publicly opposed C. Everett Koop's proposals for AIDS education in schools, describing the Public Health Service approach as *"morally empty"* and opting, as usual, for the 'values-based' approach supported by his Cabinet colleagues.

And, of course, at the time of his appointment, C. Everett Koop was also rabidly anti-queer, defending anti-sodomy laws on the grounds that sodomy was *"... repugnant to the moral sensitivity of the American people"* [51] and denouncing gay rights as encouraging *"anti-family trends"*. At the time of his appointment to Surgeon General he had all the right credentials for the Reagan administration. But the emergence of AIDS was to change all of that.

147

There were also other, less prominent figures in Reagan's administration that helped to undermine a concrete and objective approach to AIDS. One of these was John G. Roberts Jr, an Assistant Counsel to the President in the Office of White House Counsel. Five days prior to the 1985 press conference where Reagan had stated that *"medicine has not come forth unequivocally and said, 'This we know for a fact', that it is safe"*, Roberts had deliberately taken the Centers for Disease Control's (CDC) statement on this out of Reagan's briefing papers. The CDC – the country's leading AIDS research unit – had, just three weeks earlier, stated that *"casual person-to-person contact as would occur among schoolchildren appears to pose no risk"*. Roberts had prepared a memorandum that stated:

"I do not think we should have the President taking a position on a disputed scientific issue of this sort. There is much to commend the view that we should assume AIDS can be transmitted through casual or routine contact, as is true with many viruses, until it is demonstrated that it cannot be, and no scientist has said AIDS definitely cannot be so transmitted." [52]

In so doing, Roberts put his personal opinion ahead of that of global AIDS experts and perpetuated the hysteria that led to children like Ryan White and Ricky Ray, who were infected with the AIDS virus, being subject to vicious physical and verbal attacks.

As C. Everett Koop was acutely aware, the prospect of any real effective action was highly unlikely, given such appalling attitudes towards HIV within the administration. In consequence, those initiatives that were debated were either extreme proposals, such as quarantining, or extreme amendments, such as restrictions on AIDS funding. Two key players in both of these areas were William Dannemeyer (Republican, California) and Jesse Helms (Republican, North Carolina).

Dannemeyer was a Christian extremist whose actions had included attempting to block funding for evolution-related exhibits at the Smithsonian and opposing the Americans with Disabilities Act. Like others in his mould, he portrayed the queer rights movement as a movement to deprive heterosexuals and claimed in his 1989 book *Shadow in the Land: Homosexuality in America* that gay rights would:

"... plunge our people and, indeed, the entire West into a dark night of the soul that could last hundreds of years." [53]

With the advent of AIDS he became a leading advocate of testing and the quarantining of those found to be HIV positive. In *Shadow in the Land* he included his own list of priorities for controlling HIV/AIDS. As well as testing and quarantining, his other proposals included *"the restoration of laws against sodomy" and "the rejection of anti-discrimination laws"* (54) Apart from his own attempts to introduce legislation to this effect, he also backed other extremists seeking similar measures, such as Lyndon LaRouche and his Proposition 64 in California in 1986 (covered later in this book).

Dannemeyer also led opposition in the House of Representatives to the removal of HIV from the list of 'dangerous and contagious diseases' that can be used to bar someone from entering the USA. As part of this he circulated a letter to members of the House claiming that the American Medical Association opposed the removal of HIV from this list. In fact the exact opposite was the case.

And while his public statements were disturbing enough, it seems his private views were even more dangerous. For example, it is alleged that he told C. Everett Koop that HIV positive people should be *"wiped from the face of the earth"* (55).

Jesse Helms is generally acknowledged as one of the most extreme conservative politicians ever elected to Congress. He was, among other things, an anti-integrationist opposed to civil rights, women's rights, disability rights, affirmative action and, of course, queer rights and would go to great lengths to block or undermine any legislation that ran counter to his beliefs. His position on queer issues was effectively summarised in his quote:

"Nothing positive happened to Sodom and Gomorrah and nothing positive is likely to happen to America if our people succumb to the drumbeats of support for the homosexual lifestyle." (56)

One manifestation of Helms' extreme homophobia was during a debate on a federal AIDS appropriation bill in 1987. He proffered a gay men's safer sex comic published by Gay Men's Health Crisis in New York and claimed that it had been produced with federal funds. This was completely untrue but he used this deception to push through an amendment to the bill prohibiting the use of federal funds for AIDS education materials that *"promote or encourage, directly or indirectly, homosexual activities"*. In other words, the government would not act to educate the population most affected by HIV and AIDS.

Also in 1987, Helms slipped in an amendment to the Supplemental Appropriations

149

Act, adding HIV to the list of 'excludable diseases' that prevented people from entering the United States. It was added shortly after President Reagan had added AIDS to the list and was, in consequence, passed with very little debate with few politicians realising the potential impact at that time. That impact became clear the following year when an overseas delegate to an AIDS conference was detained by immigration officials after HIV medication was found in his luggage.

But there was no quick fix to this problem: supporters of the ban argued that, because the ban had been voted in by Congress, it could only be rescinded by them – and the innate conservatism of Congress prevented this from happening. This led to a boycott of the 1990 International AIDS Conference in San Francisco by a range of organisations including the International Red Cross, the British Medical Association and the European Parliament.

In 1988, when Democratic Congressman Edward Kennedy and Republican Congressman Orrin Hatch presented a bill to Congress seeking funding for a wide range of AIDS services and research Helms made repeated attempts to undermine it. He opposed spending on AIDS research on the grounds that *"there is not one single case of AIDS in this country that cannot be traced in origin to sodomy"*. He also proposed amendments calling for mandatory prenuptial testing, HIV testing in all federal hospitals, criminal penalties for transmitting HIV through blood donation, and a ban on the funding of needle exchanges. Most of his amendments were rejected but succeeded in slowing down the approval process significantly. On the issue of needle exchange funding, however, he was victorious. Congress approved a funding ban *"unless the surgeon general finds that such methods will curb the spread of AIDS"*. The reality is that extensive evidence has been produced on the efficacy of needle exchanges yet, with the exception of a very short-lived lifting of the ban in 2009, no administration – Republican or Democrat – has had the political courage to lift the ban once and for all.

Helms also sought to end funding to the National Endowment of the Arts (NEA) as a result of their alleged support for the explicit and homoerotic work of Robert Mapplethorpe. Specifically, a retrospective of Mapplethorpe's work 'The Perfect Moment' had been organised by the Institute of Contemporary Art in Philadelphia in 1988 and the NEA had contributed $30,000 towards this. The exhibition was due to be toured to five US cities and had already been displayed in Philadelphia and

Chicago without incident. However, in June 1989, following a campaign by the American Family Association, congressmen threatened to cut the NEA's budget and Helms again positioned himself at the forefront of this campaign.

The immediate effect was that the Corcoran Gallery in Washington D.C. cancelled its planned exhibition of the work. But there was also a longer-term impact as Helms and his allies sought to implement a ban on federal funding. In July Helms introduced an amendment to the NEA appropriations bill to ban the NEA from sponsoring *"obscene or indecent art"*. The amendment did not get through the House of Representatives so the conservatives tried again, achieving some success when a clause was inserted into NEA appropriations that banned federal funding for art that *"may be considered obscene, including but not limited to, depictions of sadomasochism, homoeroticism, the sexual exploitation of children, or individuals engaged in sex acts and which, when taken as a whole, do not have serious literary, artistic, political or scientific value."*

Anti-gay Lobbyists
The Moral Majority

In the USA, politicians often rely on wealthy backers as well as connections to powerful lobbying organisations to get into power. Helms, for example, was a founding member of the Moral Majority, an organisation that sought to increase the influence of the Christian Right – and their so-called 'Christian principles' – on government. These principles – which included opposition to abortion, queer rights, the Equal Rights Amendment, the Strategic Arms Limitation Talks and anything that was seen as 'anti-family' – were identical to those espoused by Reagan, Helms, Buchanan et al.

Their first engagement with federal politics was the 1980 presidential election when they publicly endorsed Ronald Reagan in preference to Jimmy Carter. Despite Carter being a self-professed evangelical Christian, the Moral Majority had been disappointed by his refusal to apply his personal beliefs to his political role. Reagan, on the other hand, had no such problems: he recruited the Moral Majority's first executive director, the Rev. Robert Billings, to be a religious adviser on his campaign then, on coming to power, gave him a job in the Department of Education.

151

On a local level, their network of chapters around the country campaigned on specific local issues such as prayer in schools and gay rights ordinances, and supported political candidates whom they thought best represented their views. This included candidates for local positions such as State Lieutenant Governor as well as congressional candidates. During presidential elections they all worked together to garner local support for their chosen candidate, which in 1980 and 1984 was Reagan. In 1988, however, they chose George H. W. Bush despite another Republican contender – the Rev. Pat Robertson – being perceived as more in tune with the organisation's ethos. Robertson was, like Moral Majority founder Jerry Falwell, a right-wing 'televangelist' and it has been suggested that it was this perceived rivalry that lost him Falwell's support.

The Moral Majority never missed an opportunity to make moral and political capital from the AIDS crisis. For example, when Falwell declared that *"AIDS is not just God's punishment for homosexuals; it is God's punishment for the society that tolerates homosexuals"*, he wasn't just declaring that God didn't like queer people; he was advocating active intolerance of queer people – something that often manifested itself in violence.

And Falwell and his organisation had no problem with lying to their followers in order to gain support. Thus, the July 1983 cover of *Moral Majority Report* was dominated by a photograph of a 'typical' (and white) American family of Mom, Dad and two kids, wearing face masks. The caption screamed: *"AIDS: Homosexual Diseases Threaten American Families."*

By 1987, Falwell was sending out fundraising letters with the claim that gay men were deliberately donating blood *"... because they know they're going to die – and they are going to take as many people with them as they can"* [57]. It was another of the Christian Right's 'truths', much in the vein of Anita Bryant's declaration that *"homosexuals have to recruit because they can't raise children"*.

It has often been claimed that Falwell made bigoted or misleading statements to one audience in order to gain support and would then deny having made them elsewhere. Thus, in March 1980 he told a rally in Anchorage that he had taken President Jimmy Carter to task for having *"practising homosexuals"* among senior White House staff. When a tape of the actual conversation proved this to be completely false Falwell declared that his previous statement had not been *"intended to be a verbatim report"* but rather *"an honest portrayal"* of Carter's position [58]. Similarly, he claimed he was misquoted when reports emerged that he had claimed that *"God does not answer the prayers of Jews"* [59].

But he came unstuck in July 1984 when, in the course of a television debate with queer activist Jerry Sloan, he was accused of making derogatory comments about the pro-gay Metropolitan Community Church. Sloan had claimed that Falwell had called the Church *"brute beasts"* and *"a vile and Satanic system"* that will *"one day be utterly annihilated and there will be a celebration in heaven."* When Falwell denied making such statements Sloan declared that he had a tape of Falwell's remarks. Falwell, in turn, claimed that no such tape existed and promised that he would pay $5000 if Sloan could produce it.

When Sloan did produce it Falwell refused to pay so Sloan successfully sued him for the money. But, never knowing when to admit defeat, Falwell still refused to pay and lodged an appeal, arguing that Sloan had only won his case because the presiding judge was Jewish and therefore prejudiced against him. Falwell lost his appeal – and was ordered to pay an additional $2875 in costs.

Lyndon LaRouche

Lyndon LaRouche was a political maverick whose brand of extremism and paranoia found dangerous levels of support within the American political system. In an extraordinary political career he appears to have been associated with everyone from the Ku Klux Klan and the Republican Party on the right to the Socialist Workers Party and the Democratic Party on the Left.

Central to LaRouche's operations was his constant development of elaborate theories on everything from biology to global capitalism, most of which seemed to incorporate some type of conspiracy theory. For example, he had argued that Henry Kissinger was a Soviet agent and the Queen of England headed up an international drugs ring. In 1973 he established a 'Biological Holocaust Task Force', which predicted that an epidemic would threaten humanity at some point in the 1980s.

Unsurprisingly, he claimed that AIDS was that very epidemic and that only he had the real solution to prevent it from wiping out humanity. This he expounded in his

'Biological Strategic Defense Initiative', which was founded on the view that HIV could be spread through casual contact as well as insect bites. In consequence, people with HIV and AIDS constituted a major threat to the survival of our species.

The 'solution' contained in his 'Defense Initiative' required that anyone working in schools, restaurants or healthcare institutions, along with anyone else suspected of carrying the virus, be tested for HIV. Those who tested positive were to be quarantined (presumably permanently given the absence of an effective treatment for HIV infection). The cost of his initiative – which included the building of quarantine facilities – was estimated by his followers at $100 billion a year.

Even in the extreme conservative political environment of that time it was clear that LaRouche's initiative would not be funded so he adopted a piecemeal approach instead, which he began by putting Proposition 64 onto the California ballot of 4 November 1986 (covered in further detail below).

Paul Cameron

If bizarre pronouncements such as those by Lyndon LaRouche are capable of attracting voter support, then how much more effective are those that claim to be grounded in 'real' science? Essentially this is the approach of sham researcher Paul Cameron, who makes a lot of money from right-wing organisations by finding 'scientific evidence' to support their prejudiced views of queer people.

Cameron trained as a psychologist and declared his position on homosexuality in his 1978 book *Sexual Gradualism*. In it he argued that parents should allow their children to start experimenting with heterosexual sex in order to prevent homosexuality. (*"While no parent wants his child starting the process 'too young', better too young than homosexual."*)

In 1982, while working as a psychologist in the town of Lincoln, Nebraska, he became Chair of the Committee to Oppose Special Rights for Homosexuals, a group established to oppose a proposed gay rights ordinance in the town. On 3 May 1982, in an early demonstration of his philosophy of not letting the facts get in the way of a good argument, Cameron declared at a public meeting that:

"Right now, here in Lincoln, there is a four-year-old boy who has had his genitals almost severed from his body at Gateway [mall] in a restroom with a homosexual act."
(60)

154

There was no evidence to support this claim: a police investigation came up with nothing and Cameron later admitted that he had actually only heard the story as a rumour. But his original declaration had the desired effect: people were outraged and the Lincoln gay rights proposal was defeated by a margin of four to one.

Buoyed by his success, Cameron sought to consolidate his position as sexuality expert by founding the Institute for the Scientific Investigation of Sexuality (now the Family Research Institute) that same year. In order to build up his academic credibility he had various 'research' papers published in the magazine *Psychological Reports*. Despite its impressive title, the magazine did not undertake peer review of the articles submitted – a basic practice of real academic publications – and it is also alleged that Cameron paid to have his articles inserted [61]. Nonetheless, Cameron began to claim a growing list of published 'research' and use that to validate a range of claims such as:

- A fifth to a third of gay men surveyed admitted to child molestation.
- Homosexual teachers are disproportionately apt to become sexually involved with children.
- The gay rights movement seeks to legitimise sex with children.
- Homosexuals have a median age of death 20 years below heterosexuals.
- Gay men are 116 times more likely to be murdered. The number of murdered lesbians was 512 times higher than that of the general population of white females aged 25-44.
- *"Along with serial murder, there appears to be a connection between homosexuality and murder."*
- *"A study of 518 sexually-tinged mass murders in the US from 1966 to 1983 determined that 350 (68%) of the victims were killed by those who practised homosexuality and that 19 (44%) of the 43 murderers were bisexuals or homosexuals."*
- *"... most violence involving gays is self-induced (and the gay subculture may export more violence than it absorbs)."*

The last three quotes come from his 'study' *Murder, Violence and Homosexuality*, which, in his usual 'scientific' style, features a cover image of a little girl cowering beneath an arm wielding an axe!

155

His 'research', of course, was nothing like scientific and has been widely criticised as the sham that many people believe it to be. For example, one review of some of his research practices concluded:

"A critical review of the Cameron group's sampling techniques, survey methodology, and interpretation of results reveals at least six serious errors in their study. The presence of even one of these flaws would be sufficient to cast serious doubts on the legitimacy of any study's results. In combination they make the data virtually meaningless."[62]

Cameron has also been expelled from a range of professional bodies including the American Psychological Association, the American Sociological Association, the Canadian Psychological Association and the Nebraska Psychological Association. The American Sociological Association stated: *"Dr Cameron has consistently misinterpreted and misrepresented sociological research on sexuality, homosexuality and lesbianism."*

Nonetheless, his lack of academic credentials has not prevented right-wing groups from quoting his unsubstantiated 'research' to support their own homophobic messages. Examples include the Family Research Council (for example *Homosexual Activists Work to Normalize Sex with Boys*, July 1990), the American Family Association (for example, *Homosexuality in America: Exposing the Myths*), the Claremont Institute, the National Association for Research and Treatment of Homosexuality and Colorado for Family Values [63].

With the advent of AIDS Cameron applied his 'expertise' to come up with solutions such as extermination, castration and branding or tattooing an 'A' on the foreheads of people with the illness. Anyone found trying to hide the tattoo would be banished to the former leper colony of Molokai in the Hawaiian Islands [64]. In 1986 he co-authored a book, *Special Report: AIDS*, in which he advocated the establishment of concentration camps for "sexually active homosexuals" [65].

Attacks at the Ballot Box

People like Anita Bryant, Lyndon LaRouche and Paul Cameron were but a few of those who used the ballot box to attack the rights of queer people and people with HIV/AIDS. For example, in her book *Gay Rights at the Ballot Box*, Amy L. Stone argues that with

the departure of Ronald Reagan in 1988, *"the New Right was left with a void in presi-*
dential leadership". In consequence they focused their efforts on attacking queer rights
through the use of referendums or specific initiatives:

"Of the forty-one attempted ballot measures during this time period [1988-92],
most were either legal referendums on non-discrimination legislation (48.8 per cent)
or legal-restrictive initiatives (24.4 per cent), although the Right also sponsored
initiatives to restrict the rights of people with AIDS (14 per cent) and to eliminate newly
passed domestic partnership laws (9.7 per cent). Slightly more than half of the ballot
measures made it to the ballot box and 57 per cent ended in victory for the Right."[66]

The continuing success of the New Right in these initiatives comes as little surprise
given that Reagan's successor, George H. W. Bush, maintained a very similar line to his
predecessor. While Reagan's track record of dumb belligerence towards queer people
and people with HIV/AIDS is so bad as to be unbeatable, Bush still did his best! He was
the preferred presidential candidate of the National Citizens Action Network, producers
of the Presidential Biblical Scoreboard and was happy to address conservative religious
groups. On the other hand, he declined an invitation to speak at the 1990 International
Conference on AIDS in San Francisco, choosing instead to attend a fundraising event for
Jesse Helms, whose travel ban on HIV positive people Bush continued to support [67].

Proposition 64

Proposition 64 was an initiative added to California's state ballot at the end of 1986 by
Lyndon LaRouche and his supporters. It required that AIDS be classified as a disease
that is easily spread; it required the mandatory testing of those groups identified in the
initiative; it allowed school officials to bar students with HIV or AIDS; and it required
that all those who tested positive should be named and quarantined. In order to lobby
for his Proposition, LaRouche established the 'Prevent AIDS Now Initiative Committee'
(PANIC).

He built support for the campaign by claiming that HIV had been created in a Soviet
laboratory to destroy America and repeatedly asserted that it was easily spread through
casual contact. Given Ronald Reagan's own reluctance to dismiss the casual contact idea
as well as his failure to mount an effective AIDS education campaign, it was unsurprising
that there was considerable support for this notion: as late as 1988/89 a national survey

on AIDS knowledge and attitudes reported that only 44.7 per cent of respondents said either it was *"definitely not possible" or "very unlikely"* to contract AIDS from *"being coughed or sneezed on by someone who had the AIDS virus"*. Only 42.8 per cent gave the same response for transmission by *"mosquitoes or other insects"* [(68)].

Whenever his view was challenged LaRouche simply attempted to discredit his critics. He accused both the Centers for Disease Control and the World Health Organisation of suppressing the 'real' evidence on transmission; he claimed that the Chair of the California Medical Association was 'lying' and that Dr Mathilda Krim, founder of the American Foundation for AIDS Research (AMFAR), had been involved in terrorist activities in France.

He also declared that AIDS was *"worse than the Black Death"* and *"a disease more deadly to mankind than a full-scale thermonuclear war"*. HIV-positive people were described as *"the walking dead"* and LaRouche argued that any rallies against Proposition 64 constituted a public health threat because they would attract gay men.

As absurd as these arguments may seem in retrospect, LaRouche's fear campaign, assisted by the sustained absence of an effective and rational HIV/AIDS education programme meant that voters were being influenced. In August 1986 – three months before the vote on Proposition 64 – the *Los Angeles Times* reported that nearly half of all voters supported the quarantining of people with HIV and AIDS. Two months later *Science* magazine reported that most people were still undecided.

Yet when Proposition 64 was put to the vote on 4 November it was defeated by a ratio of just over two to one: only 29 per cent voted in favour. Although the reasons for this remarkable turnaround are still unclear, there are two possible explanations for it. The first was the intense campaign of opposition from a range of organisations including the California Medical Association and the California Nursing Association. I happened to be in Los Angeles in the days leading up to the vote and was briefly involved with some of the activities of the 'Stop LaRouche' campaign, so I am aware of the amount of effort that went into it.

But I suspect the other factor was the increasing number of legal problems experienced by LaRouche and his various organisations.

In October 1986 alone, LaRouche had his California funds frozen by a judge following allegations of fraud against the elderly; a Boston grand jury indicted five

158

LaRouche groups and ten of his followers on credit card fraud charges; and the FBI seized a truckload of records after accusing LaRouche of running a violence-prone extremist empire.

On 30 October – five days before the vote – the *Los Angeles Times* reported:

"... the LaRouche-affiliated campaign behind Proposition 64 had raised about $283,000, almost all of it from the National Democratic Policy Committee and another LaRouche organization, Caucus Distributors Inc. The main opposition group, backed by the California Medical Association and gay organizations, has raised more than $2 million to defeat the measure ..." [69]

It also reported that the last media event of the PANIC campaign had seen treasurer Ted Andromidas standing outside the Los Angeles federal courthouse accusing *"the White House and the Soviet KGB of plotting against LaRouche"* [70].

The 4 November defeat did not stop LaRouche and his followers mounting a second attempt at a PANIC initiative in 1988. And even though the number of votes in favour was smaller (1.7 million compared with 2 million in 1986), the overall percentage of votes was actually larger (32% compared with 29% in 1986) [71].

Australia
Attacks from Governments and Politicians

Despite the passage of a motion in favour of homosexual law reform in Federal Parliament in 1973 the Australian government actually had no authority to implement such legislation: this was the jurisdiction of each individual state. In consequence there was immense variation in state governments' approaches to queers and queer issues during the 1980s, ranging from sympathetic (for example, South Australia) to downright hostile (most notably Queensland but also Tasmania and Western Australia).

Queensland – the Bjelke-Petersen Government

Queensland was (and, to a large extent, still is) Australia's equivalent of America's Deep South. Its treatment of the indigenous Aboriginal population, for example, has been on a par with the treatment of black people in the Southern USA and not far off South Africa's apartheid. Throughout the 70s and 80s public demonstrations and protest marches were banned, as was the sale of queer publications.

159

In 1984, when plans were announced to hold the 10th National Conference of Lesbians and Homosexual Men at the University of Queensland, the government's homophobia went into overdrive. One government MP declared that the conference *"posed a threat to social order"*, while the Minister for Welfare Services resurrected Anita Bryant's old argument when he told the State Parliament:

"Homosexuals do not reproduce; they recruit and they usually recruit children and young people, not middle-aged men and mothers with children." [72]

From 1987 to 1989 a Federal Royal Commission was undertaken into police and government corruption in Queensland. This not only exposed extensive corruption but also helped demonstrate how queers had been scapegoated to avoid the exposure of that corruption. In particular was the government's enduring assertion that most homosexuals were paedophiles. Thus, in 1985, when the local media alleged that a police officer was part of a state-wide paedophilia ring that engaged in sexual activity with young boys in illegal brothels, the government used its 'investigation' into the allegations to reassert the link between homosexuals and paedophilia. The Director of Public Prosecutions declared:

"... there is a modern phenomenon linking homosexuality, drugs and the corruption of children." [73]

As one commentator subsequently argued:

"In retrospect, it appears that the calling of this inquiry was predominantly intended to draw attention away from allegations that the Bjelke-Petersen government knew of corruption in the police force or of the existence of illegal brothels." [74]

Yet the government still refused to decriminalise homosexuality despite evidence that it would prevent corruption and help prevent the spread of AIDS. Indeed, recently released Cabinet papers from 1985 suggest that the government wanted the focus of any HIV/AIDS initiatives to be the identification of anyone engaging in homosexual acts. For example, the Health Minister at the time stated:

"Queensland wants to use the [federal AIDS] money for contact tracing, not setting up counselling centres, hotlines and clinics to pander to the homosexuals." [75]

Such an attitude placed immense pressure on those actually trying to manage the AIDS crisis in Queensland. In the words of former AIDS activist Phil Carswell:

160

"Activists I worked with then were fearful of [Queensland AIDS Council] being labelled as a 'gay' organisation even though all other state AIDS councils were unashamedly gay community organisations.

This reluctance was for two main reasons – firstly it was made clear to me that anyone openly identifying as a spokesperson for a gay organisation would be subject to Special Branch and other police scrutiny and harassment as well as problems in their workplace or accommodation if they were renting." (76)

For the Queensland government, the emergence of HIV/AIDS was merely an opportunity to supplement its paedophilia argument with one of physical and moral contamination. The perfect opportunity presented itself in November 1984 when the State Minister for Health announced that three babies had died from AIDS after receiving blood transfusions from a 27-year-old gay man. The problem was presented as a deliberate contamination of the blood supply and the donor was vilified . Issues such as the state's role in blocking AIDS information to gay men, the likelihood that the blood donation had been made as an act of social responsibility and the absence of any blood screening programmes were conveniently avoided.

In introducing amendments to the Transplantation and Anatomy Act that imposed a $10,000 fine or two year prison sentence on anyone who knowingly gave false information in respect of bodily tissue for transplant and transfusion, the Health Minister declared that the babies:

"... appear to be the innocent victims of the permissive society Australia is becoming. It distresses the Queensland government to see how some other states and Canberra support legalised homosexuality." (77)

When the AIDS crisis finally precipitated an end to the ban on sex education in schools, the Health Minister insisted:

"Young adults should be told that AIDS is a result of abnormal behaviour. There was quite a lot of pressure on them to accept abnormal behaviour until AIDS came along." (78)

And, always unwilling to consider decriminalisation as a means of AIDS prevention, the government came up with an alternative proposal that was bizarre even by its own standards. In 1985, it announced amendments to the state's licensing laws that would make it an offence to serve drinks to homosexuals.

161

When the legislation was introduced, the justice spokesperson for the government's coalition partner, the Liberal Party, told Parliament:

"Queensland should give a national lead in combating this modern scourge of promiscuous homosexuality and its associated disease AIDS by specifically forbidding the maintenance of places of regular congregation of homosexual people in licensed premises." [79]

Lest the government's line still wasn't clear enough, the Attorney General explained:

"... the amendment as drafted will allow action to be taken to ensure that these sexual perverts, these deviants, these gay bars, will not be allowed to prosper, will not be allowed to continue." [80]

Despite widespread protests – and large sales of T-shirts that read *"I am a homosexual: please buy me a drink"* – the proposed amendment actually came unstuck largely as a result of opposition by publicans. This wasn't based on any concerns for the rights of queer people: the President of the Queensland Hotels Association told the media that the proposals were unworkable because publicans would be *"unable to spot the deviant in a crowded hotel"*.

Following the Fitzgerald Inquiry's exposure of the extent of police and government corruption, the ruling National Party and its coalition partners were thrown out of power in a 1989 state election. Yet in spite of the vast amount of corruption exposed, the new National Party leader, Russell Cooper, still tried to declare the corruption as a 'secondary issue', with moral issues like homosexuality being the main problem. And in keeping with his party's sustained line of scaremongering, he argued that the Labor Party's policy of decriminalisation would produce *"a flood of gays crossing the border from the Southern states"*.

But, for once, the electorate chose to disagree: a Labor government was elected and homosexuality was decriminalised in 1990.

Tasmania – the Mass Arrest of Activists at Salamanca Markets

The last man to be executed for sodomy in the British Empire was hanged in 1867 – in Tasmania. And in 1988, while the punishments had become less severe, the same could not be said of government attitudes. Tasmania not only lagged behind in homosexual law reform, it actively persecuted those seeking it.

One particular setting for this was the Salamanca Markets in the Tasmanian capital of Hobart. This Saturday market featured the usual mix of craft, food, political and community stalls, one of which was the Tasmanian Gay Law Reform Group. As the name indicates, the group sought law reform and, in pursuit of that, the stall contained information leaflets and a petition.

Hobart's City Council, however, decided that 'there was no place for homosexuals in their family market' and, in consequence banned the stall in 1988.

Given the absurdity (and, most likely, illegality) of the ban, members of the Gay Law Reform Group continued to run their stall. The council responded by calling in the police and having the group's members arrested for trespass. In order to facilitate the arrests the council set up a yellow line at the market, delineating the point at which trespass would occur and any activists crossing the line were promptly arrested. They also instructed police to arrest anyone in possession of a petition, carrying a banner or wearing a badge that included the words 'gay' or 'lesbian' or displayed the pink triangle. It has also been suggested that police were under instructions to arrest anyone known to be homosexual.

The activists remained defiant and over the following seven weekends more than 130 people were arrested – by police wearing rubber gloves. Arrestees were held in police cells for long periods of time, banned for life from the market and threatened with immediate arrest when they left their homes on the morning of the market.

One activist, Rodney Croome, described one of his experiences:

"A burly sergeant approaches me: 'Under the authority of the Hobart City Council, as manager of this market, I ask that you leave the market at once. If you refuse you will be placed under arrest.'

I refuse and as he arrests me he grabs the gay law reform petition in my hand. He looks down the list of signatories and then rips the sheet into tiny pieces." [81]

These measures continued until December 1988 when the city council finally realised that it would not defeat the spirit of the activists and withdrew its ban. Shortly thereafter the trespass charges laid against the activists were found to be legally dubious and the charges were dropped.

The battle of Salamanca Markets had been won – but the war continued. Tasmania did not decriminalise homosexuality until 1997. Just as it had been the last Australian

163

state to execute homosexuals, it remained true to form by being the last Australian state to decriminalise homosexuality.

Anti-gay Lobbyists

In contrast to Western Australia, Queensland and Tasmania, the state government of Victoria took a more intelligent approach to queer issues, despite concerted campaigns from groups like the Concerned Parents Association, Citizens Against Social Evil, the Committee to Raise Educational Standards and the Festival of Light. These groups were at their most active in the late 70s and early 80s, focusing largely on government plans to include homosexuality in its Health and Human Relationships (H&HR) schools' curriculum. As usual, teaching about homosexuality became conflated with actively promoting it and all the social ills that would undoubtedly ensue thereafter.

After a state-wide campaign that included public meetings, petitions and the lobbying of politicians, the campaigners achieved some degree of success: in December 1980, the government declared that parents would be required to 'sign in' their children to any part of the H&HR curriculum that was determined to be controversial by a parent-dominated H&HR oversight committee in each school.

The move was opposed by the Victorian Secondary Teachers Association but it also failed to placate the Concerned Parents Association (CPA) whose President claimed in 1981 that *"pushers"* of sex education were using *"brain-washing techniques"* to impose *"un-Australian"* and *"anti-Christian"* doctrines on children [82].

But the concession on sex education was effectively the CPA's finest hour as its influence began to decline immediately thereafter. For example, despite CPA warnings of the unleashing of *"an aggressive social epidemic"*, the Victorian government decriminalised homosexuality in December 1980 anyway [83]. The Committee to Raise Educational Standards appears to have had one final fling in 1982 when it published its pamphlet, *The Continuing Homosexual Offensive: Next Target Anti-Discrimination*. This pushed the usual paranoid 'thin end of the wedge' argument and marked the beginning of their decline too.

Meanwhile, in Queensland the far-right government was barely out of office when the homophobic lobbyists sprang up to take its place. The new state government

164

established the Criminal Justice Commission's Parliamentary Committee on Reforms in Laws Relating to Homosexuality in 1990 and there were immediate objections from the Baptist, Presbyterian and Lutheran churches. As usual, their arguments reiterated the empty platitudes that have been – and continue to be – heard elsewhere:

- The incidence of AIDS and other sexually transmitted disease will dramatically increase.
- Homosexuality will be encouraged in schools.
- Decriminalisation will endanger the welfare of children.
- Decriminalisation will lead to the acceptance and proliferation of sexual 'perversion' in society.
- Decriminalisation will result in moral instability and the downfall of society. [84]

The government decriminalised homosexuality anyway.

But while it was beginning to look like the extremists were on the wane in some key Australian states, New South Wales saw an increased profile for the Christian Right, starting in September 1981 with the election to State Parliament of the Reverend Fred Nile.

As founder and self-appointed head of the Call to Australia Party (CTA), Nile had progressively built his power base from years of networking with evangelical organisations across Australia. He had, for example, been the National Director of the Christian Endeavour movement in the early 60s, then Assistant Director to the Billy Graham Crusade in Australia. In 1974 he was appointed National Coordinator and New South Wales Director for the Festival of Light (Australia) and was certainly a player in the Victorian campaigns against sex education in schools.

But these networks weren't the only factor in explaining his electoral success: from 1981 onwards Nile also had a widely-syndicated weekly slot on radio station 2GB, which has a reputation for right-wing 'shock jocks'. Supposedly filling the Sunday night 'religious slot', Nile's programme was often the subject of complaints from queer activists. In 1983, the Australian Broadcasting Tribunal declared that the programme had failed the test of being of a religious nature: it was, instead, merely a *"general discussion of social and moral issues"* [85]. Not that this bothered the management of 2GB: Nile remained until 1985.

As well as beginning his radio show in 1981 he also started writing a weekly column in Sydney's *Sunday Telegraph* newspaper. With such an extensive platform for his views then, it is little surprise that he was elected to the New South Wales Parliament later that year.

But being elected was one thing; fully engaging in the democratic process was quite another. For example, despite establishing his Call to Australia Party in 1977 it was still without a formal constitution by the mid-80s. Thus, in 1989, when he sought the resignation of Marie Bignold, one of various CTA Parliamentarians with whom he has clashed, she refused on the grounds that the CTA had no constitution requiring her to do so. Nile's response was, reportedly, *"I make the rules"* [(86)]. To underline that point he registered his party as the Call to Australia (Fred Nile) Group in 1987 (which subsequently became the Christian Democratic Party (Fred Nile Group)).

With the advent of AIDS Nile didn't miss the opportunity to step up his moral enterprise insisting – long after it had been proven otherwise – that HIV was highly contagious and that people with HIV or AIDS should be quarantined. He sought to have a Mardi Gras swimming carnival banned on the grounds that it was in a swimming pool that was used by 'members of the public' and he regularly called for the Sydney Mardi Gras Parade to be cancelled on the grounds that it constituted a health risk.

He was also not averse to a bit of street theatre to boost his profile. In fact, he and a small band of his followers became a regular feature of the parade; standing on a street corner praying for rain to wash away the sins being enacted before them. He wasn't particularly successful: in thirty years of annual prayer it only rained three times on the night of the parade – something that is particularly remarkable considering that it takes place in the middle of the state's rainy season.

He was even less successful when, in 1989, he tried to up the ante by leading a 'cleansing march' (*"For God and the Family"*) through Oxford Street, Sydney's queer heartland. It was obvious to everyone – queer and non-queer alike – that this was nothing more than a crude act of chest-thumping provocation against what he thought was going to be an easy target. But, like the rest of his views on queer people, he was seriously wrong.

In the build-up to the march Nile had claimed that he would lead 100,000 Christians along the route. On the day of the march he got less than 1500. Sydney's queer communities, however, incensed by this unwarranted invasion, mustered more than 5000 counter-demonstrators who lined both sides of Oxford Street ready to give Nile the welcome he so richly deserved. Their impact was enhanced even further by the fact that many wore cardboard masks featuring a caricature of Nile's face. Produced and distributed by Sydney's Gay and Lesbian Mardi Gras, they created a seemingly endless sea of Fred Niles, ready to face down the real man and his band of supporters.

Such was the scene on Oxford Street as the Christians arrived, carrying banners with slogans like *"What's So Gay About AIDS?"* Their pious smugness quickly vanished as the size and nature of the opposition hit them. Meanwhile, the mood of the counter-demonstrators remained upbeat – as demonstrated by the slogans on their banners; *"Repent, Rejoice, Redecorate"* perfectly summarising the camp mockery that characterised so much of the queer response.

The Christians' attempt at a post-march rally at the top of Oxford Street was, of course, futile: prayers, hymns and speeches being drowned out by angry chants of counter-protestors. But even though the bulk of the media's coverage took the view that Nile's march was a deliberate and indefensible provocation, he sought to mask his failure by claiming to be the victim. During one television interview he declared that 'the gays' had put his supporters at risk of AIDS by using the portable toilets he had had brought in for the event. The interviewer, quite rightly, derided him for such an ignorant response and Nile's credibility diminished even further.

The Usual Suspects
The Catholic Church

In spite of the Vatican's unceasing attacks on queer people there were still significant numbers of Catholic priests and nuns who found a way to offer great service to queer communities – particularly with the advent of HIV/AIDS. My own experience working on the AIDS ward of the Catholic-run St Vincent's Hospital in Sydney, for example, left me with huge admiration for the individual nuns and priests who demonstrated immense compassion to people with AIDS; particularly because they did so in the face of immense resentment and impediments from the hospital's administrators.

Such compassion ran counter to the views of those at the Vatican, presumably because they felt it represented some kind of endorsement of queer 'lifestyles'. One

167

particularly bitter individual was Cardinal Joseph Ratzinger – more recently known as Pope Benedict XVI (retired). Among other things, Ratzinger was the architect of the *Letter to the Bishops of the Catholic Church on the Pastoral Care of Homosexual Persons.*

Issued on 1 October 1986, it began by making its overall position very clear:

"Although the particular inclination of the homosexual person is not a sin, it is a more or less strong tendency ordered toward an intrinsic moral evil: and thus the inclination itself must be seen as an objective disorder. Therefore special concern and pastoral attention should be directed toward those who have this condition, lest they be led to believe that the living out of this orientation in homosexual activity is a morally acceptable option. It is not."

It then attempted to explain how this misguided sympathy for homosexuals had somehow found its way into the Catholic Church:

"Nevertheless, increasing numbers of people today, even within the Church, are bringing pressure to bear on the Church to accept the homosexual condition as though it were not disordered and to condone homosexual activity. Those within the Church who argue in this fashion often have close ties with those with similar views outside it."

"The movement within the Church, which takes the form of pressure groups of various names and sizes, attempts to give the impression that it represents all homosexual persons who are Catholics. As a matter of fact, its membership is by and large restricted to those who either ignore the teaching of the Church or seek somehow to undermine it. It brings together under the aegis of Catholicism homosexual persons who have no intention of abandoning their homosexual behaviour. One tactic used is to protest that any and all criticism of or reservations about homosexual people, their activity and lifestyle, are simply diverse forms of unjust discrimination."

Perhaps in order to establish that this wasn't just some silly philosophical argument, the letter went on to argue that this was about saving lives – and lots of them:

"There is an effort in some countries to manipulate the Church ... This is done in order to conform to these pressure groups' concept that homosexuality is at least a completely harmless, if not a good, thing. Even when the practice of homosexuality may seriously threaten the lives and well-being of a large number of people, its advocates remain undeterred and refuse to consider the magnitude of the risks involved."

The letter then had a brief respite from its condemnatory tone, presumably to try and demonstrate some compassion:

"It is deplorable that homosexual persons have been and are the object of violent malice in speech or in action"

Which it immediately undermined by adding the rather disturbing disclaimer:

"When such a claim is made and when homosexual activity is consequently condoned, or when civil rights legislation is introduced to protect behaviour to which no one has any conceivable right, neither the Church nor society at large should be surprised when other distorted notions and practices gain ground and irrational and violent reactions increase."

And so, having made its case, the letter made it clear what must happen next:

"No authentic pastoral programmes will include organisations in which homosexual persons associate with each other without clearly stating that homosexual activity is immoral ...

All support should be withdrawn from any organisations which seek to undermine the teaching of the Church, which are ambiguous about it, or which neglect it entirely. Such support, or even the semblance of such support, can be gravely misinterpreted. Special attention should be given to the practice of scheduling religious services and to the use of Church buildings by these groups, including the facilities of Catholic schools and colleges. To some, such permission to use Church property may seem only just and charitable; but in reality it is contradictory to the purpose for which these institutions were founded. It is misleading and scandalous."

One consequence of this directive was that many gay and HIV/AIDS support groups were barred from premises owned by the Catholic Church. Another was that Catholic-run hospitals like St Vincent's in Sydney became even more reluctant to provide AIDS services, despite the ready availability of government funds, as well as an urgent need for such services.

"Increasing bed numbers was resisted for some time by St Vincent's hospital administration for two reasons. The first was the pressure put on other units in the hospital by increasing the intake of people with AIDS ... the second was discomfort among hospital administrators and some surgeons with homosexuality, in part because St Vincent's was a very prominent Catholic institution, and in part from

169

homophobia per se. This failure to open more beds despite the availability of funding from the state government was the focus of ongoing community anger." [86]

My own experience of working in such an organisation showed me that the imposition of a rigid Catholic dogma as a response to the 'sexual baggage' that came with HIV/AIDS was done at the expense of both staff and service users. This is discussed in more detail in the section *Taking AIDS Personally*.

The Salvation Army

It was the provision of HIV/AIDS services that brought the Catholic Church's homophobic doctrines into sharp relief in the 80s. For the Salvation Army (SA) – who also provide a range of 'human services' – it was their political lobbying that highlighted their homophobia.

For example, in 1985, when the New Zealand government declared its intention to decriminalise homosexuality, the Salvation Army played a very active role in building opposition, arguing the usual line that it would lead to a decline in moral standards as well as the spread of AIDS. Acting in concert with other members of the Coalition of Concerned Citizens, the SA took a lead role in coordinating a petition against the bill. On 24 September 1985 the Coalition – Salvationists included – delivered to the New Zealand Parliament what they claimed was an 800,000 signature petition in 91 boxes – one for each electorate. The petition was subsequently rejected by Parliament's Petitions Committee due to a number of irregularities, including near-empty boxes and some petition sheets containing several signatures written in the same hand.

Two years later, the Salvation Army in the UK was a strong supporter of the Thatcher government's Section 28 – as well as a leading and vocal opponent of its repeal in 2000. In San Francisco in 1998 the SA shut down homeless and senior citizen support services rather than accept government funding because this would have required them to recognise same-sex relationships. It threatened to do the same thing in New York.

The debate as to whether the SA has taken a more enlightened approach in recent years continues to this day. [87]

References:

1. Easton, Susan. 2005. *The Problem of Pornography: Regulation and the Right to Free Speech*. London: Routledge.

2. Obscene Publications Act. 1959. Section 1.

3. Robertson, Geoffrey. 2011. *The Justice Game. Sydney:* Random House.

4. GTW defendants kept waiting. *Capital Gay*, London. 5 July 1985.

5. *The Justice Game.*

6. *The Justice Game*, p155.

7. Comment by Jonathan Cutbill, former director of Gay's the Word, posted in response to my post *The Trials of Gay's the Word* at
    www.gayinthe80s.com/2012/10/1984-the-trials-of-gays-the-word

8. *R v. Brown*. 1994. United Kingdom House of Lords Decisions, 2 WLR 556.

9. *DPP v. Morgan*. House of Lords. [1975] 2 WLR 913: [1976] AC 182.

10. *R v. Wilson*. 1996. 2 Cr App Rep 241, Court of Appeal.

11. Editorial. The Sun, London. 28 September 1984.

12. Hansard, House of Commons, 8 May 1987, cols 997-998. Quoted in Sanders, Sue and Spraggs, Gill. *Section 28 and Education*. In Jones, Carol and Mahoney, Pat (eds). 1989. *Learning Our Lines: Sexuality and Social Control*. London: The Women's Press, p48.

13. Chandwani, Seema. How Haringey and Bernie Grant stood up for sexual equality. *Tottenham, Wood Green and Edmonton Journal*. 4 November 2013.

14. Petley, Julian. *Positive and Negative Images,* in Curran, James, Petley, Julian and Gaber, Ivor (eds). 2005. *Culture Wars: The Media and the British Left*. Edinburgh: Edinburgh University Press, p166.

15. Hall Carpenter Archives. 1989. *Walking After Midnight: Gay Men's Life Stories*. London: Routledge.

16. Hansard, HC Deb 23 April 1987 vol 114 cc791-800.

17. Hansard, HC Deb 08 May 1987 vol 115 cc997-1014.

18. Hansard, House of Lords, 18 December 1986, Col. 310.

19. Hansard. House of Lords, 18 December 1986, cols 335-336.

20. Smith, Anna Marie. 1994. *New Right Discourse on Race and Sexuality: Britain 1968-90.* Cambridge: Cambridge University Press, p188.

21. The Local Government Bill [HL]: the 'Section 28' debate. Bill 87 of 1999-2000. House of Commons Library Research Paper 00/47 6 April 2000.

22. Gay rights outcry highlights new Labour line. *The Independent.* 10 December 1987.

23. Labour in two minds over ban on teaching about homosexuality. *The Guardian.* 15 December 1987.

24. Labour in two minds over ban on teaching about homosexuality.

25. See for example, *"In fact it is clear from subsequent statements by Cunningham's office and colleagues that while the position adopted by the Labour leadership was to some extent naive, in the sense that the possible implications of the clause had certainly not been fully grasped, it was also disingenuous in that the debate around the clause was initially seized as an opportunity to distance the Labour Party from what was perceived as a vote-losing association with pro-gay policies. This was implicit in the way that Cunningham, during the debate at Committee stage, made only a very half-hearted effort to defend Labour-run authorities such as ILEA and Haringey from the viciously misleading charges which were brought against them by David Wilshire and by Michael Howard, Minister for Local Government."* In Sanders, Sue and Spraggs, Gill. Section 28 and Education, p14.

26. *Section 28 and Education,* p20.

27. HL Deb 06 December 1999 vol 607 cc1042-125.

28. Davidson, Roger and Davis, Gayle. 2012. *The Sexual State: Sexuality and Scottish Governance 1950-80.* Oxford: Oxford University Press.

29. *Homosexuality and the law.* Letters, Glasgow Herald. 27 August 1980.

30. *The Sexual State: Sexuality and Scottish Governance 1950-80,* p86.

31. UK Government. 1982. Cabinet file *'Draft Homosexual Law Offences NI Order'.*

32. Shilts, Randy. 2005. *Conduct Unbecoming: Gays and Lesbians in the US Military.* New York: St Martin's Griffin, p368.

33. Rimmerman, C. and Wilcox C. (eds). 2007. *The Politics of Same-Sex Marriage*. Chicago: University of Chicago Press, p182.

34. Etzioni, Amitai. Testimony before the US Senate Subcommittee on the Family and Human Services, 22 March 1983. Quoted in *The Family: Preserving America's Future*, Report to the President from the White House Working Group on the Family. 1986. Washington, p13.

35. *The Family: Preserving America's Future*, p27.

36. *The Family: Preserving America's Future*, p27.

37. Centers for Disease Control. *Acquired Immune Deficiency Syndrome (AIDS) Weekly Surveillance Report*. 30 December 1985.

38. World Health Organisation. Global Statistics. *Weekly Epidemiological Record* 62 (49), 372. 1987.

39. The American Presidency Project: Ronald Reagan. The President's News Conference 17 September 1985.
[Online] Available at
http://www.presidency.ucsb.edu/ws/?pid=39125
Accessed July 2014.

40. See, for example, Helms Calls for AIDS Quarantine on Positive Tests. *Chicago Tribune*. 16 June 1978.

41. *Current Trends Update: Acquired Immune Deficiency Syndrome (AIDS)* – United States, MMWR September 09, 19 83/32 32(35); pp465-7.

42. *The Early Days of AIDS As I Remember Them*. Speech by C. Everett Koop, National Institutes for Health Archive. p7.
[Online] Available at
http://history.nih.gov/archives/downloads/koopceverett.pdf
Accessed July 2014.

43. *The Early Days of AIDS As I Remember Them*, p15.

44. *The Early Days of AIDS As I Remember Them*, p16.

45. Remarks at a Luncheon for Members of the College of Physicians in Philadelphia, Pennsylvania. April 1 1987. University of Texas online archive.
[Online] Available at
http://www.reagan.utexas.edu/archives/speeches/1987/040187e.htm
Accessed July 2014.

46. *Critics unimpressed with Reagan's AIDS gambit.* Website of Rep. Henry A. Waxman, 33rd Congressional District of California.
    [Online] Available at
    http://waxman.house.gov/critics-unimpressed-reagans-aids-gambit
    Accessed July 2014.

47. Fox, Daniel M. 1988. *AIDS and the American Health Polity: The History and Prospects of a Crisis of Authority.* In Fee, Elizabeth, and Fox, Daniel M. (Eds). 1988. AIDS: *The Burdens of History.* Berkeley: University of California Press, p329.
    [Online] Available at
    http://ark.cdlib.org/ark:/13030/ft7t1nb59n/
    Accessed July 2014.

48. Knight, Robert and York, Frank. 1999. *Homosexual Behavior and Pedophilia.* Family Research Council.
    [Online] Available at
    http://www.splcenter.org/get-informed/intelligence-report/browse-all-issues/2010/winter/the-hard-liners
    Accessed September 2014.

49. Webber, David W. Roberts's Queer Reasoning on AIDS. *The Nation*, 10 October 2005.

50. Rimmerman, Craig A. Presidency, U.S. The Body. 1998.
    [Online] Available at
    http://www.thebody.com/content/art14034.html]
    Accessed July 2014.

51. Koop, C. Everett. 1981. *The Right to Live, the Right to Die.* Toronto: Life Cycle Books. Quoted in New Republic obituary, 26 February 2013.
    [Online] Available at
    http://www.newrepublic.com/article/112530/c-everett-koop-obituary-reagan-surgeon-general-abortion-and-aids
    Accessed July 2014.

52. *Roberts's Queer Reasoning on AIDS.*

53. Dannemeyer, W. 1989. *Shadow in the Land: Homosexuality in America.* San Francisco: Ignatius Press, p228.

54. *Shadow in the Land: Homosexuality in America.*

55. See, for example, Gill, Peter. 2006. Body Count: *How they turned AIDS into a catastrophe.*

174

London: Profile Books or Roberts's Queer Reasoning on AIDS.

56. Quoted in Jesse Helms Dies at 86; *Conservative Force in the Senate*. In the *New York Times*. 5 July 2008.

57. Hubner, John. Putting Their Faith in the Ballot Box. *The Washington Post*. 7 October 1996

58. See, for example, Falwell apologizes to Carter. *Dallas Times Herald*. 13 October 1980.

59. *Falwell apologizes to Carter.*

60. Harkavy, Ward. Slay it with a Smile. Denver Westword News. 3 October 1996.

61. *Slay it with a Smile.*

62. Herek, Gregory M. *The Cameron Group's Survey Studies: A Methodological Critique.* [Online]. Available at http://psychology.ucdavis.edu/faculty_sites/rainbow/html/facts_cameron_survey.html Accessed August 2014.

63. A more detailed listing is available at *The Religious Right and Anti-Gay Speech: Messengers of Love or Purveyors of Hate. Wired Strategies website.* [Online] Available at www.wiredstrategies.com/relycameron.html Accessed August 2014.

64. See, for example, the allegation that he recommended extermination to Surgeon General C. Everett Koop in 1983 in Pietrrzyk, Mark E. The Man Behind the Myths: A Report on the Chief Anti-gay Researcher of the Theocratic Right. *News-Telegraph*, St Louis, Kansas City. 10 March 1995.

65. Noebel, David A., Lutton, Wayne C. Lutton, and Cameron, Paul. 1986. *Special Report: AIDS, Acquired Immune Deficiency Syndrome.* Manitou Springs, CO: Summit Ministries.

66. Stone, Amy L. 2012. Gay Rights at the Ballot Box. Minnesota: University of Minnesota Press, p18.

67. Taffet, David. A preliminary assessment of Bush 41's legacy on LGBT issues and HIV/AIDS. *The Dallas Voice.* 27 December 2012. [Online] Available at http://www.dallasvoice.com/george-h-w-bush-legacy-mixed-lgbt-community-10135322.html Accessed July 2014.

68. Hardy, A. M. *National Health Interview Survey data on adult knowledge on AIDS in the*

United States. Public Health Reports, 1990 Nov-Dec; 105(6): pp629-634.

69. Strange Twists Mark Prop. 64 Campaign. *Los Angeles Times.* 30 October 1986.

70. *Strange Twists* Mark Prop. 64 Campaign.

71. Tourney, Christopher P. 1996. *Conjuring Science: Scientific Symbols and Cultural Meanings in American Life. New Jersey:* Rutgers University Press, p93.

72. Robinson, Shirleene. Homophobia as Party Politics: The Construction of the 'Homosexual Deviant' in Joh Bjelke-Petersen's Queensland. *Queensland Review,* Number 17, No.1.

73. *Homophobia as Party Politics: The Construction of the 'Homosexual Deviant' in Joh Bjelke-Petersen's Queensland.*

74. *Homophobia as Party Politics: The Construction of the 'Homosexual Deviant' in Joh Bjelke-Petersen's Queensland.*

75. Alexander, David. Released cabinet documents of former Bjelke-Petersen government reveal Qld AIDS response "bastardry". *The Sydney Star Observer.* 7 January 2016.

76. *Homophobia as Party Politics: The Construction of the 'Homosexual Deviant' in Joh Bjelke-Petersen's Queensland.*

77. *Homophobia as Party Politics: The Construction of the 'Homosexual Deviant' in Joh Bjelke-Petersen's Queensland.*

78. *Homophobia as Party Politics: The Construction of the 'Homosexual Deviant' in Joh Bjelke-Petersen's Queensland.*

79. *Homophobia as Party Politics: The Construction of the 'Homosexual Deviant' in Joh Bjelke-Petersen's Queensland.*

80. Croome, Rodney. Do LGBT people need a *Bill of Rights?* Address delivered at the University of Technology, Sydney. 25 October 2002.
[Online] Available at
http://www.rodneycroome.id.au/other_more/54_0_2_0_M14/
Accessed October 2014.

81. Victoria's sex education under fire again. *The Age,* Melbourne. 6 August 1981.

82. Rights activists recall when gay sex was a crime. *The Age,* Melbourne. 19 December 2005.

83. Bull, Melissa, Pinto, Susan and Wilson, Paul. Homosexual Law Reform in Australia.

Australian Institute of Criminology: Trends and Issues in Crime and Criminal Justice No. 29, January 1991, p4.

84. Griffin-Foley, Bridget. 2009. *Changing Stations: The Story of Australian Commercial Radio.* Sydney: UNSW Press, p198.

85. Smith, Rodney K. 2006. *Against the Machines: Minor Parties and Independents in New South Wales.* Sydney: Federation Press, p184.

86. *Van Reyk, Paul. Life during war time: nursing on the frontline at Ward 17 South at St Vincent's Hospital.* Paper presented to the Australian Homosexual Histories conference, Melbourne University. 15-16 November 2013.

87. See, for example, www.noredkettles.com

177

Chapter Five

Then Along Came HIV/AIDS

Part One - Taking It Personally

Like most gay men of my age, AIDS first came into my consciousness via newspaper reports of a 'gay cancer' that was affecting American gay men. It was too vague and too distant a threat to be taken seriously: the notion of such an illness – or the lifestyle that apparently lay behind it – ever crossing the Atlantic to reach the sleepy town of Nottingham where I lived was inconceivable.

I became a little more focused towards the end of 1982 when I initiated the establishment of a local queer community newspaper, *Gay East Midlands (GEM)*, in response to the seemingly imminent demise of our only national gay newspaper, *Gay News*.

In planning the content for Issue 1 we tried to identify the relevant issues for queer people. Along with the proposed Police and Criminal Evidence Bill, the comeback of Tom (*"Sing If You're Glad to be Gay"*) Robinson we also had *A.I.D.S. (The so-called 'Gay Plague')*. Published in June 1983, the AIDS article now serves principally as an illustration of how little we knew, even as its toll was quickly rising. For example, I wrote: *"No one really knows what causes it, but as 75 per cent of AIDS victims are gay men the researchers have tended to look at gay lifestyles for clues."* But I did discount the notion that it was caused by the use of 'poppers' as well as so-called 'promiscuity':

"All that can be said at this stage is that, as with other sexually transmitted diseases, the greater the number of sexual contacts the greater the risk – although a reduction in sexual contacts does not give immunity from AIDS."

I reported the current prognosis – *"a 65 per cent mortality rate"* – then outlined the symptoms: things like swollen lymph glands, long periods of tiredness and reddish-blue spots on or beneath the skin (Kaposi's sarcoma (KS)). From that moment on I, along with thousands of other gay men, interpreted every minor skin blemish as the first signs of KS and every period of fatigue as the beginnings of that 'long period of tiredness'. In my case, this would continue until I finally plucked up the courage to take an HIV test in 1988.

Between Issue 1 and Issue 2 of *GEM* I visited friends in San Francisco; a visit that was to transform my view of AIDS and, arguably, my life as it set me on a course for a long career in the AIDS field.

178

The San Francisco Experience

Despite having arrived two days *after* the huge Lesbian/Gay Freedom Day Parade, just being in gay Mecca was enough for me: there was nowhere in the UK that was even half as upfront and unapologetic as this place. For this small-town early 80s gay boy the sight of seemingly endless queer enterprises – bookstores, bars, shops, clubs, cafes, newspapers, magazines, posters and so on – was just affirming beyond belief.

Of course, as the days rolled on, I grew increasingly aware of another element of San Fran gay life – the emerging AIDS crisis. I was aware of AIDS before I even got there but had yet to encounter 'the real thing'. Up to now, AIDS had been something that happened somewhere else. And now I was in that 'somewhere else'.

People were either talking about it or – presumably out of fear of the unknown – trying to trivialise it. Walking through the Castro one night we passed a group of drunken young guys horsing around. One of them climbed atop a bus shelter and pretended to start pissing on his friends. *"Look out,"* screeched one of his friends with mock hysteria. *"She's got AIDS!"*

At the other end of the spectrum the fear, coupled with the lack of government action, was also generating a number of conspiracy theories. I regularly came across one sticker in the Castro area declaring, *"It's not your lifestyle: AIDS comes from a government lab!"* Another, more substantial, poster began by declaring, *"AIDS is Germ Warfare by the U.S. Gov't Against Gays and Blacks!"* then again argued that the causative agent was genetically engineered in US government laboratories.

Unsurprisingly, it was also on Castro Street that I got my first 'serious' information about AIDS. As I walked down the street with my friend Rena one Saturday afternoon a smartly-suited man smiled at me and handed me a bright orange leaflet. The cover read, *"Can We Talk?"* Assuming it was Evangelical Christian propaganda, I smiled politely and refused.

Thankfully Rena took a copy then thrust it at me. *"I think this is for you, not me!"* she asserted. And indeed it was!

It was published by The Harvey Milk Gay Democratic Club. Such was the extent of my ignorance at that time I didn't even know what that meant: shamefully, I had not heard of Harvey Milk. For all I knew, 'Harvey Milk' could have been some dairy. But why would it have its own Gay Democratic Club?

Dairy or not, the leaflet's purpose soon became abundantly obvious to me as I unfolded it. A cartoon of a young man in a 'So Many Men, So Little Time' T-shirt announced the intent:

"We've got a real problem guys. AIDS is striking gay men in ever-increasing numbers. Everyone must make his own choices about how to be sexual during this epidemic. The Harvey Milk Gay Democratic Club believes that the gay community must have the best available information in order to make those choices. We don't have to give up sex but we do have to be careful."

There then followed the most positive message I had seen since the start of the AIDS crisis. It began by acknowledging that *"there is as yet no laboratory proof of how AIDS is transmitted"* – but went on to draw out some really practical suggestions on the basis of very limited information. And it used humour to put those messages across effectively. This included cartoons of a lovelorn frog trying to deep kiss a prince and an adventurous gay man bedecked in everything from leather to fishnet tights simultaneously trying out phone sex, porn videos and 'The Butch Book'!

Can We Talk? taught me lessons about AIDS education that I was to carry with me for the rest of my career in that field. I was so inspired by it that I ended up taking dozens of copies home for distribution to gay and nascent AIDS organisations. It also set me off on a mission to find out even more about AIDS while I was still in San Francisco.

It wasn't difficult: the community was already well organised. For example, in addition to the distribution of AIDS education brochures, there were articles in the gay press, alongside ads placed by gay businesses and organisations. I still have a copy of one by the Sutro Co-Ed Bathhouse – a *"Guide to Good Clean Fun"* consisting of six cartoon cells illustrating different aspects of good physical and sexual health. These included regular sleep and exercise, communicating about sex with your sexual partners and having regular health check-ups.

There were also regular public meetings that were organised by AIDS organisations and health services and I took the opportunity to attend one of these. It consisted of presentations by various doctors, educators and people with AIDS, followed by small group discussions on various issues. I went to the group on 'Living with AIDS', run by a man called Bobbi Campbell. I had no idea who he was at the time but I was to come across his name repeatedly for years afterwards. He jokingly referred to himself as

180

'The AIDS Poster Boy' because he was one of the first people with AIDS to come out publicly. He was subsequently immortalised in Randy Shilts' book on the AIDS crisis, *And the Band Played On.*

Much to my shame, I was actually too embarrassed to ask him questions – even though that was really the whole point of the group! I cringe about it even now but I remember thinking at the time that it would be 'impolite'! Of course, it was just one huge missed opportunity to learn more and pass on that information back in the UK.

I was able to bring myself to talk to Mitch Bart, a worker from the AIDS/Kaposi's sarcoma Foundation and made an appointment to interview him a couple of days later for an article in *GEM*. (It's interesting to note that, at that time, Kaposi's sarcoma was still being seen as a potentially separate condition to AIDS.)

During our interview he told me how the fear of AIDS was leading gay men to avoid social contact. Attendance was dropping at bars and bathhouses alike: self-isolation, rather than safer sex, seemed to be the strategy of choice for many gay men. While this may have seemed like a sensible strategy in the first instance, in practice it meant that those at risk were also cutting themselves off from education and support. This, in turn, made them vulnerable to the hysterical mythology generated by a homophobic mainstream media.

On my return from San Francisco my suitcase was bulging with AIDS information in the form of pamphlets, articles, newspapers and magazines. I also had a copy of the first AIDS book I had ever seen, *The AIDS Fact Book* by Ken Mayer and Hank Pizer, which covered psychological and social issues as well as clinical and medical ones. I read most of it on the flight home.

I put some of the general information to immediate use in my articles for *GEM* but by Issue 3 I was accused by one 'community leader' of scaring people by writing about AIDS too much!

At the time I was immensely rattled by his comments although, in retrospect, I think it was an indication of the levels of anxiety that were already setting in among British queers. Had I not been to San Francisco and seen the impact as well as the efforts to curb it, I might have taken the criticism to heart. Instead I wrote a rather angry riposte to the accusation for Issue 4.

I used more complex material such as *The AIDS Fact Book* in my studies – I was undertaking a Master's Degree in Social Work at that time. Perhaps unsurprisingly, when we were required to submit a dissertation topic I submitted *'AIDS as Metaphor: Some social work issues arising from popular conceptions of Acquired Immune Deficiency Syndrome'*. It was promptly rejected by the Head of School on the grounds that 'AIDS is a medical issue, not a social work one'! This seemed to be an extraordinary and hugely misinformed response so I duly marshalled an array of evidence and recruited a sympathetic lecturer who was willing to be my dissertation supervisor. Somewhat ironically, in order for him to get up to speed on AIDS issues so that he could tutor me he had to read a series of articles on AIDS – written by me! Nonetheless, the strategy worked and the Head of School finally consented to my dissertation topic.

The dissertation title *AIDS as Metaphor* was inspired by Susan Sontag's book *Illness as Metaphor*, in which she argued that illness is often viewed in moral and social rather than physiological terms. For example, cancer has been seen as the consequence of repressed emotions and classical composers often used tuberculosis to suggest 'retribution' for the moral waywardness of its victim (for example, Mimi in Puccini's *La Boheme*, Violetta in Verdi's *La Traviata*). Central to this perception, therefore, is the notion that the individual is in some way responsible for their illness – a notion that was never far from the surface in relation to AIDS: homosexuality has either been a sin, a crime or an illness for most of our history.

The theory that was described in my dissertation was played out in reality in the ensuing years. Moral entrepreneurs such as the Moral Majority were not slow in resurrecting the notion of sin to explain 'God's judgement' on gay and bisexual men. But, more significantly, it informed the notion of the 'innocent' and the 'culpable' AIDS victim that, too often, came to underscore government policy.

The most obvious example is the Reagan administration, whose lack of response was underpinned by an intense homophobia. But a similar theme was played out elsewhere – such as the British government's disproportionate allocation of resources for supporting and 'compensating' haemophiliacs despite the far greater number of gay men impacted by the disease.

Despite the evidence in the USA, the UK government adopted a 'wait and see' approach, so there were no jobs in the AIDS field – nor, indeed, was there an AIDS field

– by the time I finished my course in 1984. In consequence, I began to focus on a new goal – moving to Australia. Triggered initially by an extended holiday in 1982 then fed by an increasing need to get away from the doom and gloom of Thatcherism, it seemed like a far more positive option. Sadly, its appeal wasn't matched by an ease of access: it would take me almost three years to finally get there.

Early Adventures in the British AIDS Field

During the first year of my wait I volunteered my services to the nascent Terrence Higgins Trust which, at that time, was operating out of a small office in London's Mount Pleasant district and was dependent entirely on volunteers. I was their first full-time volunteer and, as such, had some level of involvement in more or less everything that was happening, apart from the medical group. On my first day I had been advised to bring a book to read on the grounds that very little happened during the day time.

We started out with only one phone, which served a range of purposes from telephone helpline to contact number for volunteers and media. For the first few weeks it was relatively quiet; we advertised the helpline as an out-of-hours number so most of those calls came in during the evening. Nonetheless, the level of anxiety around AIDS was so high at the time that some people couldn't wait until evening and rang during office hours. Some would be reassured after one conversation; others would ring back hours or days afterwards with a variation on their original query. Some of the calls were about sexual practices (for example, one man wanting to know if he could contract AIDS from swallowing his own semen after masturbating) but the majority were more concerned with casual contact. One repeat caller's initial concern about contracting AIDS from ballpoint pens progressed over a number days to cover everything from chairs to billiard balls. And some of the callers became quite legendary, not least 'the belt and Dettol man' who, sadly, I never encountered because he always rang in the evenings. In consequence, I never discovered the role of either the belt or the Dettol.

Even as late as September 1984 we had relatively few 'unsolicited' calls from journalists: most media contact at that stage was initiated by us trying to getting sensible stories across. On one occasion I took a call from a journalist on a local London newspaper, keen to talk about 'married gay men'. His perspective was that married men who also had sex with other men were simply trying to get the best of both worlds.

183

I tried to explain that the situation was a lot more complex than that: for example, many of these men had got married simply to fulfil family and social expectations and were driven to furtive and anonymous sex with other men to avoid being found out.

It was a long and painful discussion with the journalist: I repeatedly suggested that he would end up ignoring everything I said in favour of a 'good story' and he repeatedly assured me that he wouldn't. When the article was published it was exactly as I had expected: I was described as a 'spokesman for the Terrence Higgins Trust' and I had 'admitted' that some married men were putting their wives at risk by secretly 'having gay sex'. The use of the word 'admitting' suggests that he had managed to force from me some hideous secret that I would have preferred to have kept hidden. More to the point, it suggested that I – and, by implication, the Trust – was colluding on some dangerous secret that was putting 'innocent' lives at risk. The article bore no relation to our actual conversation and I learned quickly that reflecting reality was not a priority for some newspapers. As another journalist subsequently told one of my Terrence Higgins Trust colleagues: *"AIDS sells more newspapers than bingo."*

We were to find that out not long after my 'interview', as AIDS hit the front pages of every newspaper in the country at the end of 1984. I can't remember what triggered this particular outburst but the key message that was being given out could be summed up by *The Sun's* ridiculous strapline, *"It's spreading like wildfire"*. It wasn't but at least it shifted papers, which was the main objective.

Having led people to believe that AIDS was highly infectious, the press often printed our phone number – presumably this was their idea of 'social responsibility' – and we soon felt the impact. As press coverage intensified, so too did the number of phone calls until we got to the point where there was, quite literally, not a second's break between them. As soon as we put the receiver down on one call, the phone rang again. Anxious callers from around the country were being channelled towards one phone number. What was worse, the bulk of the anxiety was unfounded; triggered by sensationalist press coverage of the 'plague' about to be inflicted on 'innocent' people. And while the papers were happy to throw our phone number into their articles when it suited them, they were never forthcoming with donations or even details on how their readers could donate.

We installed an additional – and unlisted – phone line as a matter of urgency, not least so that we could contact the many volunteers who were providing all of the services that the Trust offered at that time. And, despite the ongoing press hysteria, the number of calls gradually receded, although they never went back to anything like the levels of September 1984. By the time I left the Trust in June 1985, we had expanded to two offices and a lot more telephones, although still no permanent staff, as our first funding – from the Greater London Council – was only just beginning to work its way through to us. It was stalled by a challenge from Westminster Council who felt it was abuse of ratepayers' money. The challenge was eventually dismissed by the High Court.

With no prospect of an early departure for Australia, I returned to Nottingham to work on Plan B (the first step of which was to develop a Plan B). While I waited for inspiration (and employment) to strike I continued to involve myself in AIDS work, in this case a local initiative, Nottingham AIDS Information Project, founded by staff at the local Sexual Health Service and an HIV+ man (who had actually been congratulated by his GP for being 'his first patient with AIDS'!).

With a total budget of £1000 the project sought to offer information, education and support to people affected by or concerned about AIDS. Once again, it was run entirely by volunteers who put in an enormous number of hours to deliver a range of vital services. Nonetheless this did not stop the local Health Authority repeatedly expressing its concern that the £1000 be used 'responsibly'. Given that a certain percentage of the money was already being used to rent an office and a telephone helpline, there wasn't a great deal left with which to be irresponsible. However, it soon became obvious that the underlying anxiety was that funds might be used to produce 'explicit' materials: even the purchase of a book of gay erotic safe sex stories had triggered resignation threats from two Health Authority employees on the project's management committee on the grounds that the project was becoming 'dominated' by gay men's issues.

Meanwhile, in the continuing climate of AIDS hysteria, our landlord forbade us from putting the name of the project on our office door, after our next door neighbour complained that it would frighten people away from his business. Both offices were at the end of a labyrinthine corridor on the first floor of a building full of small businesses and charitable enterprises: the likelihood that any of our neighbour's potential customers should turn and flee in terror upon seeing 'AIDS Information Project' was minimal. However the culture of that time – pander to, rather than

185

challenge, ridiculous prejudices – prevailed and we operated anonymously from 'Office 1'.

By 1986 I had become Chair of the Project: it didn't even seem like a good idea at the time then but I told myself that if somebody had to do it, it might as well be me. This was the beginning of a very bad habit that took more than a decade to get out of!

No sooner had I been elected than the original Chair threatened to sue the project for 'breach of natural justice' because he was voted out of post. Had his suit been successful it would have closed down the project since the case would have used up the few resources we had. As it was, it put enormous stress on the management committee, ever mindful that the Health Authority might pull the plug on the project. Thankfully the legal threat was – very begrudgingly – withdrawn at the last minute and we continued with our work. But this respite was short-lived: a few weeks later the Health Authority decided it was going to cut our budget to £500 due to 'financial pressures' and 'concerns about project management'. In fact, we'd already addressed the management issue; that was what had precipitated the 'breach of natural justice' threat. But it made a convenient excuse for imposing budget cuts.

So now I had to show my 'concerned' face on television and in the local and gay press as we mounted a campaign to stop the cuts. In fact it wasn't just a concern, it was an insult. The project had been running for less than a year and in that time had developed and delivered education and support to hundreds of people. Information stalls had been staffed at gay clubs, talks had been given to a range of professional and community organisations, a special AIDS awareness week had been developed with the local radio station and other newspaper and radio interviews had been given throughout the year. Support had been provided face-to-face and over the telephone helpline, and dozens of volunteers recruited and trained up to do this work. The Health Authority had got a very healthy return on their £1000 investment, especially in the face of the growing AIDS crisis.

These and various other points were put to them – and anyone else who would listen and, thankfully, they backed down from their threat, although not without a further speech on 'responsible financial management' and suchlike. We smiled politely and said thank you (albeit it through gritted teeth) and carried on in the same responsible way that we had always done.

186

The Los Angeles Experience

It was during this troubled period that I undertook my second visit to the USA – on this occasion to visit a friend in Los Angeles. I arrived as the campaign against Lyndon LaRouche's Proposition 64 was reaching its climax. Proposition 64 required mandatory testing of identified groups such as gay men, the barring of school students with HIV or AIDS, and the naming and quarantining of people with HIV or AIDS.

I spent a couple of memorable days working in the 'Stop LaRouche' campaign office and an equally memorable morning stood by a major intersection with placards that read *"No on 64"*. It was a fascinating insight into American politics since it bore absolutely no similarity to the restrained campaigning of the British political system.

Given the lack of an American accent (and probably the look of terror on my face when I saw some of the volunteer tasks), I was assigned to purely manual labour in the campaign office. All around me dozens of volunteers sat at phone banks, systematically working their way through telephone directories and calling everyone listed to talk to them about Proposition 64. I don't know what kinds of responses they got; occasionally I witnessed a call so brief that the nature of the conversation – such as it was – was blindingly obvious. But my colleagues persisted for hours on end while I sat nearby forging the signature of the Campaign Director on thank you letters to organisations that had donated up to $1000 to the campaign.

One of my other jobs was packing up T-shirts, placards and stickers to be shipped out to people 'in the field'. My opportunity to be part of that field came on polling day when I, along with two friends, stood at a designated road junction from around 6:30 till 10:00 a.m. Wearing yellow T-shirts with the slogan printed in blue, each of us held a large placard which contained one of the three words that make up 'No on 64'.

The morning was generally uneventful. Apart from the occasional supportive honk of a car horn, the only other event was a visit from a young couple running a petition demanding a new series of 'The Monkees'. It was hardly the greatest political deal in the world but we all signed in return for their assurance that they would vote against 'Prop 64'.

As it turned out, we got the best part of the deal as LaRouche's initiative was defeated by a majority of more than two to one (see the previous section on this).

187

I don't need to spell out the fate of the Monkees petition. To celebrate, we attended a 'No on 64' victory party in West Hollywood. The final result wasn't known when we arrived that evening – although it was pretty obvious which way it was going from the early returns, which showed LaRouche failing to gain a majority in any part of the state. Thelma Houston was the big name performer then a queer choir that sang lots of patriotic songs. The latter event prompted the man standing beside me to lean across and apologise, which surprised me far more than the rendition of 'God Bless America'. I was pretty much acclimatised to Americans being demonstrative about their patriotism – even if I did think it was a little over the top. For me, the LaRouche episode illustrated how America's political system seemed to favour dangerous bigots: the choir seemed to be praising that same system for its ability to keep people like him at bay.

With LaRouche defeated my next port of call was the AIDS Project Los Angeles (APLA). My overriding memory of that visit was their Chief Executive, a man of boundless energy and warmth who greeted everyone with a big smile and a supportive hug. Given the grim realities of their day-to-day business, I found that extremely impressive.

It was during this visit that someone enthusiastically recommended that I attend one of the HIV/AIDS support groups taking place that night, just across the road from the APLA offices. It was run by someone that I'd never heard of at that point – Louise Hay (although I was later to discover her writings on the 'causes' and 'cures' of AIDS: see the 'Brief Natural History of AIDS' section below).

And so it was that I turned up that night at the duly appointed time and place ready to experience a 'Hayride'.

The venue was a large meeting hall and there were at least two hundred people already there by the time I arrived. Everyone was sitting on the floor with the exception of one or two men in wheelchairs and the facilitator, who wandered around the room microphone in hand. From memory, the session began with the facilitator – whom I now assume to have been Louise Hay – inviting individual participants to offload any negative thoughts or emotions they may have been experiencing. A very emaciated man in one of the wheelchairs began, telling everyone that he'd had some vast quantity of urine catheterised from his body that very afternoon in hospital. Hay undoubtedly spoke for everyone in the hall when she expressed shock at the amount of urine: it shocked me too, but what disturbed me even more was how such a vast amount of urine had been allowed to build up in the first place. What kind of healthcare was this man receiving?

At some point in the proceedings we were asked to form small groups and I ended up with a gay male couple who didn't seem overly keen on welcoming a stranger into their midst. Nonetheless, we all went through the motions of the icebreaking exercises, which, as I recall, included sitting foot-to-foot in triangle formation, joining hands and alternately pulling or being pulled in a circular motion by our companions. The physical discomfort wasn't a patch on the social discomfort: the unconditional positive regard just wasn't flowing in our section of the hall that night, made even more obvious by the expectation that we should all be up to our eyeballs in warm and fuzzies by now.

Perhaps it was because I'd not long finished studying psychology as part of my social work degree, but it felt distinctly like being back in playschool as we sat shoeless on the floor, being urged to play nicely with the others. That sense was only compounded when we finished with 'the song'. Song sheets were handed out and we all sang *I Love Myself the Way I Am* – a song that, particularly in that context, felt uncomfortably like a nursery rhyme. Nearly three decades later, the opening lines are still burned into my brain:

"I love myself the way I am, there's nothing I need to change. I'll always be the perfect me; there's nothing to rearrange."

For my part, I was experiencing some sort of cognitive dissonance: saying (or, more accurately, singing) one thing and feeling exactly the opposite. My self-esteem is fragile at the best of times and this experience – feeling marginalised in a group of supposedly caring people – did nothing to help. The whole process seemed superficial and childish: a 'one size fits all' approach for those whose inner child might well have been hurting for a variety of reasons. Acknowledging the hurt child is certainly important but, for adults, there is also a need to develop the mature, rational, adult response too. This session didn't even come close and I was glad to leave – although not before giving my two new 'buddies' the most frigid of parting hugs possible, of course.

A New Life in Australia

I returned from LA to find some good news waiting – my Australian visa had finally been approved. Maybe loving myself in Los Angeles had improved my karma after all!

189

Or it could have been that my repeated applications finally pushed the Australian immigration authorities into submission. Who knew?

Either way, I wasted little time in organising my migration and set off for my new life Down Under on 9 January 1987.

My timing turned out to be fortuitous: Australia's largest AIDS unit – at St Vincent's Hospital in Sydney – was expanding and they were advertising for an additional Social Worker. I couldn't believe my luck – and even more so when I actually got the job. It would, however, turn out to be a mixed blessing.

Like many Australian hospitals, St Vincent's was established and run by an order of Catholic nuns, in this case the Sisters of Charity. Its location in the suburb of Darlinghurst placed it at the centre of Sydney's queer communities, meaning that it was well placed to play a key role in the emerging AIDS crisis. Not that it was overly keen to do so. The hospital was ambivalent about taking on this role and insisted on incredibly inappropriate restrictions such as a ban on the distribution of condoms to AIDS patients. It was against this belligerent background that doctors, nurses, social workers – and even some of the nuns – delivered their services to people with AIDS.

As a non-Catholic queer/AIDS activist coming into such a system, it was clear that the potential for conflict was huge – and that potential was largely achieved in the course of my time there.

The Social Work Department reflected the conservative values of hospital. The Head of the Department was given the rather adolescent title of 'Social-Worker-in-Charge' and her 15 or so underlings were all female. I gathered she wanted to keep it that way and only agreed to appoint me after doctors and other social workers in the AIDS unit insisted that a gay male social worker was essential.

The unit itself was a different world: everyone delivered their services to the highest possible standards, with the greatest possible compassion and without any sense of judging or otherwise patronising the patients. Some staff members were queer, others weren't; some were HIV positive, some weren't and others, like me, didn't know their status. It made no difference: everyone was committed to the best care of the patient.

At the time I joined the unit there was no anti-viral treatment whatsoever: nursing and medical care was focused entirely on managing AIDS symptoms such as Pneumocystis pneumonia or cytomegalovirus infection. In practice it was little more than a waiting game: wondering whether someone would pull through this particular illness, how long it would be before the next one, and how severe that one was going to be. Grief and bereavement counselling was a key part of my work, with the second most common task being the counselling of those newly diagnosed with an AIDS-defining illness.

The likely progression of a person's illness was unpredictable: in some cases people seemed to survive in the face of insurmountable odds; in others, people would be admitted to the ward directly from Friday's outpatient clinic with relatively minor symptoms and be dead before Monday. Nor was there any correlation between a person's lifestyle and the duration of their illness: for example, one of our guys was in an almost permanent state of drug or alcohol intoxication when he wasn't an in-patient and he lasted for years. Another took regular exercise, meditated and paid strict attention to his diet: he was admitted to the ward with relatively mild symptoms on Friday afternoon and died less than 24 hours later.

The uncertainty took its toll on the patients as well as their partners, families and friends, but it was also immensely difficult for the staff. Doctors and nurses enter their professions because they want to make people better; dealing with a relentless stream of deaths – no matter how anticipated – inevitably goes against that instinct and making people more comfortable in their final days comes a very poor second to keeping people alive. As a social worker I had no aspirations as to saving lives: my focus was on helping people manage the issues that their illness presented as well as supporting the partners and others who were affected by the illness and subsequent death. It was immensely painful in practice: no death, no matter how prepared for, is ever a good one. When they occur at a production line pace – one or two a week, on average – they take their toll. Irrespective of the 'professional detachment' that we were supposed to maintain at all times, it was simply not possible to put personal feelings to one side. This was particularly so as a gay man, where the thought *"Will I be next?"* was never far from my mind.

Some deaths had a greater impact than others; we are, after all, talking about real people, each with their own life stories, personalities and individual response to their illness. Some people took their anger out on the staff since we represented a concrete manifestation of their illness. For example, it was a well-established practice that a social

191

worker would never give a patient news about their condition since this triggered the 'shoot the messenger' syndrome: the patient would hold us responsible for the bad news and resent us, thus destroying any potential 'therapeutic' relationship.

Other people chose to minimise their interaction with our services as a way of compartmentalising their illness and not letting it take over their lives. They attended and fully participated in their physical treatment regimes but got their emotional and psychological support from within their own social networks.

Others still integrated their treatment regime into their lifestyles to the point where the ward, the out-patient clinics and the healthcare staff were, more or less, part of their social lives. In some cases this was by choice, in others it was a matter of necessity as their original social networks – including their families – dropped (or ran) away upon learning of the AIDS diagnosis.

Integration was facilitated, at least in part, by the high level of interaction between the queer communities and the unit itself. Many queer organisations and venues raised funds for the unit, a significant percentage of the unit staff were gay or lesbian and those that weren't would generally have ties to the communities through friendships, flatmates and so on. In consequence, there were often shared topics of interest, including the social scene and the Gay and Lesbian Mardi Gras in particular. So it was no surprise, for example, that my getting extremely drunk in one of the local gay pubs one night was common knowledge at the following morning's out-patients clinic, before I even got there!

The Gay and Lesbian Mardi Gras was always an important time on the unit. Any staff member attending the party in costume was required to come in and show the patients in the unit first. And there was, of course, the inevitable post mortem for days afterwards where the parade, the party and the participants were described and analysed in minute detail!

But the interest in Mardi Gras extended far beyond a bit of gossip about a dance party: for so many of our guys, Mardi Gras represented a very real sense of connection with their communities and identities. Participation was so important that it was not uncommon for quite seriously ill men to seek temporary leave from the unit in order to attend the all-night party. One guy, for example, spent most of his days connected to a variety of tubes that were pumping medications and other fluids into his ravaged body. But come Mardi Gras, he was disconnected in order that he could attend the festivities and dance the night away.

192

Mardi Gras also demonstrated to me the power that we have, not only over our lives, but also our deaths. It is the case that people who are close to death can and do hang on until something that they are waiting for has happened. Sometimes this can be the arrival of a loved one or a particular event: on the AIDS unit people would hang on until the Mardi Gras in February or the other major community event, Sleaze Ball in October. I don't know what the dynamics are behind this; perhaps it is sheer coincidence that people declared that they were determined to hang on until Mardi Gras and that actually happened. But there did seem to be quite a high number of such coincidences.

My views are also influenced by my experience with another one of my guys, whom I literally 'talked to death'. I'll call him John, although that wasn't his real name.

John was a pretty typical patient: in his early 20s, he loved social interaction and was a particularly big fan of disco music. As his condition deteriorated, his only social outlet was the Friday morning out-patient clinic, where he would sit in the waiting room long after he had been seen by the doctor and chat to all and sundry. It was through this interaction that he became particularly friendly with one of the other guys, whom I shall call Carl (again, not his real name). While John had a huge and friendly personality, he wasn't one of the most intelligent people in the world and this often manifested in his inability to develop insight into a lot of things. One of these was his relationship with his long-term partner, which was so volatile that it became necessary for two community nurses to evacuate him from his home to a place of safety while his partner was out at work. But, in spite of the risks, John moved back in with his partner a week later.

Another area where his lack of insight became problematic was when he was, quite literally, on his death bed. For want of a better expression, John didn't know how to die. It wasn't helped by his partner visiting him at the hospice and pleading with him, as he lay unconscious, not to leave him. Given the circumstances, this was extremely unfair to John; his physical health had deteriorated beyond the point of no return. I believed then, as I believe now, that the only thing that was stopping him from dying was that he didn't know what to do.

So, during one of my visits to the hospice, I suggested to his partner that he might want to take a break by stepping outside and having a cigarette. Thankfully, he complied.

Then I moved my chair beside John's bed and took his hand in my hands. I told him that he had nothing to be afraid of and that it was time to do what he needed to do and

193

not what other people wanted. I told him that it was alright to let go and that that was all he needed to do. I still wasn't sure if he'd believe that it was that simple so I mentioned his friend Carl, from the out-patient clinic, who had died a few weeks earlier. And, even though I don't actually believe in an afterlife myself, I told him that Carl was waiting to help him: I didn't want John to feel that he was going to be alone.

John remained completely unresponsive and, after a couple of minutes, his partner came back from his break. I told John that I was going to leave and said my farewells. I talked to his partner briefly about getting himself some support but I told him nothing about what I'd said to John.

It was a ten minute drive back to the hospital from the hospice where John was. When I got to the ward, John's name was up on the whiteboard under the 'recent deaths' section.

In contrast to the death of John and the others who had hung on, I also encountered a man whose own self-hatred brought on his early death. For Australians, it will probably come as no surprise to learn that he was Aboriginal. He too had been admitted to the ward after attending the out-patient clinic on the Friday morning. While he had a formal diagnosis of AIDS, the main condition with which he had presented was a fungal infection of the mouth and throat: this, in itself does not generally constitute a life-threatening condition. The main reason for his admission was because he was homeless and it was necessary for him to have daily treatment to get rid of the fungal infection.

When I spoke to him on the ward he came across as a very bitter man. Despite identifying himself as gay he repeatedly interrupted our conversation with detrimental comments about other men of the ward that he perceived to be gay. Every detrimental term that is likely to come out of the mouth of a well-seasoned queer-basher came out of his mouth during our conversation: 'fucking queers', 'dirty pooftahs' and so on. While never denying his own sexuality he wanted to make it perfectly clear to me that he was nothing like those 'other' queers. Clearly, he had assessed me as a heterosexual and, under the circumstances, it would have been counterproductive to correct his perception.

Then his attention turned to the Aboriginal community and with an equal amount of vitriol he trotted out a string of racist stereotypes and insults. He didn't want any help

194

from the Aboriginal Medical Service because he didn't want anything to do with those black bastards, nor did he want any help from any other Aboriginal welfare organisation because they were all dirty black fuckers. He definitely didn't want any accommodation near any of the Aboriginal communities because they were all lazy bastards who did nothing but get drunk all day. Once again, he didn't deny his Aboriginality but went to great pains to stress that he was nothing like 'the rest of them'.

Such a conversation – where so much bile is being expressed – is exhausting and not particularly productive other than to release some of the obviously pent-up emotions. In consequence we agreed that we'd meet again on the Monday: my excuse being that the treatment would have begun to kick in by then – but the reality being that I was hoping that some of the negativity would have dissipated by then.

But we never had a second conversation: on returning to the ward on Monday I discovered that he had deteriorated rapidly and died over the weekend. I further learned that as his health had declined he began to have delusions that the flames of hell were springing up around him. It transpired that this Aboriginal man, like so many other indigenous Australians, had been taken from his parents as a child and brought up on a Christian mission in outback Australia. Like the others, he was taken from his parents because Aboriginal people were deemed incapable of raising children 'properly'. Such was the 'success' of this strategy that, in the last days of his life, this man was sick, homeless, alone and hating himself as much for being Aboriginal as for being gay. And in those final hours as his life slipped away, he genuinely thought he was about to burn in hell.

This man effectively imposed his own isolation on himself as a result of his self-hatred but there were many more who found themselves isolated by their friends and families. And it was often done in the most brutal way. Many gay men had moved to Sydney from isolated outback towns in order to escape the bigotry and extreme conservatism that were such strong features of Australian rural life. The distance between Sydney and their home towns also served to keep parents at bay. But when an AIDS diagnosis came along it raised the difficult issue of whether and what to tell the folks back at home.

In some cases the guys would ask the nurses on the unit to call their parents and break the news, believing that the impact might be reduced if Mum and Dad heard it in the safety of their own home. The responses varied: in some cases there was initial upset then unambiguous expressions of support; in others there was an angry instruction to tell the son to never darken their door again; and others still where the only sound was the click of the phone being put back in its cradle.

For a variety of reasons – including those above – some of the guys chose not to tell their families over the phone and saw a face-to-face announcement as the lesser of the two evils. And in some cases they had no choice: the parents caught the first train or flight to Sydney on hearing their son was in hospital. Then, as the unwitting parent walked onto the ward, everyone's hearts were in their mouths. There was anxiety as to whether they would guess the nature of the illness simply by virtue of the other patients on the ward – no other disease hospitalised this many men in this age group. There was anxiety that someone in hospital reception might have unwittingly blurted out *"the AIDS unit"* when the parents had sought directions to 'Ward 7 South'. And there was anxiety that they might have heard a reference to it while travelling up in the lift: even though there were no signs within the hospital referring to AIDS or the AIDS unit, it was common knowledge who was cared for on Ward 7 South.

Should the parent's ignorance still be intact by the time they had reached their son an immediate meeting was organised in a side room so that the news could be broken as sensitively but as quickly as possible. Sometimes it was the son himself who would do this; sometimes it was the son with the backup of a staff member; and sometimes – occasionally at short notice after the son had panicked – it was left to a staff member. I was asked to undertake this duty by one of my guys: he was shy and timid at the best of times and Dad was the exact opposite. He would have found any hesitation by his son infuriating and would have demanded he 'spit it out'. Thankfully, my role as a healthcare professional earned me a lot more respect – as well as a bit of patience!

The minute Dad arrived on the ward I met him and, on the pretext of helping him find his son, took him into the six-bed ward where he was waiting anxiously. The initial exchange was brief and relatively strained: Dad being a country bloke who wasn't big on displays of emotion and his son simply being stressed almost to the point of paralysis. I invited Dad into a side room so that I could bring him fully up to date on his son's condition and Dad unquestioningly obliged.

In preparation for tasks such as this I would go through a mental list of issues

196

I needed to cover and the order in which I should say them. Part of this involves trying to predict what kinds of questions, comments or other reactions my explanation is likely to trigger – including anger and possible abuse – and preparing a response. And so it was that I had my speech and supplementary information ready to roll when I explained as carefully as I could that his son had AIDS.

Dad's exact words were, *"Well, that's it then."* Then he got up, shook my hand and said, *"Thank you very much Colin"* and opened the door. When I asked him if there was anything he wanted to ask or say he simply shook his head. Then without a trace of emotion on his face, he turned and walked off the ward without as much as a sideways glance into his son's ward. We never heard from him or his wife again. It's impossible to imagine the impact on his son, who lay sick in a hospital bed while his father literally walked out of his life without so much as a single word. When his son died, the Staff Nurse rang the parents to let them know: once again Dad said, *"Thank you very much,"* – and hung up.

Family responses ran the whole gamut of possibilities: some were instant and outright rejection; some were immediate rejection then subsequent reconciliation; and some were unconditional support from the outset. What often complicated the situation was the strength of the family's legal position when compared to that of the life partner or others who had actually undertaken all the caring during a person's illness. For this reason alone it could actually be a good thing if a disapproving family walked out for good since it allowed the real carers to make the decisions – from the type of care to the type of funeral. Sadly, things weren't always as clear cut as that.

During my time at the Terrence Higgins Trust I attended a workshop called 'Where There's a Will, There's a Relative'. Run by two gay men it had been put together as a consequence of the lack of legal recognition of same sex partners, especially in the event of the death of one of them. It was often the case that relatives who had had no contact with the deceased during their life time would appear once they had died and successfully claim parts of the estate that rightfully belonged to the surviving partner. This same lack of recognition also affected the determination as to who constituted next of kin when it came to making decisions about treatment when the patient was no longer able to do so.

Changes that addressed this issue were beginning to occur in the health field; in

197

particular the increasing recognition of 'de facto' relationships (both heterosexual and homosexual), which gave partners significantly more say than they had previously. This didn't entirely eliminate conflicts between partners and relatives on the ward, however, and it was usually the nursing staff who tried to manage it:

"The staff modelled the idea – that is that the partner is like the spouse and therefore had primacy but it often required some careful negotiation around visiting times etc." [1]

But these changes were largely at an institutional level: the law still gave precedence to blood relatives so that, beyond the confines of the hospital ward, the partner often lost control of the situation. This impacted in a number of ways, from blatant asset grabs by relatives who had rarely or never seen the deceased during their lifetime to hijacking of the funeral.

"If the patient died, however, it got really ugly and there are some terrible stories about the behaviour of the family (both close and estranged) following someone's death." [2]

Thankfully, I never had to manage a bitter family dispute but I did attend one funeral where the family had overridden the wishes of the deceased and his friends in order to impose their own version of reality. Their son had been perfectly well-balanced and unapologetically gay: indeed, I believe he had been a bit of a queer activist in his time. In consequence, his funeral was packed with queer and queer-friendly people, all of whom were somewhat shocked by the priest's eulogy. The priest declared that, shortly before his death, the deceased man had 'realised the wrongfulness of his lifestyle and repented for his sinful ways'. This was absolute nonsense: my colleagues and I had been with the man during his last days and notions of sin and repentance were never raised. It was clear that the priest wanted to help the family bury the whole uncomfortable reality of the man's homosexuality along with his corpse.

It was episodes such as this that brought into focus the value of the AIDS Memorial Quilt: a project established to give partners, friends and carers the opportunity to truly represent and memorialise the person that they had known and loved in the face of the denial, distortion and concealment of others. (This is covered in much greater detail in the 'How Queers Communities Responded', below.)

Desperately Seeking Spirituality

Working with relentless caseloads of debilitating illness and death took its toll on everyone: for example, it is estimated that in the early days of the AIDS unit, the average length of service for nurses was three months [3]. As a gay man of unknown HIV status with few social networks in my newly-adopted country, I ticked most of the boxes in the stress profile but tended to ignore this in the rather naive belief that it was my duty to 'serve my community'.

I did try to deal with it on a spiritual level, in the first instance attending classes at a Buddhist Centre. I've never considered myself religious but it is hard to be surrounded by such immense levels of human suffering and death without trying to make some sense of it all. Unfortunately, I didn't get any answers at the Buddhist Centre.

During the meditation sessions every attempt at visualisation was swamped by an all-consuming blackness; when I sought guidance from the teacher I was told not to question but simply accept. When I sought some explanation for the ever-increasing number of deaths I was told the same thing. This seemed irrelevant to the point of absurdity: accepting the deaths of so many young men was nothing like what I needed at that point. My dalliance with the Buddhist Centre came to an abrupt end.

I'm still not entirely sure how I ended up at a Reiki weekend but I'm sure there was some good reason for it. Either that or the balance of my mind was now completely disturbed! Reiki is essentially a rebranded laying on of hands where the power of the universe is channelled through the practitioner's hands into the body of the recipient. I've always been somewhat cynical about this 'universal power' stuff and being prepared to be transformed into a 'channel' didn't do much to disabuse me of this – especially when accompanied by the sight of the course leader, Beth Gray, constantly refreshing her hot red lipstick throughout the proceedings. Nonetheless I do feel there is value in physical contact – particularly with people with AIDS who were the lepers of the late 20th century. Nor did Reiki seem to require adherence to any particular set of beliefs such as Louise Hay's 'you're not loving yourself enough'.

Admittedly, it was a little embarrassing when, in the course of proceedings, I was required to turn to the complete stranger sitting next to me and say to them, *"I forgive you, please forgive me"*. And I did struggle to hold back a giggle when Beth 'connected'

199

me to the universe. This involved sitting with my eyes closed while she made various squiggles on my back with her finger, concluding with one sharp poke just under the ribs. This final act brought to mind images of an aerial being plugged into the back of a TV but I quickly put that notion aside as I tried to concentrate on my new status as universal energy franchisee.

I did actually use Reiki over the next year or so, mainly on the guys attending the AIDS Day Centre. I don't think anyone had any real expectations that it would bring about any physical improvements, nor did we see any evidence of that. But I think the real value was in the process: it was administered to one person by two or three people in a nice, tranquil side room. Often that person had just arrived from the hectic environment of the out-patient clinic, which was a stressful experience in itself. And, as I've already said, physical contact often had added significance for a person with AIDS.

My final attempt at finding a spiritual solution was a weeklong residential course of Vipassana meditation. This was a year into my role in the AIDS unit and I was seriously beginning to feel like I was running out of options. The Vipassana course had two things going in its favour: it had been heartily endorsed by 'non-spiritual' friends and it was free. Well, it wasn't actually free: you paid at the end of the course but you only paid what you wanted and only if you thought the course had been of some value to you.

The downsides were that you had to get up at 6 a.m., only have two meals a day and not talk to, make physical contact or even establish eye contact with other people. Nor were you allowed to read, write or listen to music as these were all deemed to be distractions from your inner contemplation. And, as if that wasn't enough, we weren't allowed leave the compound until the end of the course because our minds might be too fragile to cope with the shock of the outside world. It seemed like a good idea at the time!

Every day followed the same pattern: woken at 6, shower, go the meditation hall for the first meditation session, have breakfast, go back to the meditation hall, break for lunch, go back to meditation hall ... and so on. The day finished with a talk from one of the teachers who then remained behind afterwards to answer any questions on a one-to-one basis.

In the meditation hall itself women were required to sit on the right-hand side of the room and men on the left. This, we were told, was to further minimise the risk of distraction by segregating us from members of the opposite sex. I'm sure the other five gay men on the course found that as amusing as I did! And while we were expected to remain totally silent throughout the hours of meditation, we were allowed to leave the hall and walk around the grounds if we were struggling with our focus.

I didn't struggle with the silence so much as the images that started to pop into my head from the second day onwards. Clearly, I was tapping into a lot of subliminal stuff as the first set of images had much to do with death, with skulls and skeletons recurring frequently. As disturbing as that was, I knew where it was coming from and just went with it. The more worrying images began a couple of days later.

These were the most extraordinarily vivid images of naked men having sex: I was streaming the most pornographic of gay porn movies in my head! And yet, despite the intensity and clarity of this internal sex-fest, I remained totally unresponsive too it. No erection, not even a raised heart rate.

These images continued for another day or so until they took a disturbing turn: no longer were these very cute men energetically fucking each other, they were sitting around me. And, one by one, they got up, waved goodbye and walked away! In retrospect, it was probably another subliminal thing about the loss of so many young men. However, after so many days of restricted stimulation, my mind chose instead to conclude that I was turning straight! Since I hadn't signed up for sexual reorientation I was first in the queue for the question and answer session at that night's lecture.

I didn't go into too much detail when I raised my concerns, keeping the issue fairly broad and talking about 'disturbing images'. Some reassurance that this was fairly common at this stage of the course would have been welcome; perhaps a little something to help me understand the bigger processes underlying these events. Instead, I got the Vipassana version of what appeared to be the universal spiritual response: *"We don't try and analyse these things; we simply accept them and let them pass."*

This left me feeling incredibly short-changed. It didn't feel like it was coming from a place of deep spiritual insight; more like the 'How to Respond to Students' Questions' page in the Vipassana 101 training manual. Nothing I said could elicit a more elaborate response than that. Perhaps it was the counsellor in me telling me that something a little more person-centred was required in these kinds of situations but I was neither enlightened nor reassured by this experience.

The naked men came back – and left – again the next day, at least during the morning session. After that there was nothing and I spent increasing amounts of time wandering around the grounds, avoiding eye contact with all and sundry. I had another attempt at getting a response at that evening's question time; wording the question differently but still getting the same, disappointing response.

The following day we were allowed to speak to each other, in preparation for a return home the day after that. This was just as well since my meditation sessions had become completely uneventful, resulting in my spending even more time wandering the grounds. And with the lifting of the speaking ban it seemed that ever-increasing numbers of my fellow inmates were joining me.

Thankfully, by the time I reached home my concern about my sexual orientation had vanished, replaced with a preoccupation with finding a strong coffee and large piece of chocolate cake. In the days that followed there was no sense of enlightenment but, instead, a state of severe depression that kept me house-bound for the entire week.

Homophobia Rears Its Ugly Head

I returned to work to find preparations underway at the AIDS Day Centre for the first ever Mardi Gras Parade entry by people with AIDS. I had initiated the centre (known as the Maitraya Centre) as a facility for the many people whose only social contact was the Friday morning AIDS out-patient clinic. In 1987 Area Health Services weren't required to provide treatment and care for local people with AIDS so many people had to travel long distances just to attend the out-patient clinic at St Vincent's. It was a bit of a double-edged sword: on the one hand they got to meet up with other people for a bit of gossip and support but, on the other, it was a long way to travel for a long wait then a ten minute consultation. The fact that many of them were already seriously debilitated by AIDS simply added to the stress.

And so I began to talk to the guys about creating a space where they could go after clinic to rest, relax and socialise. Central to this idea was getting them to put to use the many skills they had developed in the course of their varied careers but now no longer had the opportunity to use. Since Sydney already had a well-developed AIDS support network, information about the proposal was quickly and widely disseminated, a working party was established and the centre was open within a matter of weeks, reliant almost entirely on voluntary input.

The centre provided a range of benefits. For people with AIDS it offered an end to their isolation, peer support, access to community nurses and social workers and a sense of community and purpose. For their partners and significant others it also offered support, a break from non-stop caring and, quite often, an end to their isolation too. For social workers and community nurses it allowed an ongoing contact with far more people than we would have been able to see during home visits or in the out-patient clinic. It was also the first day centre of its kind in Australia so it served as a model for AIDS services around the country. And, because I'd initiated it, I was invited to present papers about it to the Third National Conference on AIDS and the National Conference of AIDS Social Workers.

So my boss – the 'Social-Worker-in-Charge' – forbade me from working on it!

It came as little surprise; it was but another manifestation of the administration's hostility to our work that had pre-dated me, although I suspect it had intensified with the arrival of an openly gay man. From the outset there had been a prohibition on the distribution of condoms to our clients. Needless to say we ignored it, although doing this involved a routine not unlike an illicit drug drop.

Condoms were smuggled into the hospital by workers from another AIDS clinic during their weekly visit to the out-patient clinic. These were duly locked at the back of the bottom drawer in the filing cabinet in the AIDS social workers' office. Whenever we identified anyone in need at the out-patients clinic it was necessary to brief the client first that we were about to engage in a furtive act so they didn't reveal the condoms while they were still in the hospital. Then we walked to the office, locking the door behind us before unlocking the filing cabinet. Condoms were then put into plain brown envelopes and sealed. The filing cabinet was then duly locked, the office door unlocked and a brisk walk back to the clinic followed. The envelope was then passed to the waiting client with a reminder that it should not be opened until they had left the building!

The prospect of delivering condoms to someone on the ward was risky beyond contemplation; they certainly couldn't be held in the unit's office and having them secreted in the bedside cabinet was also felt to be too dangerous.

In reality, this petty rule seriously affected our work. From a prevention perspective, it is glaringly obvious that a key strategy should be giving condoms to people carrying the virus – not just to protect others from the virus but also to protect them from cross-infection. From a psychological perspective, a common response to an AIDS diagnosis is a sense of loss – for example, a loss of control, a loss of mobility and a loss of sexual being. To deny people condoms is to be complicit with that loss of sexual being; it is saying 'we refuse to give you the means to allow you to continue being sexual'. The Catholic position on condoms in the AIDS crisis was always indefensible; the fact that it was imposed on Australia's largest AIDS unit was criminal.

In tandem with the ban on condoms was an unspoken ban on the promotion of safe sex. Presumably this was somehow linked to the notion that it was 'promoting' homosexuality, although the reason was never actually explained to me. I first became aware of it with an embarrassed exchange between me and the Social-Worker-in-Charge in relation to a sticker I had on my work diary. The black and white sticker had been produced by the AIDS Council. On first glance it merely read 'PSST!' but on closer scrutiny the small print turned it into 'Practice Safe Sex Today!' As we assembled for our weekly team meeting she saw the sticker and loudly enquired as to what 'PSST!' meant. It felt a lot like being asked the same thing by my mother: I knew it would end with an embarrassed silence since both my mother and my boss were squeamish when it came to acknowledging sex. But my mother never went into the field of social work where people's emotions and behaviours are pretty fundamental to the job.

The tense silence was only broken by one of my more mature colleagues changing the subject – although that was far from the end of the matter.

A few weeks later I was called to my boss's office where she told me that she 'had been informed' that I had some inappropriate material on my office walls. The inappropriate materials were two posters advocating safe sex. Given the range of explicit material that was available on this subject, these were remarkably tame: one was entirely text (with nothing more raunchy than the words 'safe sex') and the other featured a cartoon-strip of two men ('Greg and Brad', if I remember correctly) eyeing each other up. There was no nudity – partial or total. There was no 'street language'. Nor was there any 'homosexual propaganda' – my clients were heterosexual as well as gay and I wanted them all to feel equally at ease in my office. But both posters did contain those 'highly offensive' words 'practice safe sex'.

It was gob-smackingly petty. I had been called down from my duties dealing with sick and dying patients on the ward to be chastised for an 'offence' that must have

204

required an immense effort to create. For the first few minutes I put my case as rationally and calmly as I could: encouraging discussion of safe sex as a harm reduction strategy was central to my job; it was about the well-being of the clients and their partners; it was about acknowledging that people had sex as well as the psychological benefits of them continuing to have sex; and it was about reinforcing a message that was central to our work.

As if completely deaf to these arguments I was told that *"some people might find the posters offensive"*. When I responded that only my clients and the other AIDS social workers used my office I was told that passers-by might see them when the door was open. When I pointed out that there were few passers-by because my office wasn't on a major thoroughfare I was told that it wasn't my office anyway. At this point I was expecting to be told that it was God's office and that he could see everything but, thankfully, it didn't descend quite to that level of farce. I was told instead that the office belonged to the hospital administration and I had no right to put material on the wall. The fact that every other social worker had material on their walls – from health information to Snoopy posters – was irrelevant. Seeing little point in continuing this absurd conversation, I walked out.

Sadly, this didn't put an end to the madness: a few days later I was instructed to be in my office at a certain time as my boss had reported me to the hospital's Sister Administrator who now wished to 'inspect' the material. The fact that three of my clients had died in the previous seven days was irrelevant: the grief and bereavement issues would have to wait until this far more important matter was sorted out.

About an hour before the appointed inspection time I broke down on the ward and was guided gently into a side room by the unit's pastoral care worker, one of the Sisters of Charity, Sister Margaret Mines. After listening intently to my blubbered tale, Sister Margaret declared that, if I was agreeable, she would attend the inspection with me *"for moral support"*. This was an immensely brave thing for her to do: none of my social work colleagues had offered such support yet this nun was prepared to stand beside me while her boss was passing judgement on me for my waywardness.

And that is exactly what she did as the Sister Administrator and her grim-faced entourage were conducted by the Social-Worker-in-Charge into the office to view the pornographic filth with which I had desecrated the walls. There was no real need for

205

me to be present during this inspection: I wasn't the only one with an office key, for example, nor was I ever asked to comment or 'explain'. In reality it was nothing more than an attempt at humiliation: a flock of uber-nuns interrogating the posters intensely, nodding in collective disapproval and disdain, and my boss echoing their mannerisms at the rear. Throughout it all, Sister Margaret – who undoubtedly also had better things to do with her time – stood quietly supportive by my side.

A combined nodding of heads confirmed that the inspectors had seen enough; the Sister Administrator thanked me and the entourage marched off. I subsequently received a letter summoning me to a meeting with the Sister Administrator and the Social-Worker-in-Charge where I would be advised of their decision. I decided that enough was enough and contacted my trade union.

When I arrived at the disciplinary meeting with union representative in tow, the managers were somewhat taken aback; particularly my boss, who had up until that time taken great pride in praising the union to new members of staff. Suddenly she found herself on the wrong side of the argument. Nonetheless, the meeting proceeded with a formal but unsurprising declaration that the posters had been found to be inappropriate and an instruction to take them down. My union representative chose to disagree: she advised the meeting that the posters were clearly appropriate and relevant to my work. Then she upped the ante: she declared that the actions taken to date clearly suggested victimisation since no other social worker had been subject to the same treatment and finished by advising the meeting that the union had formally advised me to leave the posters in place.

And so I achieved a victory of sorts: since I was now acting on union instructions, the hospital could not proceed with disciplinary measures against me without precipitating a wholesale dispute with the union. Not that they were prepared to withdraw their demand for the posters to come down: they'd painted themselves into a bit of a corner on that one since they had to be seen to be supporting one of their departmental heads (even though they probably wanted to throttle her for creating such a trivial issue in the first place). But they made no attempt at seeking a compromise solution and the matter was left unresolved.

In fact, I took the posters down the next day: victory or otherwise, the whole matter had become an unnecessary stress in a job that was already stressful enough.

And I began looking for jobs elsewhere, as well as seeing a counsellor for my depression. My boss, on the other hand, continued her war of attrition: she excluded me from any decisions about social work on the unit in favour of the other two – female – social workers and constantly tried to call me to account for my activities. At one point I ran safe sex workshops for gay men with HIV/AIDS – but these had to be advertised only by word of mouth and held away from the hospital. In order to provide the best service for my clients, I had to keep my activities secret from my boss.

And then she forbade me from working on the Day Centre – a project that I had established and something that was highly regarded within the AIDS field. I chose instead to ignore her completely: as much as her constant sniping was wearing me down, I was pretty confident that the posters fiasco would make her think twice about initiating disciplinary proceedings again.

But the politics around the Day Centre were also beginning to build as the prospect of Health Department funding seemed increasingly likely. The AIDS Council felt they were the rightful recipients of this, arguing that they represented the community of people living with AIDS as well as providing some of the Day Centre volunteers through the Community Support Network. It wasn't a view that I supported: the local health service that had put in much of the mileage in getting the project going in the first place – providing the premises for the project as well as community nurses and social workers such as myself. Additionally, many of the guys we worked with felt that the health service represented their needs better than the AIDS Council – and not all of the volunteers came via the AIDS Council.

So, while my experience at St Vincent's had hardly enamoured me to the health service, I also felt that the AIDS Council were being a bit presumptuous about their claim to the Day Centre funding. Somewhat naively perhaps, I put those thoughts in writing when the AIDS Council sent their draft funding proposal to the Day Centre Steering Committee. And the next thing I knew I was visited by the AIDS Council heavies – the Chief Executive and two senior managers – letting me know of their displeasure and threatening everything from public meetings to a formal complaint to my boss. I could have told them that a formal complaint wouldn't have been necessary; the slightest hint of criticism would have been sufficient grounds for her to instigate disciplinary measures.

But I didn't. I apologised – rather too profusely, in retrospect – then wasted an entire weekend stressing about it. But the stress was short-lived: on Monday morning I went in to work and resigned. It was one of the most liberating sensations I have ever experienced!

My boss gave me a width berth for the remainder of my stay, even taking the day off on my last day so she didn't have to make the traditional 'Thank You and Good Luck' speech that she had made for everyone else who left her department. The other social workers were left to organise the traditional afternoon tea instead; a polite affair where no one mentioned the elephant in the room.

On the AIDS unit my send-off was low-key because the staff were almost constantly engaged in patient care. Yet it had significantly more meaning since I knew they had recognised and valued my work.

And, in spite of all the stress, the AIDS unit is still one of the best places I've ever worked in my life. I met some amazing people – staff, 'patients', carers and volunteers. I saw the best – and worst – elements of human nature and I like to think I made a difference for a lot of people struggling with the physical, psychological and social aspects of this horrible disease.

Immediately after my departure, my physical and mental health went into decline. I was pissing blood the very next day; then my skin erupted in boils and rashes for several weeks thereafter. These symptoms were nothing more than a physical response to the stress that had accumulated during my time on the AIDS unit. It would be nearly two months before I felt ready to take an HIV test and another month before I felt capable of holding down a job.

That job was as an HIV/AIDS educator. It necessitated writing about HIV/AIDS but – I told myself – safely away from the hospital and 'community' politics and the hard realities of the disease itself.

It seemed like a good idea at the time.

References

1. Personal communication from former Staff Nurse Bill Paterson to Colin Clews, 18 February 2015.

2. Personal communication from former Staff Nurse Bill Paterson to Colin Clews, 18 February 2015.

3. van Reyk, Paul. *Life During Wartime: Nursing on the AIDS Ward*. Conference paper presented at Australian Homosexual Histories Conference, Melbourne, November 2013. Published on Nurse Uncut website. February 2014.
    [Online] Available at
    http://www.nurseuncut.com.au/life-during-wartime-nursing-on-the-aids-ward-part-2/
    Accessed May 2014.

Part Two - A Brief Natural History of HIV/AIDS
First Detection

The alarm bells around AIDS only began to go off in February 1981, when Dr Michael Gottlieb noted two fatal cases of *Pneumocystis carinii pneumonia* (PCP) in gay men at the UCLA School of Medicine in Los Angeles. Up until that time PCP had not usually affected younger people nor were the effects usually fatal.

Over the next few months Gottlieb and other colleagues also noted cases of Kaposi's sarcoma (KS) in gay men – again something not previously seen in this group and not previously as aggressive as it now was. A third factor – cytomegalovirus (CMV) – was also found to be prevalent within this same group of patients. In March 1981 Dr Constance Wolfsy diagnosed the first case of Central Nervous System toxoplasmosis – a condition more prevalent in cats than humans – in a gay male patient at San Francisco General Hospital (SFGH).

On 5 June 1981, the US Centers for Disease Control (CDC) in Atlanta, Georgia, published the first official notification of the five Los Angeles cases of PCP, including the deaths of two of them [1]. The following month it published its first report of KS in gay men [2].

At this early stage, with little to point to a clear link between the various conditions, clinicians described the phenomenon as KSOI. This stood for 'Kaposi's sarcoma and Opportunistic Infections' and was used for the CDCs first meeting of the 'Kaposi's sarcoma and Opportunistic Infections (KSOI) Task Force' on 8 June 1981. As more information was received about the condition the acronym changed to GRID – Gay Related Immune Deficiency – at the beginning of 1982 and then, on 27 July 1982, the CDC adopted the acronym AIDS – Acquired Immune Deficiency Syndrome (or Acquired Immuno-Deficiency Syndrome).

The name changes reflected not only the changing theories of causation but also the speed at which these theories changed. KSOI was in part a reflection of the view that KS and other conditions such as PCP and CMV might be connected but in a way that was yet to be fully understood. GRID, unfortunately, marked the point at which 'the gay lifestyle' was examined as a possible cause. And AIDS represented a greater confidence in the view that the causative agent was something transmissible from one person to another (rather than the 'self-generating' agent that the lifestyle theories imply).

210

While the condition had first been identified in the USA at the beginning of 1981, by the end of that year it was clear that it had also reached the shores of the UK. In December, the British medical journal *The Lancet* published details of the first AIDS diagnosis in the UK: a 49-year-old man admitted to Brompton Hospital in London suffering – and quickly dying – from PCP [3]. Almost a year later the first AIDS diagnosis was made in Australia: this was an American gay man who was on holiday in the country, diagnosed in October 1982. The first Australian to be diagnosed – in April 1983 – was a gay man who had recently returned home after living in the USA for a number of years.

As larger numbers of people presented with symptoms, it became apparent that some were suffering from conditions that were severe but didn't fully constitute a formal AIDS diagnosis. Such symptoms included recurring fever, swollen lymph glands, severe and unexplained weight loss and fungal mouth infections. In consequence, the term AIDS-related complex (ARC) was coined in an attempt to better define and manage this condition, which was seen by many at that time as a transitional stage towards a full manifestation of AIDS. The term was dropped in 2000 in light of more accurate diagnostic procedures.

Kaposi's sarcoma and 'The Gay Cancer'

Despite the name change to AIDS, there was still frequent use of the term 'gay cancer' in reference to Kaposi's sarcoma. In the earliest days it was seen as a distinct condition in itself but even when it became a diagnostic indicator of AIDS, the label persisted.

This may be because early theories around KS in gay men had a distinct link to perceived 'lifestyles' – and particularly the use of 'poppers' (alkyl nitrites). It was – and, indeed, continues to be – argued that the regular use of these depressed the immune system, thus facilitating the transmission of infectious agents such as the KS virus.

The prevalence of KS in gay men who did not use poppers has been explained by the theory that anal sex conducts the KS virus significantly more readily than vaginal sex. There is still some debate about this theory but its existence serves, again, to imply a role of 'the gay lifestyle' in the development of AIDS.

This, along with terms like 'gay cancer' and 'Gay Related Immune Deficiency' was to prove unfortunate, both in terms of a search for causation as well as the scapegoating of gay men. For example, long after the CDC changed the name to AIDS, the tabloid press continued to refer to it as 'the gay plague' or a 'gay bug'.

211

The Cause(s) of AIDS

While the early indicators of AIDS had been the appearance of conditions like PCP and KS in previously unaffected populations, clinicians were fairly confident from the outset that these were merely symptoms rather than the actual cause of this new condition.

As the acronym 'KSOI' suggests, the earliest theories sought to explore a possible inter-connection between KS and opportunistic infections like cytomegalovirus, PCP and toxoplasmosis. For example, on 15 September 1981 the CDC and National Cancer Institute sponsored a workshop on KS and Opportunistic Infections where CMV was considered to be *"a leading candidate for cause"* [4].

Another theory suggested that repeated exposure to a number of different agents like viruses and toxins simply overloaded the immune system, making it incapable of responding effectively to these pathogens. This was, essentially, one of a number of theories that sought answers from the perceived lifestyles of gay men.

Of the overload theory, leading researcher Dr John Ziegler was later to explain:

"One was a sort of concatenation theory, where everything seemed to be conspiring in these people to suppress their immune system. We thought this might be a cumulative effect of multiple exposures to sperm and to viruses and to hepatitis and CMV, and that was sort of a major immune overload. But nobody could really buy into that, including us, because it never happened historically, that you would get a whole lot of different agents conspiring at once in the same person. And then it certainly didn't explain why other people were getting AIDS from blood. So that theory quickly fizzled out." [5]

Another 'lifestyle' theory was the aforementioned hypothesis of a link between the recreational use of alkyl nitrites – more commonly known as 'poppers' – and the onset of Kaposi's sarcoma. The debate on this continues to this day [6].

Central to the discounting of the 'lifestyle' theories was the realisation that a lot of people with AIDS – gay men included – did not share the same lifestyle. For example, not everyone had multiple sexual partners that might lead to repeated and high-level exposure to viruses nor did everyone use poppers.

By early 1982 researchers were giving increasing attention to the idea of an infectious agent that was spread by sexual and other means and that attacked the body's immune system:

"Then we realized that there was something profoundly wrong with the immune system, that was obviously acquired from sexual and other exposures, and that it was predominantly attacking the T4 cells, the CD4 helper lymphocytes ... I would say by the spring of '82, everyone was pretty much convinced we were dealing with an infectious agent. CDC by that time had published their very nice homosexual network paper, showing that in Orange County L.A., everybody was having sex with everybody else, and you could see the network drawing of these multiple sexual contacts." [7]

This narrowing down of the focus away from the broad brush concept of 'lifestyle' to a specific causative agent wasn't just an immense breakthrough in terms of medical research; it also offered a beleaguered, frightened and confused gay community the first opportunity to identify – and thus avoid – 'risk' behaviours. In practice, it was also the first step in dismantling the notion that simply being gay put people at risk of AIDS. Contracting or avoiding AIDS was about what people did, not who they were and this gave educators their first opportunity to identify safer practices. After so much mystery and bewilderment about transmission, it was a small but hugely significant breakthrough when educators could advise people to *"avoid the direct exchange of bodily fluids"*. This was the starting point for one of the most influential education publications in AIDS history – the leaflet *Can We Talk?* produced by the Harvey Milk Gay Democratic Club in 1984. The leaflet didn't just say 'Don't do this', it also suggested a range of safer options to make the point that finding new ways to have sex could be a very real opportunity to have fun.

And while gay and bisexual men were encouraged to find safer means of sexual expression, the search for the causative agent went on. Sadly, this would be marred by the non-scientific qualities of ego, power and greed. Two of the key players who were to become central in this issue were Dr Luc Montagnier of the Pasteur Institute in Paris and Dr Robert Gallo of the National Institutes of Health in the USA.

At the end of 1982, Montagnier and his colleagues were already working on the effect of retroviruses on the body's defence mechanisms. In consequence, they chose to extend this study to see if retroviruses played a role in the onset of AIDS. By January 1983 they had isolated a new retrovirus that they felt had such a role and they named it LAV (Lymphadenopathy Associated Virus).

On 20 May 1983 they published a paper in the journal *Science* announcing their

213

findings and suggesting it had some role to play in the development of AIDS. They did not, however, state outright that LAV was the cause of the disease; they noted that it had been found in people with AIDS and, from that, speculated some kind of relationship.

In July and September 1983, Montagnier shared samples of the virus with Gallo in the USA. In April 1984, the US Secretary for Health and Human Services, Margaret Heckler, held a press conference where she announced that Robert Gallo and his colleagues had discovered the cause of AIDS – a virus that they named HTLVIII (human T-cell lymphotropic virus III). At the same time, Gallo filed a patent application for a diagnostic blood test for AIDS based on 'his' discovery.

Gallo subsequently claimed that he wanted to hold a joint press conference with Montagnier and his team but when the press had got wind of their discovery he felt compelled to proceed without them. *"If I could relive those days, I wish they had been at the press conference ... I was a little swept away."* Although not too swept away to forget his patent application.

He did manage to participate in a joint French–US press conference in June 1984, where both Gallo and Montagnier agreed that HTLVIII and LAV were probably the same. But this event marked the beginning of a prolonged dispute between the two parties during which AIDS research was effectively slowed by their refusal to cooperate with each other.

It was quickly established that the virus that Gallo had 'discovered' had, in fact come from samples provided by the French. But that didn't really settle the argument. Gallo's side argued that even though Montagnier's team had identified the virus, they had not demonstrated conclusively that it was the cause of AIDS: their paper in *Science* magazine had actually said as much. It was the Americans who had proven that it caused AIDS.

It may seem like a pedantic argument but few people doubt the financial benefit that would flow to the 'discoverer' of the virus from licensing fees for diagnostic tests. Gallo's rush to get his patent in first was not science's most glorious moment.

As part of the prolonged dispute, neither side would agree to one specific name for the virus: the French wanted to call it LAV, the Americans HTLVIII. In the end it became necessary for the International Committee on the Taxonomy of Viruses to intervene and name it the Human Immunodeficiency Virus (HIV) in May 1986.

But the vested interests were still so strong that it took an out-of-court agreement to

214

share licensing fee royalties AND a joint statement by the presidents of both countries declaring Montagnier and Gallo as joint discoverers of the virus before cooperation was re-established.

In 1995, the United States' House Energy and Commerce Committee's Subcommittee on Oversight and Investigations released a report entitled *Institutional Response to the HIV Blood Test Patent Dispute and Related Matters*. It found that Gallo and his staff *"knew or had reason to know that the virus they were working with and claimed as their own was the IP virus"*.

It went on to declare that the Department of Health and Human Services had *"conducted a parody of an investigation; they did not seek the truth but rather sought to create an official record to support the claims of Gallo et al"*.

The report also criticised the US Patent and Trademark Office for awarding the patent *"despite the fact that another patent application for substantially the same invention, the IP application, had been submitted to the PTO months before the submission of the Gallo application"*.

As if to further clarify who really discovered the AIDS virus, the Nobel Prize Committee decided in 2008 to award the Nobel Prize for Physiology and Medicine only to Dr Montagnier.

Other Theories of Causation

Even after Gallo and Montagnier had reached their agreement there were still those who doubted that HIV was the cause of AIDS.

From the outset the climate of fear and uncertainty forced people to come up with their own notions of causation in an attempt to gain some sense of control over the situation. In some cases the theories revealed people's deepest fears but in others they revealed the nastiest and most exploitative motives.

One of the ways the fears came to the surface was in the form of conspiracy theories. For example, during my first visit to San Francisco in June 1983 I remember seeing stickers declaring, *"It's Not Your Lifestyle! AIDS Comes From a Government Lab!"* There were a number of variations around this theme, for example substituting Soviet lab for US government lab.

More complex variations included the African swine fever theory. This was based on early speculation that the causative agent may be a mutation of the African swine fever virus. At some point in the 60s or 70s the CIA had deliberately infected Cuba's pig population with African swine fever in an attempt to destabilise both the economy and President Castro. The AIDS theory was based on the notion that the swine fever virus had subsequently been carried from Cuba to the nearby island of Haiti, where it had infected Haitian pigs. From there it had been transferred to a pig farmer after he had had sex with his pigs and then subsequently to gay American tourists after he had had sex with them too.

Of course anything that can be linked to sex – and gay sex in particular – inevitably brought out the moral entrepreneurs. This was a particular breed of individual who happily ignored all the evidence to engender fear and hatred – usually in the name of 'Christian love'. Thus, the UK's *Sun* newspaper was ready to give a high profile to the Reverend Owen Leigh-Williams when he declared, *"AIDS Is the Wrath of God"* [8] and claimed that *"... homosexuals offended the Lord ..."* – and this was more than a year after it was known that AIDS wasn't restricted to homosexual men. This convenient but erroneous moral shorthand was echoed repeatedly around the globe by the likes of Jerry Falwell and Pat Buchanan in the USA and Fred Nile in Australia.

That political and moral opponents to homosexuality should come up with crack-pot theories came as no surprise. What was more puzzling was those theories formulated by those who claimed to be allies. Such was the case with Louise *("You Can Heal Your Life")* Hay, who built a hugely profitable empire on a strange combination of superficial psychology and a 'self-help' ethos that any right-wing politician would be proud of. In essence Hay argued that illness was your own fault and if you were a good enough person you should be able to heal yourself.

Riding the wave of sugary sentiment and naive thinking that characterised the so-called New Age, Hay told us that love was the answer and, incredibly, many people swallowed it hook, line and sinker. Such is the vulnerability of a community in crisis. Drawing on very real psychological issues that affect queer people (such as guilt and low self-esteem) Hay declared these to be the *"probable cause"* of AIDS in her global bestseller *You Can Heal Your Life*:

"Feeling defenseless and hopeless. Nobody cares. A strong belief in not being good enough. Denial of the self. Sexual guilt." [9]

216

She went on to explain how queers had, in effect, set themselves up for this:

"... gay men ... have created a culture that places tremendous emphasis on youth and beauty ... Because of the ways gay people often treat other gays, for many gay men the experience of getting old is something to dread. It is almost better to die than get old. And aids [sic] is a dis-ease that often kills." [10]

But it wasn't just Hay; a number of 'somatic therapists' were also pushing this line that the 'dis-ease' was the consequence of unresolved emotional conflicts. And, unlike Hay's happy-clappy saccharine simplicity, they developed a quasi-scientific jargon that, on the face of it, implied some genuine scientific validity.

A more scientifically based – although no less controversial – theory on the causation of AIDS is that from Professor Peter Duesberg, Professor of Molecular and Cell Biology at the University of California. In 1987 he began to challenge the notion that HIV was the cause of AIDS, arguing that:

"... there is no virological, nor epidemiological, evidence to back up the HIV-AIDS hypothesis. Instead the virus is biochemically inactive and harmless, and AIDS is not a contagious disease." [11]

As a scientist his arguments are, of course, incredibly complex but part of his argument seemed to be that neither Robert Gallo nor Luc Montagnier – the 'discoverers' of HIV – had actually published a scientific paper documenting the processes that led them to the conclusion that HIV causes AIDS. In rejecting the notion that HIV causes AIDS Duesberg seemed to be postulating a range of other causes including 'lifestyles' and anti-viral drugs:

"There are only two explanations for a new epidemic of 'acquired' diseases: germs or lifestyles, associated with chemical or physical health risks. Hardly anyone remembers that in 1981 AIDS researchers had already advanced the lifestyle-AIDS hypothesis in the 'prestigious' New England Journal of Medicine (Durack et al. NEJM 1981). According to this hypothesis the massive use of recreational sex and party drugs, like nitrite inhalants, amphetamines and cocaine is causing AIDS.

Since viruses or microbes do not transmit AIDS, the recreational and anti-viral drugs 'must be the truth'." [12]

Duesberg appeared to be espousing a 'lifestyle' theory of causation that was discounted 25 years ago. He has also claimed that he is being shut out of the AIDS debate

217

by those who feel intimidated by his 'uncomfortable' questions. Unsurprisingly, there are many other people who would argue that he is not being shut out; he's not being listened to because he won't acknowledge evidence that contradicts his own theories.

For non-scientists the complexity of the debate means that it is close to impossible to come to a conclusion. As Charles Bremmer wrote in *The Times* newspaper:

"It may not take long for history to judge whether he is a brilliant visionary or a dangerous distraction in the pursuit of a remedy to the most mysterious and terrifying disease of this era." [13]

Bremmer's quote highlights a fundamental issue about all theories of causation: are they helpful or harmful? As long as a cure – and even a vaccine – remain elusive it is essential that we continue to ask questions and consider new perspectives. But it is also crucial that, in the process, we don't lose the few gains that we currently have.

Clearly theories around 'God's judgement' are nothing but small-minded nonsense aimed at making moral capital at the expense of people with HIV/AIDS. That Louise Hay's books continue to espouse the 'blame the victim' approach – 'the reason you're unwell is because you don't love yourself enough' – is equally indefensible, particularly this far into the AIDS crisis and in the complete absence of supportive evidence.

And while there may be scientific evidence to support Duesberg's arguments, the 'anti-viral treatment is poison' line is a dangerous one given the lack of demonstrable alternatives. During my time working at St. Vincent's Hospital in Sydney, Australia, I met a man who was a very vocal advocate of the 'AZT is poison' argument. He was living with AIDS and he never missed an opportunity to espouse his opinion in meetings and the queer media. Yet what was less well-known was that he was taking the treatment that he was simultaneously denouncing. Clearly he had every right to but there is something seriously unsettling about this 'do as I say, not as I do' approach – particularly when it comes to a life-threatening illness.

The Implications of the 'AIDS Virus' Discovery

Prior to the discovery of a causative agent, the first indication that a person was infected with AIDS was the appearance of the associated symptoms. For those perceived to be most at risk this meant, in practice, a constant scanning of one's body in search of any such signs. I know I wasn't the only gay man who went into a panic at any

218

blemish on my skin or the slightest shortness of breath. Another key sign we were all urged to look out for was 'night sweats'. In the earliest days we didn't know that these were indicators of 'sero-conversion' – that is, the body's initial attempts to fight off HIV infection. We knew only that it was another sign of AIDS and, as with the skin blemishes or shortness of breath, any nocturnal perspiration was quickly interpreted as an AIDS symptom. This generated much anxiety – which just happens to be one of the other causes of 'night sweats'!

The discovery of HIV provided us with a more tangible indication of infection (or lack thereof) although it was neither an instant nor ideal solution. While the discovery of the causative agent was announced in 1984, it would be another year before the first so-called 'AIDS test' would become available.

The test – the Enzyme-linked immunosorbant assay (ELISA) test – detected antibodies to HIV in the bloodstream. Since antibodies are part of our body's response to HIV rather than a part of the virus itself, the test told us that HIV had been in our body and our body had produced a response to it. What the test didn't tell us was whether or not our body had successfully fought off the infection, since antibodies continue to be produced long after the toxin that triggered their production has disappeared. And even if the test failed to detect antibodies, this did not eliminate the possibility that the body simply hadn't got around to producing them yet. In the most severe cases there was also a theoretical possibility that AIDS had already damaged the body's immune system so badly that it was no longer capable of producing antibodies.

So the ELISA test certainly gave us another piece of the jigsaw but it still didn't give us the full picture. We still had to wait for the emergence of symptoms before an AIDS diagnosis was possible. And while the development of the Western blot test in 1987 increased the reliability of HIV testing, it was still based on the detection of antibodies. It wasn't until 1989 that the first test to detect actual proteins from the virus itself was licensed.

But even as evidence of HIV infection became more certain this did not necessarily translate into certainty as to how the disease might progress. The introduction of HIV tests gave us a much clearer idea of the number of people infected: it also triggered speculation as to how many of them would go on to develop AIDS. The estimates began at around 10 per cent then began to climb as more people presented with AIDS-defining conditions.

219

To Test or Not to Test?

While the first HIV tests were introduced in 1985, there were no anti-HIV treatments until the introduction of AZT in 1987. This influenced not only the progression of HIV infection but also the number of people coming forward for HIV testing.

I, for one, didn't have an HIV test until late 1988. Like many gay men at that time, I saw little purpose in knowing my HIV status when there were no treatments available. I was already practising safer sex, didn't donate blood and was looking after my general health: knowing my HIV status wouldn't have made any difference to what I did – other than induce regular bouts of panic and anxiety. Even when AZT was introduced in 1987 it was, in the first instance, available only to those with AIDS-defining illnesses and so I still would not have been eligible for it. Also, in 1987 and 1988, working as a social worker at St Vincent's Hospital in Sydney, I saw on a daily basis the grim realities of how AIDS was taking its toll. I simply couldn't have done that work if I'd had a positive HIV test (and I have huge admiration for the HIV positive healthcare staff that did). It was some two months after I left that role that I had my first HIV test.

AIDS Treatments

In the earliest days of the AIDS crisis the only medical treatments that were available were for the symptoms; for example, pentamidine was used for the treatment of the AIDS-related *Pneumocystis carinii pneumonia* (PCP), but Kaposi's sarcoma was essentially untreatable.

Since the cause of the disease was unknown until 1984 it was, understandably, virtually impossible to develop a 'cure' before that. There was always the possibility that, purely as a matter of chance, something might have been found that would eliminate all evidence of symptoms. But this would very much have been a shot in the dark. For example, without knowing the actual cause it would be impossible to determine whether the cause had been eliminated or just suppressed – to return once treatment was stopped.

Against all of those concerns, of course, was the sense that, left unchecked, AIDS was likely to be terminal. In consequence, a range of approaches – ranging from the

220

unconventional to the more scientific – were taken to try and make some impact on its progress.

One of the earliest was based on the view that, if your body is under attack, then you should do everything you can to bolster its natural immune response. 'Clean living' was the order of the day: for example in 1983 San Francisco's Sutro Co-ed Bath House ran its *Guide to Good Clean Fun* in local newspapers. This included everything from safer sex (*"avoid the direct exchange of bodily fluids"*) to a healthy diet, plenty of exercise, getting sufficient sleep and having regular health check-ups.

Of course, healthy living meant different things to different people: some decided to 'detox' – everything from the usual suspects of alcohol and recreational drugs, to coffee, food additives and other perceived toxins that might put a strain on the body's immune system. Stress was also identified as a potential 'immuno-suppressant' and, again, this produced a variety of responses from the sensible to the suspicious. A number of AIDS projects developed stress management information and workshops and many people took up various forms of meditation, yoga and massage.

And, as previously mentioned, a number of people developed 'somatic' therapies based on the notion that unresolved emotions were depressing the immune system and causing AIDS.

Louise Hay's approach was to develop a *"new thought pattern"*:

"I am part of the Universal design. I am important and I am loved by life itself. I am powerful and capable. I love and appreciate all of myself." [14]

In all fairness, I should point out that, in spite of her seriously superficial theories, Louise Hay still attracted a large number of followers from within the queer communities, including people with HIV/AIDS.

We were still well into the so-called 'New Age' when AIDS emerged. This was, essentially, a growth in interest in 'alternative' lifestyles (although not as radically 'alternative' as those advocated in counter-culture of the late 60s). It manifested itself in a variety of forms from wind chimes and synthesised music to philosophy, meditation and holistic healing. And, again, some of these approaches – such as meditation and massage – were of real value to people with HIV/AIDS: meditation, for example, was a valuable stress management tool in itself and it often gave people a sense of spirituality that helped them better manage the issues around illness and dying. But then there were others that can only be described as a 'clutching at straws' approach: for example, in the movie *Common Threads*, queer activist Vito Russo describes how his lover Geoffrey would talk about placing an invisible blue protective cloak around himself.

At the end of the day, people were desperate for a way to get a handle on this mysterious and frightening condition, particularly in the early days when no cause had been identified. In consequence, it would be very wrong to point an accusatory finger at those who adopted what would, in retrospect, seem to be such obviously ridiculous strategies. The desperation of those times can never be overstated.

Sadly, some people were only too willing to exploit that desperation; for example, in 1985 a former worker in a UK tractor factory began selling 'Excine 8531' tablets at £1.50 each. He claimed that *"Excine 8531 greatly reduces the risk of AIDS on the basis that a healthy body will always resist attacks by a virus far better than an unhealthy one."* [15] Unsurprisingly, there was no evidence of any type to support his claims. As late as 1999, a Florida couple Kenneth Thiefault and Mardol Barber were selling an 'Ozone Generator', which they claimed oxidised toxins in the body and cured AIDS. Happily, in both cases the perpetrators received jail sentences and/or large fines [16].

The Development of New Treatments

With the identification of HIV as the putative causative agent, an additional approach to treatment was added to those already underway. In essence, the approaches to treatment could be categorised as follows:

1) **Anti-viral treatments.** These are treatments that seek to either destroy the virus or prevent it increasing by blocking various stages of its reproductive cycle.

2) **Immuno-therapy.** These approaches seek to stimulate the body's natural immune system to mount a more effective response.

3) **Symptom management.** This was how the management of AIDS first started – treating the associated illnesses such as PCP or cytomegalovirus infection.

4) **Prophylaxis.** This is essentially a proactive version of symptom management, where individuals who are perceived to be vulnerable to particular types of illness are given smaller doses of medication at regular

intervals to keep the illness at bay. For example, 'aerosolised' pentamidine was given to people who had contracted or who were thought to be at risk of pneumonia.

Mainstream Treatment Options

Anti-virals

Once HIV was identified the search began for treatments that targeted the virus itself. The first anti-viral treatment to be adopted was AZT (azidothymidine, also known as zidovudine). Originally developed in the 60s as an anti-cancer drug, it had been shelved in the 70s when it failed to show sufficiently strong results. With the advent of AIDS it was brought off the shelf and tested in relation to HIV. The results were deemed to be sufficiently promising that it was patented by Burroughs-Wellcome in 1985 and approved by the US Food and Drug Administration (FDA) for use against HIV and AIDS in March 1987.

I was working at St Vincent's Hospital when AZT was introduced in Australia and remember that it was administered in very high doses. In fact the dosage was so high that it triggered various side effects, the most common being severe anaemia. In consequence, it was not only necessary to set up a clinic for the administration of AZT it was also necessary to bring recipients on to the ward at regular intervals to receive blood transfusions. If I remember correctly, AZT also had to be taken every four hours, which meant that it was impossible for anyone taking it to get a decent period of sleep. Unsurprisingly, this too took its toll on the health of those who were taking it.

Thankfully research soon showed that AZT was just as effective at much lower doses and that lowering of the dose saw the anaemia (and loss of sleep) disappear. However, even at a significantly lower dosage, AZT was still proving to be too toxic for some people. This was addressed in part by the FDA approval of a second anti-viral drug dideoxyinosine (ddI) in September 1989 and then dideooxycytidine (ddC) in May 1991. The approval of these new drugs also resolved another developing problem – HIV's increasing resistance to AZT. Obviously, being able to change drugs from time to time helped avoid this but there was an even greater breakthrough when it was realised that using the drugs in combination rather than one at a time greatly increased their impact. 'Combination therapy' has been the standard approach to HIV treatment ever since, with new anti-virals continuing to come onto the market.

Immunotherapy

Mainstream approaches to immunotherapy began as early as 1983, with the transplantation of bone marrow [17]. Other attempts have included transplants or injections of thymus tissue, frozen T4 cells, alpha interferon and Interleukin 2 [18].

Symptom Management and Prophylaxis

Symptom management and prophylaxis has also developed with new drugs being approved for the treatment of a range of conditions including PCP, cytomegalovirus and herpes simplex.

Self-administered Treatments

Given the speed and severity with which AIDS hit gay men as well as the slow progress in finding an effective long-term treatment it was more or less a necessity for people to find their own ways of minimising the impact. As well as the 'healthy living' options discussed earlier, people with HIV and AIDS were also researching and trying a range of alternative/additional treatments to those offered through mainstream health services.

They fall mainly into two of the aforementioned four categories – anti-viral and immunotherapy – although since a number of them have also been held to alleviate symptoms they could arguably be seen as symptom management and prophylaxis.

The list of alternative treatments is both extensive and ever-growing. Additionally, there is no universal agreement as to either the practice or the benefits of the various treatments, therefore a comprehensive summary is close to impossible. Nonetheless, here is a list a few of the substances and their claimed benefits to give some indication of the magnitude of the practice:

- Aloe vera – anti-viral and immunotherapeutic.
- Bitter melon – a Chinese vegetable; drinking juice extracted from the leaves is said to have anti-viral and immune-modulating effects.
- Chinese cucumber – from the same family as bitter melon, also known as Compound Q. This is said to have anti-viral effects.
- Hypericin – the active ingredient in St John's wort. Said to have anti-viral properties.

224

- Citrus seed extracts – said to have anti-viral, anti-bacterial and anti-fungal properties.
- Curcumin – an active ingredient of turmeric. Said to have anti-viral properties.
- DNCB – a benzene-based chemical used in photo finishing and air conditioning. Its main benefit is that it is immunotherapeutic but it has also been used to treat certain types of wart associated with HIV infection.

That so many alternative or supplemental approaches to HIV/AIDS management have been and continue to be used is indicative of the level of frustration at the paucity of 'conventional' treatment. But it is also indicative of the extraordinarily high level of participation in, and 'ownership' of, the treatment agenda by people with the disease. This is something that has characterised HIV/AIDS from the outset; that the people affected by it have educated themselves to the very highest levels about the nature of the condition and sought a central role in its management. This was particularly the case in the early days when it was very common for people with HIV/AIDS to have to educate their GPs and other clinicians about it so that they could then 'manage' the patient. Since levels of ignorance (and accompanying prejudice) were often quite profound, it was virtually a necessity for the 'patient' to present well-armed with the most up-to-date clinical and epidemiological information.

Of course, this role reversal of patient informing the doctor about a medical condition was not always welcomed by some practitioners who felt it undermined their role as 'medical expert'. Nonetheless, it happened and left many gay men and people living with HIV/AIDS with an expectation of a more participative model of medical management thereafter.

Route of Transmission

On 9 September 1983 the CDCs *Morbidity and Mortality Weekly Record* (MMWR) explicitly identified all major routes of HIV transmission as well as ruling out the possibility of transmission through casual contact:

"The occurrence of AIDS cases among homosexual men, IV drug abusers, persons with hemophilia, sexual partners of members of these groups, and recipients of blood transfusions is consistent with the hypothesis that AIDS is caused by an agent that is transmitted sexually or, less commonly, through contaminated needles or blood.

225

About 91 per cent of reported cases have occurred in these patient groups. Among the remaining cases, there has been no evidence that the disease was acquired through casual contact with AIDS patients or with persons in population groups with an increased incidence of AIDS. AIDS is not known to be transmitted through food, water, air, or environmental surfaces."[19]

Given the CDCs central role in coordinating and developing the response to the emerging health crisis, this article constituted the definitive statement on the issue. Sadly this prevented neither the deliberate scaremongering of moral entrepreneurs nor, even worse, Ronald Reagan's uninformed exacerbation of the prejudice against school student Ryan White when, in September 1985, he told a press conference:

"It is true that some medical sources had said that this cannot be communicated in any way other than the ones we already know and which would not involve a child being in the school. And yet medicine has not come forth unequivocally and said, 'This we know for a fact', that it is safe. And until they do, I think we just have to do the best we can with this problem. I can understand both sides of it." [20]

Epidemiology

The world first became aware of AIDS when it was detected in gay men in Western countries; shortly thereafter it was discovered in injecting drug users, haemophiliacs and, in the USA, people from Haiti. It was referred to by some people as 'the four H's' – homosexuals, heroin users, haemophiliacs and Haitians – and, of course, by others as 'the gay plague'. But not all Western cases of AIDS fell neatly into these groups; for example, in 1983 in France and Belgium the majority of cases were heterosexuals from, or with links to, Central Africa [21].

In that same year, the World Health Organisation's (WHO) first meeting to assess the global AIDS situation also showed different patterns of spread around the world. AIDS cases were reported across a broad range of continents and countries including North and South America, Europe, Australia, Japan, Haiti and Zaire (now the Democratic Republic of Congo). However, while this meeting marked the beginning of the WHO's global surveillance of AIDS, the lack of appropriate screening facilities in poor regions such as Africa meant that any accurate assessment of the situation was virtually impossible. For example, there was considerable debate as to whether the

226

so-called 'slim disease' that had been prevalent in Kinshasa in the late 70s and Uganda and Tanzania in the early 80s was, in fact, a manifestation of AIDS (22).

Nonetheless, a greater focus was placed on Africa in light of established connections with the French and Belgian cases as well as some of the Haitian cases diagnosed in the USA. And while the numbers remained vague, studies of specific African outbreaks repeatedly identified heterosexual transmission as the main route. For example, in Rwanda:

"... an association of an urban environment, a relatively high income and heterosexual promiscuity could be a risk factor for AIDS." (23)

In the Democratic Republic of Congo:

"... a strong indication of heterosexual transmission ..." (24)

The focus on Africa also resulted in the theory that the virus had been present in humans on that continent for several decades – possibly as early as the late 19th or early 20th century. Furthermore, it was argued that HIV was a transmutation of simian immunodeficiency viruses (SIVs) – that is, viruses that infect monkeys – and that its emergence in humans was as a result of it crossing the animal/human barrier:

"Our best estimate for when HIV entered humans is 1908, but it could have been from 1884 to 1924." (25)

This is generally thought to have occurred through the preparation and/or eating of infected monkey flesh.

It has been further estimated that by the 1960s some 2000 people in Africa were infected with HIV (26). A United Nations report has also suggested that:

"Most of the available epidemiological data indicate that the extensive spread of HIV started in sub-Saharan Africa in the late 1970s. By the early 1980s HIV was found in a geographic band stretching from West Africa across to the Indian Ocean." (27)

A sudden increase in the numbers of opportunistic infections such as cryptococcal meningitis, KS, and PCP in Kinshasa in Zaire (now the Democratic Republic of Congo) in the 1970s has been taken as evidence of the first 'AIDS epidemic'. Zaire is also suggested as the virus's 'departure point' from Africa, being transported by migrants to the Caribbean island of Haiti and the former colonial powers of Belgium and France. From Haiti it reached the USA either through Haitian migrants or American gay men holidaying in Haiti.

227

The history of AIDS in Africa raises some interesting issues, not least of which the fact that apparently large outbreaks of the disease occurred almost a decade before its detection in the West with little apparent global awareness or concern. In a similar vein, it is interesting to note that the first two recorded AIDS diagnoses in Africa were two white, gay South African men in 1982 [28].

In 1990, the United Nations estimated that there were some 8.1 million adults and children living with HIV globally, with 5.7 million of those living in sub-Saharan Africa, approximately one million living in the United States and 360,000 living in Western and Central Europe [29]. Of these figures:

"... the predominant mode of transmission worldwide continues to be heterosexual contact (75% of total spread)." [30]

References

1. Pneumocyctis Pneumonia – Los Angeles. *Morbidity and Mortality Weekly Report*. 1981 June 5, Vol. 3 No.21.

2. Kaposi's sarcoma and Pneumocystis pneumonia among homosexual men – New York City and California. *Morbidity and Mortality Weekly Report*. 1981 Jul 3; 30(25); 305-8.

3. duBois, R.M., Braithwaite, M.A., Mikhail, J.R., Batten, J.C. Primary Pneumocystis carinii and cytomegalovirus infections. *The Lancet*. 1981 Dec 12; 2(8259):1339.

4. Hughes, Sally Smith. AIDS Chronology in *The AIDS Epidemic in San Francisco: The Medical Response, 1981-1984, Volume IV*. San Francisco AIDS Oral History Series, Online Archive of California.
   [Online] Available at
   http://archive.org/stream/aidsepidemicinsf01chinrich/aidsepidemicinsf01chinrich_djvu.txt
   Accessed February 2015.

5. Ziegler, John. *Early Theories of Etiology in The AIDS Epidemic in San Francisco: The Medical Response, 1981-1984, Volume IV*. San Francisco AIDS Oral History Series, Online Archive of California.
   [Online] Available at
   http://archive.org/stream/aidsepidemicinsf01chinrich/aidsepidemicinsf01chinrich_djvu.txt
   Accessed April 2014.

6. See, for example, the view that the virus now known to cause KS is transmitted much more efficiently through anal sex than vaginal sex in Chandan, Kira., Madnani, Nina, Desai, Devendra, Deshpande, Ramesh. AIDS-associated Kaposi's sarcoma in a heterosexual male. *Dermatology Online Journal*, 8 (2) 2002.
   [Online] Available at
   http://escholarship.org/uc/item/2304k6w2
   Accessed April 2014.

7. Ziegler, John. *Early Theories of Etiology*.

8. Whittow, Hugh. AIDS Is the Wrath of God, Says Vicar. *The Sun*. 7 February 1985.

9. Hay, Louise. 2009. *You Can Heal Your Life*. London: Hay House, p147.

10. *You Can Heal Your Life*, pp133-134.

11. *Brief History* from the website *Duesberg on AIDS*.
    [Online] Available at
    www.duesberg.com/about/index.html
    Accessed April 2014.

12. Duesberg, Peter. A multibillion $ quiz: *Is AIDS a viral or a chemical epidemic?* Powerpoint presentation given at Lew Rockwell conference, Foster City. 1-2 December 2006, p22.

13. Bremmer, Charles. Cast Out for an AIDS Heresy. *The Times*, London. 11 May 1992.

14. *You Can Heal Your Life*, p147.

15. Fake anti-AIDS pill sold to gays. *The Sun*. 7 March 1985.

16. See, for example, *HIV/AIDS Historical Time Line 1995-1999*, US Food and Drug Administration website.
    [Online] Available at
    http://www.fda.gov/ForConsumers/ByAudience/ForPatientAdvocates/HIVandAIDSActivities/ucm151079.htm
    Accessed April 2014.

17. Hassett, J.M. et al. Bone marrow Transplantation in AIDS. *New England Journal of Medicine*, 309:665, 1983.

18. See, for example, Vadas, Mathew. 1988. Immunoregulation in Management of HIV Infection. In *Report of the Third National Conference on AIDS, 4-6 August 1988*, Hobart, Australia, Australian Government Publishing Service, pp539-542.

19. *Current Trends Update: Acquired Immunodeficiency Syndrome (AIDS)* – United States, MMWR September 09, 1983/32 32(35); pp465-7.

20. The American Presidency Project. *The President's News Conference, September 17 1985*.
    [Online] Available at
    http://www.presidency.ucsb.edu/ws/?pid=39125
    Accessed April 2014.

21. Weller, I., Crawford, D.H., Iliescu, V., MacLennan, K., Sutherland, S., Tedder, R.S. and Adler, M.W. 1984. Homosexual men in London: Lymphadenopathy, immune status, and Epstein-Barr virus infection. *Annals of the New York Academy of Science*, Volume 437, edited by Selikoff I.J, Teirstein A.S. and Hirschman S.Z., The New York Academy of Sciences, pp248-249.

22. See, for example, Serwadda D., Mugerwa R.D., Sewankambo N.K. et al. 1985. *Slim disease: a new disease in Uganda and its association with HTLV-III infection. The Lancet*, 2:849-52 compared with Kamradt, T., Niese, D., Vogel F. 1985. Slim disease (AIDS). The Lancet 1985; ii: 1425.

23. Van de Perre, P., Rouvroy D., Lepage, P. et al. 1984. Acquired Immunodeficiency Syndrome

in Rwanda. *The Lancet*, 2:62-5.
[Online] Available from
http://www.avert.org/history-aids-1986.htm#footnote79_y3cy11m
Accessed April 2014.

24. Piot P., Quinn T.C., Taelman H. et al. 1984. Acquired Immunodeficiency Syndrome in a heterosexual population in Zaire. *The Lancet*, 2:65-69.
[Online] Available at
http://www.avert.org/history-aids-1986.htm#footnote80_gd2t3nm
Accessed April 2014.

25. Worobey, M. et al., Direct evidence of extensive diversity of HIV-1 in Kinshasa by 1960. *Nature*, 455, pp661-664, 2 October 2008, DOI:10.1038/nature07390.

26. Sample, Ian. Hunt for origin of HIV pandemic ends at chimpanzee colony in Cameroon. *The Guardian*. 26 May 2006.
[Online] Available at
http://www.theguardian.com/world/2006/may/26/aids.topstories3
Accessed April 2014.

27. Department of Economic and Social Affairs, United Nations Secretariat. 2003. *A History of the HIV/AIDS Epidemic with Emphasis on Africa*, paper from the Workshop on HIV/AIDS and Adult Mortality in Developing Countries, New York, 8-13 September 2003.

28. Ras G.J. et al. Acquired Immunodeficiency Syndrome: A report of two South African cases. *South African Medical Journal* 64, 23 July 1983.

29. HIV estimates with uncertainty bounds. *UNAIDS Report of Global AIDS Epidemic 1990-2013*.
Retrieved from
www.unaids.org/en/dataanalysis/knowyourepidemic, April 2014

30. Gayle, Helene D. and Hill, Gena L. 2001. Global Impact of Human Immunodeficiency Virus and AIDS. *American Society of Microbiology Clinical Microbiology Reviews*, Clin. Microbiol. Rev. April 2001 vol. 14 no. 2 pp327-335.

Part Three - Press Coverage

On 5 June 1981 the *Associated Press* and the *Los Angeles Times* covered the MMWR's first report on the five gay men with PCP. The following day the *San Francisco Chronicle* covered it in *A Pneumonia That Strikes Gay Males* [1].

One of the first uses of the term 'gay plague' in the US press seems to be *'Gay Plague' Baffling Medical Detectives*, which appeared in the *Philadelphia Daily News* on 9 August 1982.

The first article on AIDS in the UK's mainstream press is thought to be a report about the establishment of the CDC's Kaposi's Sarcoma and Opportunistic Infections (KSOI) task force, *Inquiry Into Cancer and Gays*, in *The Guardian* newspaper on 29 August 1981. *Gay News* ran its first story, *"Gay Cancer" Scare*, on 12 November 1981. The first recorded use of the term 'gay plague' in the UK press seems to be a *Sunday Times* article of 27 March 1983 *(What Killed Gay Plague Man?)*. On 2 May 1983 there was a bit of a rush to use the term: *The Daily Mirror* reported *Alert Over "Gay Plague"*; the *Daily Telegraph* announced *"Gay plague" May Lead to Blood Ban on Homosexuals*; and *The Sun* advised *Watchdogs in "Gay Plague" Blood Probe* [2]. This may have been a result of the heightened awareness of AIDS generated by the broadcast of the BBC's 'Horizon' documentary *Killer in the Village* on 25 April.

In Australia, *Time (Australia)* magazine ran a story, *Opportunistic Diseases: A Puzzling New Syndrome Afflicts Homosexual Men*, in December 1981 with *The Sydney Morning Herald* publishing *Fatal Homosexual Disease Linked to Lack of Immunity* on 2 January 1982. The term 'gay plague' appeared in *The Australian* newspaper – *"Gay Plague" Epidemic Sweeping US* – on 17 July 1982 and again in *The Australian* two days later with *Australia Could Be Next on the List for "Gay Plague"* [3].

AIDS in the British Press

During my time as as a full-time volunteer at the Terrence Higgins Trust (THT) in London I witnessed a huge increase in the volume of phone calls.

And yet there had been no significant changes in the spread of AIDS: the rate and method of transmission remained the same; there had been no sudden jump in the number of AIDS diagnoses.

232

What had changed, however, was that AIDS – as 'the Gay Plague', of course – had become the preoccupation of the mainstream press. It appeared in front page headlines on an almost daily basis and dominated much of the content on other pages too. Sadly, the degree of coverage wasn't matched by the degree of factual accuracy; for example, according to *The Sun* newspaper, AIDS was *"Spreading like wildfire"* (this claim being made in an article entitled *20 Things You Didn't Know About AIDS!*). [4] To get a better understanding of this, I looked at hundreds of British press cuttings for the period October 1984 to October 1985 to see what kind of messages they were sending out. The most obvious message, simply by virtue of the huge increase in media coverage, was that AIDS had suddenly become 'a problem': exactly what that problem was would be up to the reader to decide – ably assisted by a range of vivid headlines. I identified a number of key themes (and, indeed, a subsequent study of Australian press coverage identified identical themes, which leads me to suspect that these were fairly global).

1. **Infectivity**

   AIDS was presented as being more far more infectious than it actually was. The use of the word 'plague' implies a level of infectivity that simply did not exist. This highly contagious nature was reinforced with headlines like *Cough Can Spread AIDS, Warns Doc* (*The Sun*, 31 August 1985), *It's Spreading Like Wildfire* (*The Sun*, 1 February, 1985), *Brutal Truth About AIDS: No One's Safe* (*The Sun*, 12 August 1985) *Kiss of Death* (*The Star*, 27 September 1985), *A Million Will Have AIDS in Six Years* (*Daily Mail*, 10 January 1985), *AIDS Threat to One in Five: Gays Are Warned* (*The Star*, 4 February 1985) and *March of the Gay Plague* (*News of the World*, 24 February 1985).

   As if to reinforce the notion of infectiousness, another theme implied that AIDS was everywhere. There was no escaping it: it was reaching into every corner of society, every major British institution. For example, *AIDS on the QE2* (*The Sun*, 13 February 1985), *AIDS Death Shock at BBC* (*Sunday Mirror*, 17 February 1985), *AIDS: Three British Airways Crew Die* (*The Sun*, 18 February 1985), [Government] *Minister killed by AIDS* (*News of the World*, 25 August 1985).

233

2. **The Cover Up**

Meanwhile, headlines such as *Storm Over AIDS Priest Cover-Up By Hospital* (*Daily Express*, 2 January 1985) and *Scandal of AIDS Cover Up on QE2* (*Sunday People*,17 February 1985) suggested that people had been at risk but deliberately kept in the dark. The reality was that they had not been at risk and therefore there was no reason to tell them and - certainly in the QE2 case, where the individual was still alive - they had every right to confidentiality. Indeed, it is arguable that, in the environment of press-generated hysteria, telling people unnecessarily would have been counter-productive. Would people really have accepted that they weren't at risk and were being advised merely as a matter of courtesy?

The notion of conspiracies and 'cover-ups' had already been generated by the likes of the *Daily Mail*, who had taken it particularly badly when their 1983 article *Hospitals Using Killer Blood* had been declared 'alarmist' by the Press Council. In consequence, when a second British haemophiliac died from AIDS in November 1984, the *Daily Mail* ran indignant editorials: *Those Guilty of Muffling the Alarm* on 22 November and *AIDS: This scandalous Cover-Up* (*Mail on Sunday*, 25 November 1984) three days later.

And their front page coverage of the second haemophiliac death epitomised the tabloid view of 'the real problem':

3. **'The Problem'**

On 19 November 1984, the *Daily Mail* ran a banner headline, *AIDS Virus Kills Man in Britain*. The subsequent article then described how:

"Doctors faced a nightmare problem last night after the death of a man in Britain from the mysterious disease AIDS."

It was only when readers got to the last line of the article – on page 2 – that they were told, *"There have been about 90 [cases of AIDS] in Britain, including 37 deaths."* The majority of those deaths were gay men – who had been dying since 1981 – yet the headline clearly suggested that only one man had died to date. The article made it clear that the *"nightmare problem"* that doctors faced was the fact that the most recent death wasn't a *"homosexual or self-injecting*

234

drug addict", whom the paper described as *"most likely to catch – and become carriers [of AIDS]"*. He was a haemophiliac who had contracted AIDS through a blood transfusion.

That the *Mail* quickly adds that homosexuals are most likely to become *"carriers"* after pointing out that they are most at risk speaks volumes. The impact on gay men is unimportant; their main role in this crisis is as vectors not than victims. 'The problem' therefore, was that AIDS was breaking out of its 'host' community to infect 'innocent' people.

This theme was repeated elsewhere, not least because of AIDS' designation as 'the gay plague' or 'gay bug', along with the inference that it was actually generated by the gay 'lifestyle'. But what was even more insidious was the inference that gay men were deliberately infecting the blood supplies. Thus, *Blood From Gay Donor Puts 41 at AIDS Risk* (*The Sun*, 21 December 1984), *One Man Caused AIDS Outbreak* [... *"a homosexual who was a regular blood donor*] (*The Times*, 24 December 1984), *Britain threatened by Gay Virus Plague* (*Mail on Sunday*, 6 January 1985), *Gay Plague Brings New Havoc* (*News of the World*, 5 November 1985).

4. Establishing Priorities

While gay men were portrayed as less deserving of sympathy than the so-called 'innocent' victims, another group regularly demonised by the media suddenly found themselves rehabilitated. These were young offenders: usually 'thugs' and 'hooligans' – until the prison chaplain at Chelmsford Prison died of AIDS in January 1985. Then they became *"terrified young offenders"*, *"teenagers"* and *"lads"*. (*AIDS kills teenagers' prison chaplain*, *Daily Mail*, 1 February 1985; *Barricades Threat in AIDS Fear Jail*, *The People*, 3 February 1985; *Gay Plague Seals Off Death Prison*, *The Sun*, 6 February 1985.)

But even when gay men were being viewed as social pariahs, there was one man who beat them to the position of 'lowest of the low' – the left-wing leader of the Greater London Council, Ken Livingstone. In an interview on Warwick University's closed-circuit television station, he had joked that Conservatives should be infected with AIDS. In an extraordinary show of hypocrisy, the press pounced on him for his 'insensitive' comments: *Sick Sex Jibe by Red Ken* (*The Sun*, 10 December 1984), *Red Ken's AIDS Joke Falls Flat* (*Daily Mirror*, 10 December 1984).

5. The Solution

Since the problem was AIDS escaping from its host community, then the suggested solutions were predominantly around keeping it contained. *The Sun* called for the exclusion of gay and bisexual men from blood donation: *Now Slap a Ban on Gay Donors* (22 December 1984); *AIDS: It's Time to Act – Blood Donors Should Declare That They're Not Homosexual* (9 February 1985). But even they realised that this was not as simple as it may sound:

"We appreciate that by ceasing to be donors you might make people you know suspect that you are gay. But that is surely a small price to pay."

The fact that the paper's relentless homophobia made it so difficult for gay men to come out is conveniently overlooked. Nor was there any call for additional services to support gay men, the population most affected by AIDS in the UK.

Government plans to detain people with AIDS against their will also received widespread – and uncritical – coverage (for example, *AIDS: Law to Isolate Victims* (*Daily Mail*, 22 March 1985) and *AIDS Victims Face Forced Quarantine* (*Daily Mirror*, 11 February 1985). The plans were indefensible, not least because they flew in the face of expert opinion on the subject and reinforced the erroneous notion that AIDS was highly infectious and that people with AIDS deliberately sought to put others at risk.

6. Guidelines for Public Reaction

Just in case members of the public weren't clear on how hysterical they should get, the press gave them a few examples: *BANNED! AIDS-Fear Club Ousts Gay Couple* (*The Sun*, 5 February 1985), *Gays Put Mrs Mopps in a Sweat Over AIDS: 'Work in Your Gloves' Order to Theatre Cleaners'* (*The Sun*, 19 February 1985), *Ban on AIDS Corpse* (*The Star*, 16 January 1985), *Pub Ban on Gays in AIDS 'Panic'* (*The Sun*, 8 February 1985), *Hotel Bans Gay Chef Who Took AIDS Test* (*The Sun*, 14 February 1985), *AIDS: Now Ambulance Men Ban Kiss of Life* (*Daily Mirror*, 21 February 1985), *Firemen Ban Kiss of Life* (*News of*

the World, 17 February 1985), *Warders at AIDS Chaplain's Jail Ban Transfers* (*Daily Telegraph*, 6 February 1985). Of course it is arguable that the papers were merely reporting these behaviours, not advocating them. But the reality is they often did so uncritically (and, in some cases, almost gleefully as if to vindicate their own approach to the issue). And by seeking out and reporting each isolated case of over-reaction they were engaging in what sociologists call 'amplification'; that is, giving a sense that the issue was far more common than it actually was. This, in turn, plays into the 'no smoke without fire' mentality: that is, the belief that there must be some basis to these people's actions. There wasn't, but the hysteria grew.

7. The Experience of People with AIDS

The selective use of the most lurid and severe cases of AIDS suggested that an AIDS diagnosis would, inevitably, lead to a short and tormented life: *Seven-Month Hell of Man Dying From AIDS* (*Daily Mail*, 20 November 1984), *My Doomed Son's Gay Plague Agony* (*News of the World*, 30 December 1984), *Victims Of Gay Plague Long To Die; Torment Haunts Final Sad Weeks* (*News of the World*, 6 January 1985), *The Outcast Under a Sentence of Death* (*Daily Express*, 17 January 1985), *Heartbreak Plea of AIDS Victim* ["Don't let me die"] (*Daily Mirror*, 8 February 1985), *Blind Hell of Dying Earl* (*News of the World*, 25 August, 1985).

These lurid tales were far from representative of the AIDS experience but the 'freak show' approach obviously sold far more copies than a more balanced reportage. In the process, the impact on other people living with this mysterious new condition, including those who were newly diagnosed, was ignored. Similarly, anyone considering a check-up might have deferred in case it confirmed their worst fears, thus delaying access to early – and more effective – medical management of their condition.

8. Moral Enterprise

It was impossible to get away from moral enterprise in the first decade or so of the AIDS crisis and this was certainly reflected in press reports. The most

237

obvious form was the presentation of the opinions of others – *AIDS is the Wrath of God, Says Vicar* (*The Sun*, 7 February 1985), *Joan [Collins] Blasts Sins of Hollywood* (*News of the World*, 28 July 1985), *AIDS Victims to be 'Struck Off' by the Top People's Bible,* (*Daily Express*, 25 February 1985). But sometimes the newspaper itself felt obliged to preach: the most notorious being *Permissive Hosts Must Pay the Bill* by Digby Anderson in *The Times*, 5 December 1984.

Intrinsic to this was the notion of innocence and culpability. Those who had contracted HIV through contaminated blood or blood products were repeatedly referred to as 'innocent' victims. The term was never applied to gay men or injecting drug users, all of whom were deemed – implicitly or explicitly – to be somehow responsible for their situation, as illustrated in the aforementioned *Daily Mail* article *AIDS Virus Kills Man in Britain*.

An Attempt at Improving AIDS Reporting

In May 1984 the National Union of Journalists Equality Council issued a leaflet entitled *AIDS and the Media*:

"... in the belief and hope that NUJ members will want to raise the standard of public discussion of this potentially serious health problem."

The leaflet included four specific points to avoid. These were:

1) **Inflation of figures and incidence** – *"AIDS has nothing to do with wildfires or icebergs. Such clichés should be pensioned off ... In 1983 not only The Guardian but also the Daily Express gave American figures for the number of cases as the number of deaths with AIDS."*

2) **Confusing AIDS with other diseases** – *"AIDS is not a 'plague': it's just not that infectious ... Mixed-up reporting of (genital) herpes and AIDS on television programmes such as BBC1's Panorama persuaded one Isle of Man viewer that herpes is the female and AIDS the male version of the same disease!"*

3) **Stereotyping people with AIDS** – *"The widow of the first British man with haemophilia to die with AIDS complained bitterly about newspaper reports*

describing it as a 'gay disease', as he wasn't gay. She could have added that there was no proof that the blood donation(s) which lead to his death were given by gay men."

4) **Invasions of privacy** – "In view of the stigma which sensational publicity has attached to AIDS there is a strong case for withholding the names and identifying details even of people who are dead, unless they or their relatives have given permission. One Sunday newspaper got hold of the name and address of a gay man with AIDS, interviewed his neighbours in an effort to get his 'story', and threatened to print a photo of his house if he did not cooperate. Perhaps some element of residual decency, aside from the threat of a High Court injunction, aborted this plan."

References

1. A Pneumonia That Strikes Gay Males. *San Francisco Chronicle.* 6 June 1981.

2. Meldrum, Julian. 1984. *AIDS through the British media.* London: AIDS Action Group, p5.6.

3. French, Robert and Duffin, Ross. 1986. *Mossies could spread AIDS.* Sydney: Gay History Project, p19.

4. Cliff, Peter and Toulson, Leslie. *20 Things you didn't know about AIDS. The Sun*, London. 1 February 1985.

Part Four - Government Responses to AIDS

Governments responded to the AIDS crisis in very different ways. The responses of US, UK and Australian governments, for example, ranged from appalling to exceptional. Opinions differ as to the commitment of some governments, particularly in the UK, so it is helpful to have some measures by which we can evaluate these. For my part, I would suggest these are:

- the speed of response
- the aims of the response – for example, whom it targeted and why
- the nature of the response.

The Speed of the Response

The Reagan administration's response to the emerging AIDS crisis – covered in the chapter 'Under Attack' – was by far the slowest and most ineffectual, despite the USA being the worst hit western country. Reagan's lack of political will over the issue is demonstrated by the fact that he didn't even mention the word AIDS in public until 1985.

The lack of urgency was also reflected in the limited resources that were invested in treatment research. In April 1988 Dr Anthony Fauci, Director the National Institutes of Health AIDS Program, told a White House sub-committee that research was being hampered by a lack of staff and shortage of office and laboratory space [1]. AIDS activist Vito Russo articulated the views of many when he said:

"And we read on the front page of The New York Times last Saturday that Anthony Fauci now says that all sorts of promising drugs for treatment haven't even been tested in the last two years because he can't afford to hire people to test them. We're supposed to be grateful that this story has appeared in the newspaper after two years. Nobody wonders why some reporter didn't dig up that story and print it 18 months ago, before Fauci got dragged before a Congressional hearing.

How many people are dead in the last two years who might be alive today if those drugs had been tested more quickly?" [2]

And Russo was one of many to compare the slow response to investigating AIDS to the speed with which the cause of Legionnaire's disease was established, following the death of 34 people in July 1976:

241

"Legionnaire's disease was happening to them because it hit people who looked like them, sounded like them, who were the same colour as them. And that fucking story about a couple of dozen people hit the front page of every newspaper and magazine in this country and it stayed there until that mystery got solved [in January 1977]."[3]

In the UK, the government did not act or assign additional resources for the management of HIV/AIDS until 1985, despite the first AIDS death occurring in 1981. Prior to this there appears to have been an expectation that the issue would be managed within existing health service resources – which were already subject to budget cuts – or by voluntary organisations such as the Terrence Higgins Trust. And, despite being at the front line of the emerging crisis, doctors and surgeons didn't receive official guidelines until 1985.

In January 1985, *The Guardian* newspaper published an article *'Too little, too late' to Prevent AIDS Crisis* [4], in which both the Chairman of the Terrence Higgins Trust, Tony Whitehead, and an unnamed *"leading London consultant who has experience of dealing with AIDS"* criticised the lack of resources available for the management of people with AIDS. On 7 February 1985 the Royal College of Nursing spokesperson, Richard Wells, described the government's response as *"derisory"* during a television interview:

"We need an investment in those centres which are seeing the majority of AIDS cases. It is not happening. There has been no investment in the education of the public or health staff. The only organisation disseminating information to patients, the Terrence Higgins Trust, can only afford to operate for two hours a day. That is derisory." [5]

And it wasn't until later in the year that the Expert Advisory Group on AIDS was established.

In contrast to the USA and UK, the Australian government responded immediately. In 1983 – the year of the first Australian AIDS death – Federal Health Minister Neal Blewett began to bring together community organisations, researchers and clinicians to develop an effective public health policy for the management of HIV/AIDS.

In 1984 he established the National Advisory Council on AIDS (NACAIDS):

"... to act as the government's peak advisory committee on prevention education; care and treatment of those living with HIV/AIDS; and social policy for the entire Australian population and groups at high risk of acquiring HIV infection." [6]

He also established the AIDS Task Force to bring together HIV/AIDS clinical and scientific experts to:

"... make recommendations on the allocation of HIV/AIDS budgets for applied medical, scientific and social research." [7]

In 1985 the Australian government also established the Parliamentary Liaison Group on AIDS to keep politicians up to date with the way HIV/AIDS was impacting and the policy options available to the government.

The Aims of the Response

When considering the 'aims' of Reagan's response it needs to be noted that, for the greater part of the decade, he did very little in the way of offering a concrete response. In consequence, it is hard not to conclude that the main aim was not to get involved at all. For example, in September 1985, when a journalist sought his opinion on whether children with HIV should be allowed to attend school, he manifested (or feigned) a complete ignorance about what researchers had established two years previously about HIV transmission. *("And yet medicine has not come forth unequivocally and said, 'This we know for a fact', that it is safe").*

His main concern was not losing votes and to do that he had to avoid uncomfortable realities. He deliberately evaded the sensitive –but very real- issue of HIV/AIDS-related discrimination; arguably because, on this occasion, it was being experienced by a 13 year-old boy – Ryan White - and his family. Since the White family's circumstances did not lend itself to a simplistic moral sound byte about 'innocent' versus 'culpable' AIDS victims, Reagan had no real, practical response. The closing line of his statement, *"I can understand both sides of it"* was classic 'political speak' for *"I'd rather not get involved".*

Two years later, when he finally declared a goal – to find a cure for AIDS – he left no one in any doubt as to the reasons behind his change of heart:

"Some time ago I heard the story of a man who received what turned out to be a transfusion of blood contaminated with the AIDS virus. He was infected, and in turn his wife was infected. And within two years they both died. Well, I'm determined that we'll find a cure for AIDS." [8]

In other words, it was time to act because – in his opinion, at least - 'innocent' people were now being infected.

243

While there was no doubt that Reagan's UK counterpart Margaret Thatcher was far more aware of the issue, her government's initial response seemed to focus more on containment than meeting the needs of those already affected. In February 1985, the Earl of Caithness told the House of Lords that the government was *"... strengthening its efforts to discourage those in high risk groups from donating blood"* [9]. The following week Health Minister Kenneth Clarke announced the enactment of the 1984 Public Health and Control of Diseases Act, which included powers to detain people with AIDS who were perceived to be 'a danger to others'. According to *The Guardian* newspaper, the government's Chief Medical Officer, Donald Aitchison, suggested that possible cases might include *"... a sufferer who was vomiting blood and refused to go into hospital and a patient in hospital who was delirious and attempted to leave"* [10].

In September 1985, with 2935 HIV diagnoses in the UK [11] the government gave the Terrence Higgins Trust £35,000 to produce leaflets and fund the telephone helpline. Prior to this the organisation had relied on charitable donations and a £17,000 grant from the Greater London Council (a grant challenged in the High Court by Westminster's Conservative-led Council). In December 1985, four years after the first UK AIDS death, the government allocated a further £6.3 million. This included £2.5million to London hospitals, £2.5million for a public health education campaign, £750,000 for screening blood donations, £270,000 for haemophiliac centres and £100,000 for training AIDS counsellors in the NHS.

By 1985 in Australia, the organisations created by the government were already at work developing an effective response to HIV/AIDS that would include:

- "peer-based, direct and explicit preventive education campaigns directed both at high-risk groups and the general public
- widespread introduction of subsidised needle and syringe exchanges
- rapid expansion of methadone maintenance treatment
- access to free, anonymous and universal HIV testing
- subsidised access to azidothymidine (AZT) and subsequent ARV treatment
- general advocacy of the need to adopt safer sexual practices, especially the use of condoms" [12].

The Nature of the Response

The Reagan administration's response eschewed an evidence-based approach in favour of a set of conservative moral values. This was characterised in part by the sustained exclusion of anyone who was directly affected by the virus or anyone who was believed to hold 'radical' views such as teaching sex education in schools. When Surgeon General C. Everett Koop – appointed for his extreme conservative views – disappointed his conservative masters by using evidence to challenge notions such as compulsory testing and quarantining he too was sidelined: this included exclusion from the Presidential Commission on HIV, which Reagan had stacked with pro-family, anti-condom advocates opposed to sex education in schools.

The morality line continued with the ban on federal funding of needle exchange programmes (which is still in place at the time of writing) and a ban on the use of federal funds for AIDS education materials that *"promote or encourage, directly or indirectly, homosexual activities"*.

In the UK, the government did take a pragmatic approach to tackling the issue – once it finally started to take action. The Expert Advisory Group on AIDS included representatives of all the key players involved in the AIDS field, including representatives from the Terrence Higgins Trust. But morality wasn't too far from the surface in the form of Margaret Thatcher whose repeated demands for changes to the first government AIDS education programme in 1986 led to it becoming entirely counter-productive:

"One of the drafts contained the following frank explanation: 'During sexual intercourse, minute breaks may occur in the walls of the vagina. It is through these that the infected semen passes. As the rectum is far more delicate than the vagina, it is more easily damaged. This means anal intercourse is the easiest way of being infected.' But this was excised from the final version on the firm instruction of Margaret Thatcher. On her suggestion, the term 'anal intercourse' became first 'back passage intercourse' and finally the approved 'rectal sex'.

'The department tried to keep her out of it as much as possible,' one civil servant remembers. 'At one point, after she had seen a draft, we got a message from Nigel Wicks [her Principal Private Secretary] which said, "She wants to know if they have

to go in the newspapers." We asked him where else they were supposed to go. He said, "She was wondering about lavatory walls."'

There was no mention of the words 'condom' or 'rubber', both of which were considered too explicit. Instead, use of a 'sheath' was advised, a word that many people cruising the clubs had never heard before."[13]

A few months after the first AIDS 'campaign' the British Medical Journal reported the results of a survey conducted at Southampton General Hospital. It found that:

- before the campaign 5% thought there was a vaccine against AIDS: after the campaign 10% did
- before the campaign 10% believed AIDS was transmitted through the sharing of washing, eating and drinking utensils: after the campaign 14% did
- before the campaign, 48% didn't know what the acronym AIDS stood for: after the campaign 59% didn't

Despite the obvious failure of the campaign, attitudes hadn't changed much by the time a second campaign was rolled out in 1987. This included the delivery of education leaflets to every household in the UK:

"There was talk of not sending leaflets to the elderly; before this was ruled out as too impractical it was suggested the guidelines should be withheld from anyone whose first name was Gladys, Albert or Daisy."[14]

Additionally, the government decided to put the telephone numbers of the Terrence Higgins Trust and the London Lesbian and Gay Switchboard on the leaflets – but offered no funding to either organisation to help them manage the immense workload generated by this. In consequence, Switchboard's phone lines collapsed after becoming overloaded by the number of calls generated.

By September 1987, the British government was providing £466,000 in funds to the Terrence Higgins Trust; the organisation that had managed the AIDS crisis in the UK from the outset and that the government itself had seen fit to promote in its 'educational' literature. One of the groups served by the Trust was gay and bisexual men, who made up the majority of HIV and AIDS cases in the UK. Meanwhile, in November 1987, the government gave £10 million to the Haemophilia Society to help them set up a trust fund for haemophiliacs infected through contaminated blood products [15]. This was yet another manifestation of the 'innocent' versus 'culpable' perspective on people with

HIV/AIDS. And then, of course, the government introduced Section 28 of the Local Government Act in 1988, which threatened action against local authorities that 'promoted' homosexuality. It offered the perfect excuse for conservative local authorities to avoid HIV/AIDS prevention activities and even more progressive councils became reluctant on the grounds that simply discussing homosexual behaviour might be deemed to constitute 'promotion'.

Ultimately, it's hard not to conclude that the British government's response was driven by a moral and political agenda, rather than an objective assessment of need. Certainly the failure to develop a national HIV/AIDS Strategy meant that there was no consensus on the management of the issue, nor any sense of where resources might come from. People with HIV/AIDS were already facing an uncertain future: the government's failure to commit to a national strategy meant that AIDS services were too.

By contrast, the Australian government undertook a massive campaign to involve all possible stakeholders at every stage of the development of a national HIV/AIDS strategy. This included all of the major political parties as well as each individual state, since the delivery of healthcare was shared between state and federal governments.

In 1986 a number of consultative committees were established to consult with stakeholders nationwide as part of a detailed needs assessment for the national HIV/AIDS strategy. The committees looked at a range of issues including the needs of Aborigines and Torres Strait Islanders, injecting drug users, men who have sex with other men, haemophiliacs, and sex workers. In each case a discussion document was produced detailing the findings then widely distributed to seek further input on how the issues might be addressed. Only when this stage was complete was the first draft of the national strategy produced for further comment.

In 1987 the final version of Australia's National HIV/AIDS strategy was published. As part of this each state was then required to produce its own strategic plan demonstrating how it would implement the national strategy at a local level. Another requirement was that half of the money spent by state and federal governments should go to community-based organisations.

However, despite bipartisan political support at a national level, there was a predictable reaction from right-wing state governments: Western Australia, Tasmania and Queensland refused to decriminalise homosexuality and in Tasmania

247

needle exchanges weren't established until 1993. In Queensland the government refused to provide needle exchanges, distribute educational materials or support an AIDS Council in their state. The Federal Health Minister Neal Blewitt responded by providing the money for the Queensland AIDS Council through the Catholic organisation the Sisters of Mercy [16]. Needle exchanges finally began in 1990 after the Conservative state government was thrown out of office following a major corruption scandal.

248

References

1. Kahn, Arthur D. 2005 (reprint). *AIDS, the Winter War: A Testing of America*. Lincoln, Nebraska: iUniverse, p212.

2. Russo, Vito. *Why We Fight*. Transcript of speech delivered at ACT UP demonstration in Albany, New York, 9 May 1988.

3. *Why We Fight*.

4. de Jongh, Nicholas. *'Too little, too late' to prevent AIDS crisis*. The Guardian, London. 21 January 1985.

5. Veitch, Andrew. *Government's 'derisory' response to AIDS crisis*. The Guardian, London. 8 February 1985.

6. Bowtell, William. 2006. *Australia, in Fighting a Rising Tide: The Response to AIDS in East Asia* (eds. Tadashi Yamamoto and Satako Itoh). Tokyo: Japan Center for International Exchange, p31.

7. *Australia, in Fighting a Rising Tide: The Response to AIDS in East Asia*.

8. Remarks at a Luncheon for Members of the College of Physicians in Philadelphia, Pennsylvania. April 1 1987. University of Texas online archive.
   [Online]
   Available at
   http://www.reagan.utexas.edu/archives/speeches/1987/040187e.htm
   Accessed July 2014.

9. AIDS may be made notifiable. *The Times*, London. 14 February 1985.

10. Veitch, Andrew. Detain powers for Aids. *The Guardian*, London. 21 February 1985.

11. *30 years on: people living with HIV in the UK about to reach 100,000*. Health Protection Report, Volume 5 No 22, 6 June 2011.

12. *Australia, in Fighting a Rising Tide: The Response to AIDS in East Asia*.

13. Garfield, Simon. AIDS: The first 20 years (part one). *The Observer*, London. 3 June 2001.

14. Garfield, Simon. 1994. *The End of Innocence: Britain in the time of AIDS*. London: Faber and Faber. Quoted in Garfield, Simon. Saying the unsayable. *The Independent*. 11 November 1995.

15. Schramm-Evans, Zoe. Responses to AIDS, 1986-1987. In Aggleton, Peter (ed). 2013. AIDS: *Individual, Cultural and Policy Dimensions*. London: Routledge, p227.

16. *Sin, Sex and Science: The HIV/AIDS Crisis*. History Online Courses: HST425: American-European Health Care since 1800. Michigan State University.
    [Online} Available at
    http://history.msu.edu/hst425/resources/online-essays/sin-sex-and-science-the-hivaids-crisis/
    Accessed April 2014.

Part Five - How Queer Communities Responded

Given the severity of AIDS, the slow response from most governments and the homophobic angle taken by much of the media, it is unsurprising that queer communities took the lead in responding to the health crisis. In the first instance this came from a broad range of social and community organisations as well as the queer media. AIDS-specific organisations were formed very shortly afterwards to drive forward a more focused and specialised response. This had three basic strands – getting information out, caring for people affected by AIDS (including the partners and significant others of people with AIDS) and lobbying for government action. Underpinning all of this was the crucial task of fundraising, without which very little could happen.

Within the UK, counselling and support organisations such as London Lesbian and Gay Switchboard were very much at the frontline since it was they who received the thousands of phone calls from anxious inquirers. In conjunction with the Gay Medical Association and the nascent 'Terrence Higgins Memorial Trust', London Switchboard organised a one day conference on 21 May 1983 to discuss the situation and start to plan a way forward.

When the conference came to discuss an action plan it was acknowledged that the development of a London Switchboard AIDS Hotline would detract from the other work the organisation did (as well as seriously overstretch its resources). In consequence, it was agreed that efforts should be focused on the development of the Terrence Higgins Memorial Trust as the key community AIDS organisation. In order to expedite this process a number of experienced activists from organisations like London Switchboard and the Gay Medical Association joined the Trust's board.

Within a very short time the trust was providing most of the services that it still provides today. These included producing health education literature, providing speakers across the country, providing a one-to-one befriending service for people with AIDS (named the Buddy Project after a similar one launched by New York's Gay Men's Health Crisis), working with groups such as doctors and social workers to develop professional guidelines, and running a national telephone helpline. All of this was undertaken by volunteers until late 1985 when the Greater London Council provided the first statutory funding that allowed the employment of two workers.

A similar pattern occurred around the globe. In New York, Gay Men's Health Crisis – the world's first HIV/AIDS support service – was established in 1981 when:

"... six gay men and their friends gathered in writer Larry Kramer's living room to address the 'gay cancer' and raise money for research. The informal meeting provided the foundation for what would soon become Gay Men's Health Crisis. In 1982 an answering machine in the home of volunteer Rodger McFarlane acted as the first AIDS hotline – receiving over 100 calls the first night." [1]

In April 1982 in San Francisco:

"... a group of community leaders and physicians, including Dr Marcus Conant, Frank Jacobson, Cleve Jones and Richard Keller, came together to respond to the emerging health crisis plaguing mostly gay men in San Francisco. They formed the San Francisco AIDS Foundation, then called the Kaposi's Sarcoma Research and Education Foundation, becoming the second HIV service agency of its kind in the United States. They first operated out of a small office on Castro Street with a dedicated team of volunteers providing basic AIDS medical information, resources and referral services." [2]

In Australia, the first community response was the formation of AIDS Action Councils in every state. The first – the Victorian AIDS Action Council – was established in Melbourne, at a public meeting held four days after the first Australian AIDS death in 1983. In 1984 community groups came together in Queensland to discuss ways to tackle the homophobia generated by that state's Health Minister after he announced that four babies had died after receiving blood donated by a gay donor. In Sydney a public meeting that included representatives from a range of groups such as the Sydney Gay and Lesbian Mardi Gras, the Gay Counselling Service and the Bobby Goldsmith Foundation established the New South Wales AIDS Action Committee. (As with the Terrence Higgins Memorial Trust in the UK, the Bobby Goldsmith Foundation had been established by Goldsmith's friends who had cared for him during his illness.) By 1986 every Australian state and territory had an AIDS Action Committee (which subsequently became AIDS Councils to better respond to the federal government's HIV/AIDS Strategy).

While every country developed its' 'peak' organisations that were based in the largest cities and towns, there were also a huge range of smaller voluntary organisations that sprang up to meet local needs in smaller population centres. These were particularly valuable in those areas where specialist health services were either deficient or completely absent. While no estimate has ever been made of the number of support groups that sprang up to meet the HIV/AIDS challenge it is fair to assume that no area that had any sort of queer presence would have been without some form of support network: to describe the level of queer input as immense would be an understatement.

As well as specialist HIV/AIDS services, other queer organisations played a variety of roles too. Counselling services, for example, now skilled themselves up to address HIV/AIDS issues alongside their more 'routine' issues like coming out, relationship difficulties and identity issues. Social groups supported individual members who contracted HIV, 'political' groups also produced educational material (most famously, the Sisters of Perpetual Indulgence brochure *Play Fair* and the Harvey Milk Gay Democratic Club's *Can We Talk?*) and queer venues ran fundraising activities.

The latter function was especially important, particularly in those areas where national or local government was unwilling to provide funding for even the most basic services. The range of fundraising activities was immense, limited only by the imagination of the queer communities (and therefore pretty expansive). Everything from collection tins on the bars of gay pubs to elaborate events like the Terrence Higgins Trust's 'Night of a Thousand Frocks' at London's Hippodrome club and the Bobby Goldsmith Foundation's 'Shop Yourself Stupid' in Sydney's queer suburbs. Fighting AIDS and supporting HIV/AIDS organisations rapidly became the community norm, not only mobilising existing organisations but also turning previously apathetic individuals into activists.

The Queer Media

Another key player in the fight was the queer media whose sustained coverage of the crisis from the outset had, among other things, provided a welcome and intelligent relief from the homophobia and hysteria of the mainstream press. It tracked the emergence of the disease from its 'gay cancer' roots and was generally characterised by informed commentary on the developing issue, rather than the melodramatic headline that was the approach of the mainstream press. This was absolutely critical as gay men struggled to grasp the personal implications of the mysterious and frightening condition emerging in our midst. And, again, it was one of the reasons why people with HIV/AIDS – and, indeed, gay men in general – often knew more about the condition than their medical practitioners.

The range of media was quite extraordinary – ranging from professionally-produced, high-quality national publications to the duplicated newsletters of small social groups. In the UK, the situation was summed up by Julian Meldrum in his 1984 report *AIDS through the British Media*:

"Outside London, apart from the [national] publications named [Gay News, Capital Gay, Him Monthly/Gay Times and New Gay News], publications such as Gay Scotland, Mancunian Gay (in Manchester) and Gay East Midlands (in Nottingham) have published original articles, often in as much depth and as thoughtful as those in the London gay media. A host of comments and short articles ... have appeared in newsletters and bulletins circulated within local and special interest gay organisations, political and social. Concern has been most evident among motorbike/leather and S/M clubs, many of whose members appear to have comparatively high disposable incomes, given to foreign travel and inclined towards distributive sex at a high level of physical intimacy." [3]

In London, the weekly newspaper *Capital Gay* began the world's first regular column on AIDS in 1982 (and is credited by the *Oxford English Dictionary* as being the first publication in the world to use the term HIV). When *Gay News* – the UK's only national newspaper at that time – collapsed in April 1983, *Capital Gay* temporarily extended its distribution area beyond London to selected gay clubs in Nottingham, Manchester and Newcastle-upon-Tyne:

"... specifically to circulate news about HIV/AIDS which was not being covered by the mainstream press and which was information we thought was urgently needed by gay people nationwide. We pulled back to London and Brighton [in July 1985] once other national gay titles began to cover AIDS." [4]

In addition to the queer media of one's own country, publications from other countries were also readily available in large population centres, thus offering a more global perspective on the HIV/AIDS crisis. For example, I remember buying Canadian magazine *Body Politic*, US publications *Christopher Street*, *The Advocate* and *Gay Comix* as well as the French *Gai Pied* at London's Gay's the Word bookshop.

253

Through these publications gay men learned more about causation and possible treatments of AIDS and the possible implications and impact, while the tabloids focused on scaremongering and playing the blame game, irrespective of the cost. Queer media coverage enabled people to explore and articulate often confused thoughts and feelings and, in so doing, develop their own response. Not that this was always an easy or straightforward process. These were times of very high passions: this was a life-or-death crisis, after all, not some philosophical debate on a trivial issue. In consequence, while the rest of the world was reading simplistic platitudes about 'the gay plague', the dialogue that was taking place in the queer media was more intense, challenging and broad-ranging.

One publication that exemplified this was the *New York Native*. Established in December 1980 it had the dubious distinction of being the first queer publication to print an article about the emerging health crisis. This was the Centers for Disease Control's (CDC) denial on 18 May 1981 that a 'gay cancer' was developing. (Sadly, four weeks later, on 5 June 1981, the CDC published their first ever report on the emergence of the condition that would soon become known as AIDS).

But in November 1982, the *Native* published an article by Richard Berkowitz and Michael Callen, *We Know Who We Are: Two Gay Men Declare War on Promiscuity*. In it the two men argued that AIDS was not the result of a single causative agent but was down to the combination of factors associated with gay men's 'promiscuous' lifestyles – drug use, multiple sexual partners and repeated exposure to other sexually-transmissible infections. It was widely criticised, not least because it had no scientific basis but also because it was based on the assumption that all gay men with AIDS had lived so-called 'promiscuous' lifestyles – a notion that could have come straight from Moral Majority literature.

In March 1983 the paper published a less controversial but highly impassioned article by activist Larry Kramer: *1112 and Counting* was Kramer's furious attack on the apathy and neglect from politicians, clinicians and parts of the community in the face of the emerging AIDS crisis. It was, in practice, the first public articulation of the frustration and anger that would lead to the establishment of the AIDS Coalition to Unleash Power (ACT UP) in 1987.

Unfortunately, there seems to be a general consensus (including the view of its

254

founder Charles Orteb) that the *Native* seriously lost the plot at some point and came across as paranoid and embittered. Central to the criticisms is the view that it eschewed the growing wealth of scientific data on causation and possible treatments in favour of the latest fad or conspiracy theory [5]. The newspaper, it seemed, just wanted to find the negativity in everything. On 1 June 1987, for example, it published a front page article on AZT in which the author, John Lauritsen, stated:

"*Recovery from AIDS will come from strengthening the body, not poisoning it. Do not take, prescribe or recommend AZT.*"

Such a position was quite extraordinary – particularly at a time when AZT was viewed by most people as the first faint glimmer of light in what had been years of unremitting gloom. Perhaps unsurprisingly, ACT UP was boycotting the publication by the mid-80s. Between 1985 and 1996 its circulation dropped from 20,000 to 8000 and it closed on 13 January 1997. Just how much its contrarian stance on HIV/AIDS contributed to its closure is difficult to say – very few queer publications have especially long survival rates.

It is certainly unfortunate that the *Native* seemed to get bogged down in one – particularly negative – perspective at a time when people were increasingly desperate for some certainties. The AIDS crisis generated a number of needs for queer communities: one of these was a need for dialogue to explore how best to deal with its impact; another was a need for solidarity and support when they were under attack from both the disease and, it seemed, the rest of the world. Underlying this was a huge amount of anger; generated by the losses people had experienced, the lack of government action, the intensified discrimination and homophobia, the sheer frustration at the slow pace of treatments and the fear of facing an uncertain 'illness career'. While organisations like ACT UP helped focus some of that in the right direction, a lot of it was still channelled into the debates within queer communities – and it took its most visible form in the articles of the various gay media.

The AIDS Coalition to Unleash Power (ACT UP)

ACT UP was initiated in New York following a public talk given by writer and activist Larry Kramer at New York's Lesbian and Gay Community Services Center in New York

255

in March 1987. Kramer had been one of the founders of Gay Men's Health Crisis in 1981 but had become increasingly disenchanted with what he called its 'political impotence' and resigned from its board in 1983. In the course of his speech at the Lesbian and Gay Center he asked his audience if they'd be interested in a more radical approach to AIDS politics. Two days later, a meeting of some 300 people formed the world's first ACT UP group.

A few days after that, on March 24, 1987, they held their first demonstration in front of Trinity Church on Wall Street, New York. The flyer promoting the action listed the following demands:

1. *"Immediate release by the Federal Food and Drug Administration of drugs that might help save our lives. These drugs include: Ribavirin (ICN Pharmaceuticals); Ampligen (HMR Research Co.); Glucan (Tulane University School of Medicineo; DTC (Merieux); DDC (Hoffman-LaRoche); AS 101 (National Patent Development Corp.); MTP-PE (Ciba-Geigy); AL 721 (Praxis Pharmaceuticals).*

2. *Immediate abolishment of cruel double-blind studies wherein some get the new drugs and some don't.*

3. *Immediate release of these drugs to everyone with AIDS or ARC.*

4. *Immediate availability of these drugs at affordable prices. Curb your greed!*

5. Immediate massive public education to stop the spread of AIDS.

6. *Immediate policy to prohibit discrimination in AIDS treatment, insurance, employment, housing.*

7. *Immediate establishment of a coordinated, comprehensive and compassionate national policy on AIDS."*

Seventeen people were arrested at the demonstration. Whether it was coincidence or otherwise, two months later the Federal Drug Administration issued revised drug approval regulations. These permitted unlicensed drugs to be made available *"to persons with serious and life threatening illnesses, for whom no comparable or satisfactory alternative drug or therapy is available"*, if those drugs were deemed to be promising.

At their second demonstration – outside the White House on 1 June 1987 – police wore rubber gloves to arrest demonstrators, an action that further angered the protestors. ACT UP groups sprang up across the USA in the next couple of years; for example San Francisco's AIDS Action Pledge Group re-named itself ACT UP in the autumn of 1987, Los Angeles ACT UP was founded in December of that same year and cities like Boston and Seattle established groups the following year.

In May 1988, Vito Russo gave a speech at an ACT UP protest in Albany, New York. The speech has subsequently come to be known as *Why We Fight* and, like Larry Kramer's article *1112 and Counting*, has become a key text in explaining the emergence of a direct action organisation like ACT UP. For example, in it he said:

"You know, for the last three years, since I was diagnosed, my family thinks two things about my situation. One, they think I'm going to die and two, they think that my government is doing absolutely everything in their power to stop that. And they're wrong, on both counts.

So, if I'm dying from anything, I'm dying from homophobia. If I'm dying from anything I'm dying from racism. If I'm dying from anything, it's from indifference and red tape, because these are the things that are preventing an end to this crisis. If I'm dying from anything, I'm dying from Jesse Helms. If I'm dying from anything, I'm dying from the President of the United States. And, especially, if I'm dying from anything, I'm dying from the sensationalism of the newspapers and magazines and television shows, which are interested in me, as a human interest story – only as long as I'm willing to be a helpless victim, but not if I'm fighting for my life.

If I'm dying from anything – I'm dying from the fact that not enough rich white heterosexual men have gotten AIDS for anybody to give a shit." (6)

Interestingly, ACT UP groups outside the USA did not emerge until relatively late; ACT UP London, for example, was established by Peter Tatchell in 1989: in the Australian cities of Sydney, Melbourne and Perth not until 1990. It is hard to say whether this was the result of a different political mindset among queer/AIDS activists outside the USA or a reflection of the more extreme government intransigence US activists faced.

Similarly, there was no international equivalent of ACT UP's sister organisation Gran Fury. Gran Fury came together as the result of an exhibition at the New Museum for Contemporary Art in New York. In late 1987, the Museum's curator, Bill Olander, offered ACT UP window space to promote their message. The result was *Let the Record Show*, an installation that, in essence, sought to put the likes of Ronald Reagan, Jerry

257

Falwell and Jesse Helms on trial for crimes against humanity.

Set against a backdrop of images from the Nuremberg Nazi Trials were six cardboard cut outs of key 'defendants' – Reagan, Falwell, Helms, conservative commentator William F. Buckley, Cory Servas of the Presidential AIDS Commission and an 'anonymous surgeon'. In front of each of these was a concrete slab containing various quotes that these people had made. For example, the Servas quote was, *"It is patriotic to have the AIDS test and be negative"*, while that of the anonymous surgeon read, *"We used to hate faggots on an emotional basis. Now we have a good reason"*. Only Reagan's slab remained blank – a statement about his profound silence on the issue.

Above the installation was a neon sign that read *"SILENCE = DEATH"* over an inverted pink triangle. This had been loaned to ACT UP by the SILENCE = DEATH project design collective, a group of activists whose manifesto declared that *"silence about the oppression and annihilation of gay people, then and now, must be broken as a matter of our survival"*. They posted the SILENCE = DEATH image around New York, along with other messages that included *"ACTION = LIFE"* and *"IGNORANCE = FEAR"*.

The installation received a very positive reception and encouraged a number of those involved in the project to set up a group to explore more visual means of political expression. The name they chose – Gran Fury – came from the model of car used by New York police as well as its suggestion of the immense anger activists felt about the lack of action around HIV/AIDS. Over time the group became completely separate from ACT UP – although they obviously shared the same broad agenda. Their images began to appear everywhere – from billboards and brick walls to museums and galleries – and included a poster declaring that *"Kissing Doesn't Kill"* and another that read: *"All people with AIDS are innocent."* For the 1990 Venice Biennale they created two controversial pieces – *"Sexism Rears It's Unprotected Head"*, which featured a large image of an erect penis – and another attacking the Pope for his comments that *"The truth is not in condoms or clean needles. These are lies ... good morality is good medicine"*. Alongside an image of the Pope and his quote, Gran Fury spelled out their response:

"The Catholic Church has long taught men and women to loathe their bodies and to fear their sexual natures. This particular vision of good and evil continues to bring suffering and even death. By holding medicine hostage to Catholic morality and

withholding information which allows people to protect themselves and each other from acquiring the Human Immunodeficiency Virus, the Church seeks to punish all who do not share their particular version of human experience and makes clear its preference for living saints and dead sinners. It is immoral to practise bad medicine. It is bad medicine to deny people information that can help end the AIDS crisis. Condoms and clean needles save lives as surely as the earth revolves around the sun. AIDS is caused by a virus and a virus has no morals."

The AIDS Memorial Quilt

The AIDS Memorial Quilt, or the NAMES Project AIDS Memorial Quilt to give it its full name, was the brainchild of San Francisco activist Cleve Jones. During the course of the 1985 Candlelight Memorial rally for murdered supervisor Harvey Milk and Mayor George Moscone, Jones realised that more than a thousand San Franciscans had now died of AIDS. To get some idea of the size and impact of this, he asked rally participants to write on placards the names of people they knew who had died then fasten them to the wall of the Federal Building. The effect was immediate and obvious: for the first time since the crisis had hit, people could see just how many people had been lost to AIDS. And it was the patchwork effect of the dozens of placards that gave Jones an idea of how to move this forward.

A year later Jones and some of his friends had made a quilt in memory of one of their friends, Marvin Feldman. It was three foot wide by six foot long – the size of a human grave – but decorated with items and images that they associated with their friend. The following year – in June 1987 – he and a few other people formally launched the NAMES Project Foundation and people began sending in quilts from across America. Four months after its official launch, on 11 October 1987, the quilt was put on public display for the first time on the National Mall in Washington D.C. to coincide with the National March on Washington for Lesbian and Gay Rights. Despite the relative novelty of the project, 1920 panels were displayed.

Its display in Washington was, in part, a memorial for those who had died but also a means of highlighting the government's dismal response to AIDS. In October 1988 it was displayed in its entirety again in Washington – this time with 8288 panels – as continuing testimony to the inadequacy of that response.

259

But the quilt wasn't just about political protest; it was about demonstrating the personal impact of the disease – not only on those who had died from it but on the partners, friends and family of those left behind. Because each quilt is made up from very personal items – ranging from soft toys and jockstraps to badges, vinyl records and photographs – it instantly transforms the statistics into individual human stories, underscoring the value and richness of each life that has been lost. In its early days it was often the only memorial to people who had died from AIDS since many funeral parlours and cemeteries refused to accept the bodies and many families rejected their offspring when they learned of the AIDS diagnosis. Even when there wasn't complete rejection, the stigma associated with the disease meant that families wanted to forget about it as soon as possible. Commemorating a person who had died from AIDS simply wasn't an option for a lot of relatives.

The quilt gave the friends of the deceased – who may well have been excluded from the decision-making during the person's illness because they weren't officially next-of-kin – the opportunity to remember them. People who would have been swept under the carpet continue to be remembered through the quilt. And that commemoration process – the actual construction of an individual's quilt panel – also served as a means for the bereaved to explore and express their feelings about the loss of a loved one. While some quilts were prepared by individuals in the solitude and privacy of their own homes, many more were made by groups of friends who met either in someone's house or on the premises of the Quilt Project itself. The selection of design and constituent items often served as triggers for memories of the deceased person. Discussions on the meaning of the item for both the deceased and the quilt maker were cathartic and a way of bringing people together for mutual support during their grief.

When quilts were subsequently displayed, their unwrapping was often accompanied by some form of ceremony that would involve partners and significant others. This could include things like standing silently around the panel before or afterwards or the unveiling of the quilt as the individual's name was read out from a central dais. It was extremely rare for panels to be laid out impersonally.

The Quilt Project grew rapidly in the USA, reflecting the enormity of the impact on that country. As with many other AIDS initiatives that originated in the USA it was taken up elsewhere around the globe. In Australia it was formally launched at a display in

260

Sydney's Martin Place on World AIDS Day – December 1 – 1988. At that point in consisted of 35 Australian panels as well as some that were on loan from the USA. A further 944 names were added in its lifetime, making it the largest quilt project outside the USA.

The Quilt Project appears to have played a lesser role in the UK, starting in the late 80s as the UK NAMES Project and growing to 48 panels, each of which contained some six to eight individual quilts, as was the practice with all Quilt Projects around the globe.

References

1. *About Us*. Gay Men's Health Crisis website.
    [Online] Available at
    http://www.gmhc.org/about-us
    Accessed April 2014.

2. *Our History*. San Francisco AIDS Foundation website.
    [Online] Available at
    http://www.sfaf.org/about-us/our-history/
    Accessed April 2014.

3. Meldrum, Julian. *AIDS through the British media*. Introduction and Overview.

4. Comment by former *Capital Gay* editor Michael Mason in response to article on *Capital Gay on Gay in the 80s* blog. http://www.gayinthe80s.com/2012/08/1981-capital-gay/

5. See, for example, Pogrebin, Robin. Controversial Gay Magazine Shuts Down. *New York Times*. 9 January 1997.
    [Online] Available at
    http://www.nytimes.com/1997/01/09/nyregion/controversial-gay-magazine-shuts-down.html
    Accessed May 2014.

6. *Why We Fight*.

Final Thoughts

I had originally considered putting the section on HIV/AIDS at the front of this book, since it came to over-shadow our lives, wreak havoc on our communities and serve as a handy weapon with which our enemies could attack us. And, even though I would never argue that HIV/AIDS was a good thing, it did mobilise far greater sections of our communities than would ever have become involved in 'gay rights' campaigning. In so doing, it strengthened our sense of being part of a community – albeit one that seemed to be constantly under attack.

In the end, I decided not to start the book with HIV/AIDS because there was far more to the 80s than just this hideous disease: there was queer life before - and indeed, throughout - the AIDS crisis. For one thing there were those political initiatives that had their roots in the 70s and earlier decades; most obviously, the fight for decriminalisation and equal rights. The queer social scene was already well established and becoming increasingly visible, aided, no doubt by the growing interest in the 'Pink Pound/Dollar'. And I think it is arguable that this pink currency also helped drive the growth of queer film, music and literature.

All of these things happened despite, not because of, HIV/AIDS - and our enemies would have opposed them with or without the convenient weapon of the 'gay plague'.

That is not to dismiss the immense loss our communities experienced but rather to recognise the resilience that sustained us throughout this period. When I met Bobbi Campbell, one of the first people to come out as a person with AIDS, he wore a badge that read 'I Will Survive'. It was a symbol of his determination that life would go on in spite of this disease. Sadly he was to lose his fight, but across the broader community, the fact that we chose to continue the fight for our rights, continue to make our voices heard - and continue to party – signalled that we weren't going to let an illness define us. Regardless of what life threw at us, we continued to move forward. If there's any one thing we should remember about the 80s, it's that.

About the Author

Now in his early 60s, Colin Clews still doesn't know what he wants to be when he grows up. This may explain the broad-ranging nature of both his professional and 'activist' careers to date.

His professional career includes counselling, education, communications, service development and freelance journalism. As an activist he has been involved in campaigns on a variety of issues including anti-racism, sexuality, sustainability, animal rights and Lesbians and Gays Support the Miners.

He has lived and worked in both Australia and the UK. His current interests are queer film history, food sustainability and, of course, his blog Gay in the 80s, which he has been writing since March 2012. It seemed like a good idea at the time!

www.gayinthe80s.com